"When the Last Tree Is Cut Down, the Last Fish Eaten, and the Last Stream Poisoned, You Will Realize That You Cannot Eat Money"—**Native American saying**

"It is a small part of life we really...live"—*On the Shortness of Life* by **Seneca, A.D. 49**

"It was as if LOW-KEY had married the WILD WEST...and they had a baby named KEY WEST"—**Will Soto**

"Aliens would do well to give Key West a wide berth"—**JVM Rubin**

"Not all those who wander are lost"—**JRR Tolkien**

ABOUT THE AUTHOR

JON BREAKFIELD is the author of nine books. These include the four-part Amazon bestselling series **KEY WEST**.
And **KEY WEST** Celebrities and A Splash of Scandal.

Also **PAN AM:** No Sex Please We're Flight Attendants, the naughty and eye-popping The New **NAKED EUROPE**, and the best-selling crime fiction series **DEATH** by **GLASGOW**, and its stand-alone sequel **DEATH** by **KEY WEST**. For those with a short attention span, have a wee snoop at **LIVERPOOL, TEXAS** ... **LONDON, ARKANSAS**.

When not running from hurricanes, Jon and his wife divide their time **between iconic Glasgow, Scotland, and punch-happy Key West, FL, not quite the USA.**

KEY WEST

Starting Over

by

Jon Breakfield

KW
Press

DEDICATED TO THOSE COURAGEOUS, PLUCKY AND INDEFATIGABLE SOULS...INDEED, THOSE RESILIENT DENIZENS OF KEY WEST AND THE FLORIDA KEYS WHO STARED THAT BITCH IRMA IN THE FACE, AND PLAYED MOTHER NATURE'S FINICKY VERSION OF *RUSSIAN ROULETTE*— AND WON

ACKNOWLEDGEMENTS: Special shout-out to the intuitive and eagle-eyed **Debbie Williamson**.

A "Give it up!" for **Will Soto**, **Al Subarsky**, **Sallie Foster**, **Henry Fuller**, and **Popcorn Joe**, in Key West.

Eric TCD Wilson of F, in Falkirk.

And my long-suffering editor **GL Rotocampo**.

**COVER ALERT: The cover photo was originally meant to be plucked from the sterling collection of renown photographer Henry Fuller (*Key West Through the Eyes of a Conch*) but, alas, Hurricane Irma wiped out all communication between the two of us and transfer of digital images was unable to be concluded prior to this manuscript being shipped off to the publisher. Sad face.

**And it must be repeated, for great care is always taken: No snowbirds were harmed during the making of this book.

CHAPTER ONE

Gabrielle and I are sitting in the Bull & Whistle Bar in Key West, Florida.

No surprise there, right?

We're sequestered next to the first big window by the front door. It's the bewitched, fall-down-drunk side of midnight. Humid as hell. Bare-legs-stick-to-the-barstool hot. Out of the window, a raft of colorfully, albeit scantily dressed humanity is floating by on Duval Street.

Inebriates going downstream toward the watering holes of Sloppy's, Rick's, Two Friends, and the Hog's Breath.

Gays going upstream toward 811, La Te Da, and, yes, Bobby's Monkey Bar.

Trop-a-sexuals just milling about, not knowing which way to go, upper Duval or lower.

Did I mention that it was hot and humid? Sticky, even? Many places up in America don't get this blast of balmy weather in the summer.

Key West can get this weather in the winter.

Like today.

Christmas Eve.

And, yes, a *bar* on Christmas Eve.

It's what folk do here. Perhaps not everyone, but enough so you don't feel guilty doing it yourself. In the Great White North, folk celebrate in front of the fire, within striking distance of the turkey and all that booze on the top shelf in the kitchen cupboard (*"Oh, let me just go and check on the turkey!"* *Glug. Glug*). Here, on the rock, we're more than happy to forgo the bird, not gobble till you wobble, and sit in front of an open window with night-blooming jasmine wafting in, within striking distance of the bar.

Back home you may have a Christmas tree dripping in tinsel in your living room, here—in the Bull—they have a Christmas tree, as well, but this one's in the corner— HANGING UPSIDE DOWN!

It's Key West, after all.

Up on stage, Sallie Foster is absolutely killing it with her rendition of "PIECE OF MY HEART."

Something breaches Gabrielle's attention and she points. Just outside our window, a rather shapely lassie is handing out flyers.

"Can you make out what she's pushing?" Gabrielle asks me.

"No, but she seems to be creating a fair amount of interest."

"Is it her flyers or is it the way she's dressed?"

"Not sure. I've never seen anyone with legs and a rump like that except in glossy mags and on the *Animal Channel*."

"Go!" Gabrielle tells me.

"Go where?"

"Go get a flyer. Consider it research."

"I'm not going out there, I'll get swept down Duval and never be able to wade back."

"Go!"

So I go.

I exit the Bull by the front entrance, push through two cloud-chasers vaping their lungs out, an incoming tide of pissed-to-the-gills holiday revelers, and sidle up to Miss Curves. Then my eyes grow stalks: the woman is all orchestra and balcony. I didn't know they made them like that. Perhaps they *don't* make them like that.

Miss Orchestra and Balcony hands me a flyer. "Hope it's not for you!" she teases.

I hurry back inside before I'm sucked downstream. I sit down and hand Gabrielle the flyer. Gabrielle scans it.

8

"Jeez Louise, look at this!" Gabrielle holds it up for me to see. "It offers: **15 % OFF ON BRAZILIAN BUTT LIFTS.**"

"Touting for cosmetic surgery! What has this world come to?" I say.

"It's come to this!" Gabrielle says, and she slaps the flyer with the back of her hand for emphasis. "Come to Key West, get a bum lift, learn to twerk, go home a new woman."

"Or new man."

"I wonder if you can go right back to work after having a bum lift? Can't exactly sit at your desk for eight hours, I would think."

"Wonder how much a bum lift costs? Get out your cell and Google it."

So Gabrielle Googles. "Make sure no one's looking over my shoulder. Found it. Listen to this: 'A Brazilian Butt Lift is a procedure designed to create a more prominent, sensual, enhanced buttock. It involves injecting your fat, liposuctioned from other areas into your buttocks. People of all ages can have a Brazilian Butt Lift.'"

Gabrielle stops reading.

"I can't believe it says *people of all ages can have a Brazilian Butt Lift!* What kind of message is that sending?"

Gabrielle reads on: "'There must be enough fat to be harvested for re-injection. People with limited fat may benefit from a gluteal augmentation with implants rather than a fat transfer or Brazilian Butt Lift. After surgery, you will most likely have some drainage from your incisions.'"

Gabrielle stops, jabs at her open mouth with her index finger.

"What else?" I ask.

"It says 'You must not sit directly on your buttocks for up to 3 weeks. Results take time. They can be seen in as little as 6 weeks. The time may vary considerably depending on each individual.'"

"Perhaps it's just me, buttt…"

"You trying to be fanny, I mean funny?"

9

"Ha, ha."

Then Gabrielle leans close: "I read recently that young girls are unhappy with the shape and size of their private parts and are demanding designer privates."

"Vaginal facelifts?"

"You could describe it like that, yes. They want it to look like a 'Barbie', that's what they call it."

"When you say young, what age are we talking about here?"

Gabrielle moves even closer and whispers in my ear.

"That young! Now I'm going to gag. When I was that age, I was looking for field mice and tadpoles. How can a young girl think she's not shaped right?"

"Porn."

"What! Please tell me that's not true."

"Unfortunately, it is. They're watching porn and those excuses for the female of the species are their role models."

Children watching porn. God help us.

Gabrielle studies her cell phone for a moment. "Oh, here we go. You can also get a labiaplasty done while you're down here on vacation."

"You serious?"

"I kid you not."

"Come to Key West for Christmas, start the year off with the latest, new model."

"Oh, please!"

"Oh, oh."

"Now what?"

"The prices. I found them. And are you sitting down, if you can, I mean, an average butt lift costs $11,000."

"I would take the $11,000, get it in small bills and just stuff it down the back of my pants. Get the same effect without having to fork out, or suffer the leakage."

"Funny. Oh, look, an average labiaplasty only sets you back about $3000. Unless you need the vaginal tightening."

"If you can believe what you're being told."

"And it's not just lip service."

"That's so not funny!"

We had been ignoring our drinks, so we spent some time catching up, then I said: "I've been to a gynecologist's…"

"What?!" Gabrielle almost fell off her stool.

"When I lived in France, in Normandy, I lived with a French family. The father was a doctor and the mother a teacher. I tutored their two kids in English and looked after their horses."

"Where does the gynecologist come in here?"

"It was the summer and the 24 Hours of Le Mans was on. I wanted to go see the race, so the family I was living with rang a friend who was a doctor in Le Mans and arranged for me to stay there."

"Keep going."

"When I got to Le Mans, I learned that the family lived in an old Belle Époque building above the surgery. There was no place for me to sleep, so the doctor's wife made up a bed for me down in the doctor's surgery."

"In the waiting room?"

"No, on the examining table."

"But those are small."

"You spotted the problem, right off."

"How did you manage?"

"Feet in the stirrups. Slept like a baby."

Gabrielle and I both hit our drinks BIG TIME. Needed to after all that. A bit too much information, I do believe.

Then Gabrielle comes up for air. "Go!" Gabrielle commands.

"Now where?"

"You know where."

"I do?"

"Yes, you do. Now go!"

"Oh, no, not that again. I'd rather soak my feet in boiling oil."

"You have to. Consider it research."

"You keep saying that…"

"Go!"

"But…"

"GO!"

I rise reluctantly from my barstool, very much tail between naked, peely-wally legs, and head for the back door that spills out onto Caroline Street. I step outside. Fractionally cooler out here. I don't smell the night-blooming jasmine now, but I do smell cannabis coming from somewhere. Wait! This is Key West, it could be coming from *everywhere*. I walk five feet, turn right, and begin to tentatively climb the outside wooden set of stairs. I go up two flights to the *clothing optional* Garden of Eden Rooftop Bar, passing a few buff members of the crack Key West Police Force coming down. What's the haps? As they rumble by me, I can just make out that they are speaking *sotto voce*, and in Spanish.

At the top of the steps, there's a warning sign of sorts. It's white with red lettering. It reads:

BY ENTERING THESE PREMISES YOU AGREE

TO ABIDE BY THE FOLLOWING RULES

NO USE OF CELLPHONES ALLOWED

NO STILL OR VIDEO PHOTOGRAPHY

NO SEX ON PREMISES

MUST BE OVER 21

NO GLASS ALLOWED

WE RESERVE THE RIGHT TO

DESTROY THE DEVICE(S) USED TO CAPTURE

AND SEND IMAGES IMMEDIATELY AND

WITHOUT

LEGAL RELIEF AFFORDED TO OWNERS

OF DEVICES CONFISCATED

Some scamp has stuck one of the **15% OFF BUTT LIFT** flyers on the sign. Is this aimed at any one person who frequents the establishment? All of them? Many are past their sell-by date and gravity has clearly been the victor.

There's an ambrosial, glowing female creature perched where the usual chiseled, brick-shithouse bouncer hangs (and I mean *hangs*). This vision of femininity has painted-on, red short-shorts and is sporting a skin-tight T-shirt which reads: CAME ON VACATION, WENT HOME ON PROBATION.

She *does not* need the services that the flyer offers.

But, she *does* smell of weed (the source?).

Now exceedingly loquacious owing to the vats of brew I've consumed, I form a sentence and ask: "Are *you* the bouncer?"

"No, just covering..." And then, the sweaty vixen proceeds to tell me, *in detail*, why there was no bouncer.

"Oh, my God!" I respond.

Then she tells me some more.

"Holy shit!" I say.

And she goes on.

"Not in the toilet!" I gasp.

Then she concludes, recounting the final, gory, seedy, debauched events of the evening.

And I'm struck dumb.

"You coming in?" she asks me, giving me the once over and then wishing she hadn't. "Not much going on up here since the police arrived. Scared the tourons off."

"Maybe later."

I turn to go, but she stops me by extending both hands in my direction, palms down.

"What do you think?"

"What do I think of what?"

"My fingernails."

13

"Can't see them so well. Hold them up to the light."

And she does.

And I gasp again.

"You have little paintings on each nail..."

"That's right."

"Is that what I think it is?"

"It is. One on each nail."

"Is it anatomically correct?"

"You tell me."

And she gives me a look with frightening subtext.

"I'll be back," I say, sounding a bit too much like Arnold Schwarzenegger and make a run for it.

I scarper back down the wooden set of stairs and blow back in through the aft door of the Bull. I re-commandeer my seat and Gabrielle says: "Speak."

"You won't believe it. Some Miami Beach touron called police claiming the juiced-bouncer slapped her on the ass. She wanted to file charges and she wanted the police to photograph her pink backside, so the police officer took her into the toilets..."

"Male or female?"

"Huh?"

"Male or female police officer?"

"Male."

"Male or female?"

"Huh?"

"Male or female toilet?"

"Don't know...either way it's going to be awkward, isn't it?"

"Then what happened?"

"You won't believe it. The woman hiked up her skirt, pulled her panties down and bent over at the waist!"

"In front of the police officer!"

"Precisely."

"What did he do?"

"He did his duty."

Gabrielle and I hit our drinks.

14

When we come up for air, Gabrielle asks: "Was the bouncer arrested?"

"No, the woman didn't want to press charges."

"Then why call the police?"

"Was wondering that myself."

"Then what happened?"

"She wanted to be taken to the police station."

"What for?"

"Said she'd never been to one..."

We hit our drinks again.

"Only in Key West," Gabrielle says.

"Only in Key West," I say. Then, I add: "There's more..."

"More?"

"Yes, the woman bouncer up at the Garden..."

"What about her?"

"She showed me her vulva."

"What!!!"

"She had a tiny vulva painted on each fingernail...I kid you not."

Gabrielle blew out her cheeks.

"Only in Key West," Gabrielle says.

"Only in Key West," I say.

Out the window, something breaches our attention: A transient is riding his bicycle past. He's wearing antlers, and the basket of his bike has Christmas bunting. The Christmas bunting lights up. As do the antlers.

I'm destroying yet another Bud, out of a plastic glass, as is tradition here in the Bull. Gabrielle is romancing a mojito. I would gladly tell you how many we've had, but we're ripped and I just don't know. Plus, it's Christmas, so I'm not counting. Not that I could do the math right now.

I look up at a ceiling fan and verbally plead with it to try harder. Gabrielle laughs. I look over at my wife. I've never seen her happier than she's been since we moved to the end of the world, Key West, FL, not quite the USA, with no money and no jobs.

She laughs again.

15

"What's so funny?" I ask.

Gabrielle points to a corpulent, professional inebriate with a grey ponytail sitting at the bar. He's wearing a black T-shirt with white lettering on the back. The print is large, like the man, and even I, in my addled state, can read it from all the way over here by the window. It reads: I DON'T MIND GOING TO WORK, IT'S JUST THE WAITING AROUND FOR EIGHT HOURS…THAT'S BULLSHIT!

Now I laugh.

"Remember that?" Gabrielle says. "We both had jobs that paid the bills and paid for all the toys that we thought we needed…"

"Like a snow blower."

"And a second car."

"And a flat-screen TV as big as the side of bus."

"And another one in the bedroom."

"And a portable in the kitchen."

"And an Aga…"

"A what?"

"An Aga."

"We had one of those?"

"What do you think I cooked on in the kitchen?"

"An Aga?"

"Nothing gets by you, "Gabrielle teases. Then says: "At least you didn't have a man cave."

"I had a man drawer, but no man cave."

"I remember that drawer, you had five frequent-flyer cards from long defunct airlines, two sets of miniature screwdrivers with 30 different heads, and an old stub from a Packers game. What do you have to say for yourself?"

"Aaron Rodgers passed for 305 yards and four touchdowns in that game."

An explosion of laughter comes from just outside the front entrance: A raucous herd of sunburnt fifty-something maidens are attempting to penetrate the bar. They have a sense of danger about them—their *thirst*. The lead maiden is busty and sports a tight, tight T-shirt which reads: TOO HOT FOR HEAVEN, TOO COOL FOR HELL.

"Quick! Go!" I beg Gabrielle. "Order one more before they suck the place dry! I'm numb from the waist down now and can't move my legs."

Gabrielle calmly rises. Gives me a playful look. "Grace under pressure," she says, quoting Hemingway, and beats the thundering herd to the bar by two furlongs, or was it two fur thongs, what with it being winter?

Gabrielle returns with a fresh Bud for me and a cup of something for her.

"Coffee?"

"Irish coffee. *Sláinte!*"

"*Sláinte mhaith*," I respond.

We lift our glasses, mime a toast, and we drink. Gabrielle the delicate hummingbird, me as always the parched camel.

Then we form sentences.

Me: "Now, here in Key West, it never snows, never has, and never will, so we don't need the snow blower."

Gabrielle: "We sweep up plumeria blossoms and not shovel the snow."

Me: "We pick up coconuts that have fallen and don't rake leaves."

Gabrielle: "And we have two bikes, not two cars."

Me: "We don't need the latest flat-screen, 75-inch, beast of a TV with all the sexy bells and whistles, because we go out and listen to live music."

Gabrielle: "Big Al instead of Big Brother."

Me: "Exactly!"

We lap at our drinks.

"Plus, if we want diversion at home, we can listen to Trop Rock on Radio A1A."

"Or the Fishing Report."

"We don't have the latest fancy-smancy smartphone, just throwaway ones for emergencies."

"If we want to talk to someone, we jump on our bikes and go knock on their door."

17

"And if they live up on the mainland, we write them a letter."

"And we read."

"Nothing better than falling asleep reading a book," Gabrielle says.

"Exactly," I say. "Someone just messaged me on Facebook and said much the same thing. They said my latest book about PAN AM put them to sleep."

Gabrielle laughs.

"What?" I say.

Up on the stage, Sallie is now shaking the walls and bringing down the house with "BACK TO KEY WEST." Does Sallie rock or what!

> **"I got the car loaded down,**
> **Got my suitcase all packed,**
> **I'm leaving this place,**
> **And I ain't never comin' back,**
> **Good God almighty,**
> **Lord have mercy on me,**
> **But I got a thousand miles an hour**
> **Til' I get to the Keys,**
> **I gotta get back livin'**
> **Where the livin' is the best,**
> **I'm going all the way to Florida,**
> **But down to Key West..."**

Gabrielle points to Black T-shirt Man, then Sallie Foster. "Pretty much sums it up, doesn't it? We made the right choice by moving here, struggling, never giving up, and finding ways to survive and make it all work."

I look into my wife's green eyes and they're sparkling. "Would you do it all over again?" I ask her.

"In a heartbeat," she says.

WAIT!

Having said that, Dear Reader, we *are* doing it all over again. My elderly father up in Wisconsin, who had congestive heart failure, took a turn for the worse, and we had to leave

Key West to care for him. We didn't know if we'd be gone for a week.

Or a month.

WE WERE GONE FOR A YEAR.

And now we are starting all over. Except for our two bikes which Popcorn Joe looked after for us while we were gone. And we're staying at Popcorn Joe's until we find a new apartment. Sadly, Popcorn Joe sold the Pineapple Apartments, so there's no chance for accommodation at our old hovel up in the attic.

"Tomorrow, we'll buy the Mullet Wrap and see if there are any apartments we can afford. If not, we might be sleeping at the beach."

"But a cold front is coming through in a few days, and it's going to drop down into the upper sixties."

And we both laugh.

"If we had any money, we could buy some hole-in-the-wall…"

"Have you seen how much property is going for here now?" Gabrielle asks.

"No."

"Trailers on Stock Island for $250,000, studios in the Key West Old Town with no view and resident cockroaches for $300,000, one-bedroom shoeboxes (365 sq. feet) for $400,000 and up. Never mind. It will be exciting starting all over again," Gabrielle says.

"Indeed, it will," I say.

"Uh, oh!"

"What?"

"Just thought of a problem. A *big* problem."

"What?"

"It's winter season. *High* season. It's impossible to find accommodation in Key West this time of the year. Any available apartments will be renting short-term for the big bucks. Even illegal dwellings at many of the city commissioners' houses will be booked."

We sip our drinks in a bit of a euphoric, suddenly, toilet-flushing, life-swirling stupor.

"Remember what my mother used to say?"

"What was that?" Gabrielle asks.

"There's always room for one more."

"Which means?"

"We only have to find *one* place."

"Hmmm, that's comforting. Let's see if it's still comforting in the morning."

The Bull is winding down now, pedestrian traffic on Duval is slowing to a vertigo crawl. A few pedicab drivers, who are either training for the Tour de France or high on meth, are zipping tourists back to guesthouses, upmarket hotels, and massage parlors, which offer "NUDE LAP DANCING AND BED DANCING TILL THE WEE HOURS."

Gabrielle and I rise, we wave a hand at Sallie who is now singing "DUVAL CRAWL."

**"People come to Key West
From almost everywhere…
Well, they like to run amok,
Go crazy, let down their hair…"**

Then, we wave at the bartender who is pointing out the sign behind her which reads: STAFF RESERVE THE RIGHT TO TELL YOU TO GO FUCK YOURSELF to two drunken letches, and we step out the backdoor of the Bull and into a gentle, tropical breeze. The smell of cannabis is gone and now we can smell salt in the air. Across the street, the Porch is already shuttered and dark, down on the corner of Whitehead, the lights at Kelly's are still twinkling, but there is no sign of higher life forms. We stroll a few feet down Caroline past the Lost Weekend Liquor Store and Mr. Cheapee's Liquor & Stuff. We decide we need some *stuff*, so we go in and I pick out a tube of salt & vinegar Pringles, and cheesy Tortilla Chips, and a small tub of chocolate-chip cookie-dough ice cream, and some beef jerky, and some salted peanuts, then Gabrielle puts back the cheesy Tortilla Chips, and the small tub of chocolate-chip cookie-dough ice cream, and the beef jerky, and the salted peanuts. But I get to keep the salt & vinegar Pringles, which for me is a small victory. We approach the cash register to pay, but there is no one there. The young male employee, who was there when we came in, is now outside, sucking on a fag. I'm talking about the tobacco. He finishes his ciggie and throws the butt in the gutter. Then he turns to come back in, stops in his tracks, goes back to the offending cigarette butt, scoops it up out of the gutter and brings it inside. He disposes of the stub in a suitable receptacle behind the counter.

"Can't do that anymore in Key West," he informs us. "Against the law now to chuck your cigarette butt. Hundred dollar fine. Guess I'd better take up vaping."

We pay for our *stuff*, thank the young man, who is now thumbing his cell phone and step back outside.

"A lot of things have changed since we've been gone," Gabrielle says.

"Prices, for one," I say. I'm waiting for Gabrielle to say what else had changed, but she doesn't respond, she just has a look of horror on her face.

"What?"

Gabrielle points to a pole where our bikes had been chained.

"Someone's stolen our bikes!"

21

CHAPTER TWO

Christmas morning.

We awoke at Popcorn Joe's the next morning, staring at a ceiling fan circling lazily overhead.

The bed in Popcorn Joe's guest room had a mattress called "Silent Night." Appropriate for the season but, alas, I had anything but a silent night. More like a restless night...or a slept-like-shit night. My brain was circling lazily overhead, just like the ceiling fan, albeit in the opposite direction, and I had a hellacious headache. The headache was not from an alcohol-induced hangover, and a now empty tube of salt & vinegar Pringles, rather from a stolen-bike hangover. This was the second time since we'd moved to Key West that we'd had our bikes nicked. It hurt tons the first time around, now it possibly hurt even more. Lowlife, thieving bastards, that was Key West for you. It's such an expensive place to live, to even exist, that former upstanding citizens and former pillars of a distant, points-north community lower themselves to base level and resort to criminal means to make ends meet. I'm talking about folk who never even dreamed about breaking the law before they moved here, before they got the drug problem or the alcohol problem.

Many folk had good intentions: they rode the wagon down to Key West, then fell off.

And don't forget that class of historical romantics, yes, you heard right, the *historical romantics*, those who were enamored with Key West's shipwrecking, smuggling, rum running, gun running past, they thought theft an entitlement—cool, even, and everyone and everything was fair game: bicycles, booze, food, you name it, if it wasn't bolted down, it would go missing.

* * *

So as to keep you in the loop, may I just mention that after Popcorn Joe sold off the Pineapple Apartments, he moved into Truman Annex, and now we were staying with him for a week, but only a week, so the clock was ticking for us to find our own place.

In actuality, we would love to find an affordable place to stay here in this glorious Truman Annex tropical compound—but that is highly unlikely.

CHOMP ON THIS: Truman Annex is one of Key West's most coveted places to call home-sweet-hideaway. It's located in the Old Town, it's a lush, gated community, and blooms BIG TIME with frangipani, hibiscus and jasmine. It absolutely oozes charm, history, *mucho* wealth, and hints at colonial appeal and a bygone era. It does not have a down-market area, that part of Key West is just over the back fence. Sadly, the down-market sector is rapidly becoming anything other than *down-market*, owing to greedy, rampant gentrification. I'm talking about Bahama Village, or course, and it annoys me more than just a bit that wealthy outsiders (and the odd affluent local) have bought up homes and vacant lots, and rebuilt and resold for millions, driving out the original denizens of African-Bahamian descent who can no longer afford the property taxes and can no longer live in the homes that their ancestors built with their own blood, sweat and *fears*, out of coveted Dade County pine, and the timbers harvested from ships which ran aground on the reef. See how long that last sentenced is? That's called a rant.

Anyway, back to Truman Annex. It used to be a base for submarines, it's where the Little White House is located and the home to Fort Zachary Taylor State Park. Even though Truman Annex has a gatehouse and is a gated community, everyone is welcome to stroll around, pay a visit to the Truman Little White House (where President Truman hung out in the

23

winter)…and pay to use the beach (where Gabrielle and I go snorkeling).

* * *

"Merry Christmas," I croaked.

"Merry Christmas," came the reply.

Gabrielle and I crawled out of bed and padded across a tiled floor into Popcorn Joe's *cocina*. Bare feet on tile in winter. Idyllic. There's something special about waking up in Key West, isn't there? It's the end-of-the-world, back-of-beyond, last stop on the great railway train of life—and only 90 miles from Havana. That smacks of intrigue and just a sustainable dose of danger. Sometimes I picture a map of the world in my mind, then I close in on the US of A, work my way down to Florida, down the Florida Keys to that little speck at the end in the middle of the ocean.

That's us!

Goosebumps.

"Look," Gabrielle said, pointing at the kitchen table. Popcorn Joe was already up and gone, and he'd left us a note: GONE ROLLERBLADING. CUBAN BREAD IN OVEN. HIT THE SWITCH ON THE BASS-O-MATIC FOR A CUP OF AMBITION.

Gabrielle flipped the switch on Giuseppe's Nescafe Dolce Gusto machine and then looked down at her feet.

Popcorn Joe's cat "Fausto" padded silently in and wrapped itself around Gabrielle's leg. Gabrielle bent over and stroked Fausto and that set off the purring machine.

FYI: Popcorn Joe named his cat after Fausto's Food Palace on Fleming. Joe first saw Fausto sitting out front of the market, then he noticed the stray cat would follow customers into the market to the pet food aisle. And beg. This was a cat that knew what he was doing! Popcorn Joe adopted Fausto and Fausto signed on with Popcorn Joe, and now they are leading a great life together.

"I want to go visit Mr. Leroy," Gabrielle said.

"You're on," I said. "We'll go over to Mrs. Grace's today

and see how they're both doing."

For those of you who don't know or may not remember Mr. Leroy, might I just recount that Mr. Leroy was a black cat with a white moustache and white spats, and he had adopted us when we moved into Aronovitz Lane. When we moved back into Popcorn Joe's attic on Caroline Street, Mr. Leroy stayed behind in Aronovitz Lane, sleeping on Mrs. Grace's porch, across the tropical alley. Aronovitz Lane was his domain, his territory, and it wouldn't have been prudent to turf him out.

Popcorn Joe's cat suddenly unclamped from Gabrielle and ran to the kitchen door like a dog would do.

"Giuseppe's back," I said.

On that, the kitchen door, which led to a tropical compound out back, opened, and Popcorn Joe glided in, still wearing his rollerblades, and followed by a blast of humidity.

"Merry Christmas B's!" Joe enthused. "Went around the island. Bit of a problem out by Higgs Beach. A transient wanted his usual picnic table, but an iguana with a wild hair up its ass had taken up residence and he was not about to move. The iguana was huge—*National Geographic* huge. There was a lengthy stare down, then the iguana hissed and the transient jumped on his bike and got the hell out of there. How'd you sleep?"

"Fitfully," Gabrielle said. "Someone stole our bikes last night when we were at the Bull."

"Wondered where they were." Popcorn Joe went into deep thought. "Let me just make a phone call…"

"Who you gonna call?"

"Not Ghostbusters, but someone who has his ear to the ground. He's British. Used to be with the French Foreign Legion. He's sort of picked up from where Captain Jerry left off after he kicked the bucket. His name's Johnny-Johnny."

"Johnny?"

"No, Johnny-Johnny."

"Johnny-Johnny?"

"You got it now, and don't ask. When you meet him, he'll

25

tell you all about it."

Popcorn Joe pulled his cell phone out of a back pocket and stabbed at it. Immediately, it was picked up on the other end. "Johnny-Johnny, wasssuppp?"

Popcorn Joe explained our dilemma, listened, added some more details, then finished it off with: "Yeah, I know exactly where you're talking about…"

And he slapped his cell phone shut.

"Have you ever heard about Black Cat Alley in Hong Kong?" Popcorn Joe asked.

"A somewhat dodgy area," I said.

"That's it. If anything is stolen in Hong Kong today, it will be for sale in Black Cat Alley tomorrow."

"And?" Gabrielle said.

"We have a place like that here. It's out on Stock Island."

"And we're going today, Christmas Day?"

"You're going right now. And here's what I want you to do…"

Popcorn Joe explained his game plan.

Gabrielle muttered an "Oh, my God!"

And I muttered a "Holy shit!"

* * *

Popcorn Joe drove us out to Stock Island in his old red Ford van. Gabrielle was riding shotgun, I was sitting on an upturned, blue milk crate behind the front seats. Just after the Cow Channel bridge, Joe pulled over to the right, in front of Shifting Gears automotive and shut down the engine. "See that building?" Joe pointed to a one-story structure just to the left. "That used to be the Boca Chica Lounge. Most dangerous bar in all of Florida."

Gabrielle and I were all ears.

"Police were called out here most nights. One old cop told me that when he had road duty and had to go in, he was the least-armed person in there. They had a chain-linked fence running right down the middle, protecting the bar from the shrimpers, the smugglers, drug dealers, sailors and *Marielitos*. It

26

may have lacked in charm, but it made up for it by never being closed. Eventually it had its hours cut back to 4am, 'cause parents were complaining to city commissioners that it was frightening their children going past on the school bus early in the morning and witnessing all the drunks and fighting and prostitutes out front."

Gabrielle: "You've been in there, haven't you?"

"Oh, I don't know about that," Popcorn Joe said, with a cheeky twinkle in his eyes. Then: "I'm going to drop you here. Do as Johnny-Johnny suggested."

Gabrielle jumped out the front, then I slid the side panel open and jumped out the back.

"Remember, fins to the left, you and Gabrielle to the right. Later!" Popcorn Joe said.

Gabrielle and I walked along the Overseas Highway, passing a few folk riding bicycles, then hung a right on Cross Street. It was mostly overcast but hot, and we walked down to 5th, then turned left and headed through a fugue of marl dust past Key West Brick & Tile, where two life-size statues of naked men were on prominent display. Obviously there is a calling for that in Cayo Hueso.

We carried on past Second Hand Sam's, lots of single-story homes sequestered behind chain-link fences on the right side of the street. Chain-link fences are a big deal in the Keys.

The sun peeked out and it would have been a glorious stroll in paradise if it weren't for the delicate task at hand. Just past Sam's, on the right, was another chain-link fence protecting a burnt-out lawn. The front yard was swimming with used bicycles and a few trikes, and was being watched over by a burnt-out hippie who looked as if he had been through the sixties more than once. A warning sign on the front gate hinted at the demeanor of the resident hound. The sign was in Spanish: *Cuidado con el Perro!* Snoozing in the shade on the front cement porch was a robust, steroidal pit bull-esque monster. Perhaps the warning sign should have really said: *One False Move And I Will Chew Your Face Off.*

Gabrielle does not see the appeal in killer dogs that

slabber, have bad dental hygiene, and are larger than a fifth grader. She had a bad experience with a pooch of similar ilk when she was in Primary Five back in Scotland.

"I don't want to go in," Gabrielle said.

"He's chained to the porch."

"I'm not going in."

"We are on assignment. Look! His owner is opening the front door and taking him inside…"

"Probably to feed him a dead chicken that was left over from last night's foray into Santeria and slake his own thirst with a bucket of blood," Gabrielle said.

The owner came back outside. He was not a hippie, rather Cuban. A *Marielito*? Was he packing, or was that a dog bone in his pocket?

Gabrielle sighed and we entered the compound. The gate CREAKED open.

"Close gate," Mr. Marielito said with a heavy accent. Not impolite, but not so friendly either. Why did he need the gate closed if vampire-dog was inside having a blood-smoothie?

"*Hola*," I said, in my lowest register. "Looking for a bike."

"How many? Two?" the *señor* said.

"No, just one," I said.

"Take look. All cheap."

Gabrielle and I did a walk-around.

Then we heard the gate go behind us. CREAK. We turned to see an even rougher sort of guy come in. He wasn't tall, but he was wiry. He was bare-chested, tanned black and was wearing a Santa's hat over long, shoulder-length hair.

Gabrielle nudged me. "Scarier than the dog," she noted.

"Need a bike," Wiry Dude said, in a deep baritone.

Mr. Marielito waved a hand at his fleet.

Gabrielle and I carried on looking, all the while keeping one eye on Mr. Marielito and the other eye on Wiry Dude.

All the bikes in the yard had been spray painted black to conceal original ownership.

Gabrielle put a hand on my elbow and guided me to the far side of the yard. Right there, perhaps not as big as Dallas, but for sure quite large, indeed, were both of our bikes.

They hadn't been spray painted black. No need for that as that's how they had come when we'd first got them as a gift from Popcorn Joe.

We heard conversation between Mr. Marielito and Wiry Dude. W.D. had found a bike he liked.

"Can I take it for a test drive?" he asked the Cuban.

"Sure."

W.D. checked the bike over thoroughly, saw that the tires wouldn't explode, that the seat was about the right height and that the handle bars wouldn't collapse down when you put pressure on them, chipping all your front teeth. He walked the bike to the gate. Opened it. CREAK. Mr. Marielito followed closely behind.

Wiry Dude climbed on the bike then he rode it about twenty yards down the street, made a turn, came back, then tried turning to the right and to the left.

He pulled up next to the gate where Mr. Marielito was camped.

"How much you want for it?"

"Fifty."

"I'll give you thirty."

"No deal."

"You do it for forty?"

"No deal."

"Not sure it's worth 50 bucks."

Wiry Dude dismounted, then knelt down and had another good hard look at the bike. Did some triage. He stood back up, faced the bike and then straddled the front tire as we all used to do as kids to straighten out the front wheel.

"Forty?" he said.

"No deal."

W.D. didn't seem to be too surprised by being turned down over his latest offer. I guess he expected it, that's why he just jumped back on the bike and rode off as fast as he could.

"*Oy-e!*" Mr. Marielito yelled. "*Puta!*"

Gabrielle and I watched Mr. Marielito sprint after Wiry

Dude, then we quickly snatched our bikes, walked them out through the front gate, closed it, CREAK, and road down to the corner of 5th Avenue, where Popcorn Joe was waiting for us in his red Ford truck. We loaded the bikes in the back, Gabrielle took up her position, shotgun, me on the overturned milk crate in the middle.

"Johnny-Johnny is scary," Gabrielle noted.

"And that's just one side of him," Popcorn Joe said.

CHAPTER THREE

Later that evening, we decided to celebrate Christmas and our adventure/getaway/escape and ride our stolen-back bikes around the Old Town looking at all the conch houses and cottages decorated with Christmas lights. Imagine doing that up in the Great White North? Having said that, theoretically, it *is* possible.

Here's how you can make it work:

Dress for polar exploration, scarves, gloves, mittens, earmuffs, ski facemasks, balaclavas, woolen long johns, alpaca-wool South-American Chullo winter hats with the fetching earflaps, clunky snowmobile boots for you, "Joan of Arctic" Sorels for the little lady, snow boots from Wal-Mart for the kids, and don't forget the hand warmer down the back of your underwear. Then you need to take the bicycles down from where they are hanging upside down in the garage, pump up the tires with last year's Christmas present, your Black & Decker AirStation and off you go.

*But...*that idea is not so very prudent what with there being snow and ice on the roads and it being a minus freeze-your-tits-off wind chill, so you opt for option #2—vehicular conveyance.

You get everyone out the front door and lined up outside by the SUV (there's no room to park the SUV in the garage because that's where you keep the snowmobiles, the snow blower, the George Foreman "15-serving outdoor grill," and your wife's sexy, sporty, cherry, two-door convertible, which she NEVER uses in winter, not because it's a convertible, rather on account of the body being made of fiberglass and if she even breathes on the accelerator on an icy winter road it spins with more revolutions than an Eastern European child's dreidel).

Despite the family being outfitted like the Michelin Man (or the Lake Michigan Man), they are freezing and imploring you to "Hurry up and open the door!" Your wife discreetly throws in a "damn door," just above the hearing range of most children, but within easy reach of small dogs. You thrust the beeper at the car as one who fences would attempt a deceptive lunge, and endeavor to BEEP the doors open on the SUV.

But nothing happens.

You BEEP again. Nothing. Now your youngest, the one with the hearing of a small dog, implores you to "Open the damn door!"

Frantic, but not wanting to tarnish your image of *the great protector, and the even greater provider*, you insert the key into the lock on the driver's side, but the lock's frozen and won't turn. But you are a clever man and prepared for this: you have one of those little de-icers that look like a key and can be inserted into the lock to make your life of a better quality. That's when you realize that the nifty de-icer is inside the DAMN CAR!

But you are not a quitter, you light a match (now thankful that you hadn't given up smoking...you've saved that impossibility for the New Year's resolution) and hold the match under the key and give that a go.

It works!

You pile all the kids in the backseat, mutter "oh, shit!" under your breath because you've forgotten grandma! You rush back inside the house, and grandma tells you to piss off because even though she's dressed for success, she's been hitting the Manischewitz, and she's not going anywhere anytime soon. You hustle back out to the wife and the kids. The kids are wearing their ski goggles even though it's night, and now they're fogged. Your wife tells you that the windows are frosted over and you need to go scrape them. The scraping process is slow and you would like to go back in and get some of granny's hooch and pour it on the windshield to de-ice, but grandma is in fact your mother-in-law and she would personally take pleasure in slowly incising your scrotum and exhuming your testicles, one by one, if you so much as gesture toward her guilty pleasure, and you certainly can't do what you did *last* Christmas, which was pour *hot* water on the windshield as that was damn foolish—and costly. So you scrape like a maven.

Your scraper breaks so you turn to that Mariah Carey CD, her Greatest Hits, as you are now less of a fan since her meltdown last New Year's Eve when the ball dropped, plus that recent incident with the bodyguard.

And you scrape.

The CD works better than the scraper. Was cheaper, too, what with you purchasing it at the tag sell on the other side of the tracks, by the high school.

Finally finished with the scraping, only two and a quarter hours have elapsed since you suggested "Let's take a drive and look at all the Christmas lights!" Then, you were a hero. Now you are a schmuck. Your youngest, the one with the small-dog hearing, now needs the toilet. This is a BIG problem as you will have to unwrap your mummified child from the snowsuit, use a hair dryer on the goggles and check on grandma and find out why she's now lying face down on the kitchen floor crooning "Hallelujah!"

Finally, back outside, everyone is back onboard and eager to get this party started. You say something poignant, like: "Wait till you see the Bueller's house!"

You push the ignition button to fire up the gas guzzling SUV, but there will be no gas guzzling tonight.

The battery is dead.

And you're going nowhere.

But wait!

You didn't buy this big house with the life-sucking mortgage and all the toys by being a stupid fuckwit, you have hatched a new plan: you are going to put the beast in neutral, release the handbrake, depress the clutch, rocket down your long, long *private* drive and POP THE CLUTCH.

33

"Sure, you all laughed at me when I said we wanted an SUV with a stick! But look who's got the last laugh now!"

Just before you come to the main road that runs by your property and the long, long private drive, you jerk your knee back and pop the clutch, the engine COUGHS...COUGHS again, virtually EXPLODES, and you blow through the three-foot barrier of snow the snowplow has blocked your drive with when it plowed the street to a glaze, and your gas-guzzling SUV, with the 420 horses and the eight cup holders, comes to skidding rest in the middle of the well-plowed street.

DEAD.

Shoulda, woulda, coulda parked it in the garage.

"Daa-ad?" your youngest son says. "I can see my breath! In the car!"

"Not now, son, daddy's thinking..." In reality, you're wondering how the fuck a $70,000 vehicle with overhead airbags and a nifty tow package could have become Ice Station Zebra so quickly.

"Dad?"

"Not now!"

"Daa-ad???"

"WHAT IS IT?"

"I wanna know, Dad..."

"WANNA KNOW WHAT!"

"How does the man who drives the snowplow get to work?"

* * *

Meanwhile, 1632-miles to the south, down in Key West, FL, not quite the USA, the temperature hit 82 today, and now it's plummeted to a merry, merry warm and civilized 77 degrees. Gabrielle and I have thrown on our only remaining pair of shorts, me, my trusty "northern sleep shirt" with a small-mouthed bass painted on it, Gabrielle a sweatshirt with WISCONSIN BADGERS in fetching red letters, and we're already pedaling through the Old Town, eyes wide with child-like wonder, simply besotted with all the glorious Christmas

34

decorations and lights.

"Smell that?" Gabrielle asks.

"Night blooming jasmine?" I answer.

"Don't know…bit early for that?"

"Whatever it is, it's intoxicating."

"Can't believe we're back in Cayo Hueso."

NOTE: Okay, northern folk, I'm not rubbing your nose in it by telling you all this, just cajoling you to "Come on down!" And bring granny, she's never met an alcoholic bevvy she doesn't like, she'll fit right in.

But wait!

Before we do anything else, Gabrielle and I head over to where we used to live in Aronovitz Lane to pay a visit to Mr. Leroy. Aronovitz Lane is alive with Christmas lights and floral fragrances, and the scene tugs at our heartstrings. We wished we still lived in this quirky lane with all our interesting neighbors like the Bahamian gentleman with the wooden leg.

We pull up in front of Mrs. Grace's. The cottage is dark. No Christmas lights. No Mr. Leroy sleeping on the front porch. What's going on? We ring the doorbell, but no one's home. She must be out with family.

"Let's come back later," Gabrielle says, looking up and down the lane, and we climb back on our bikes.

Just before we exit Aronovitz Lane, we see a figure bending over in between two of the cottages. It's an old crone. She's placing out food for cats on a piece of wood, and cats are slowly emerging from hiding places. The crone looks skittish and wild. She throws furtive looks our way. Just like the feral cats she's feeding.

"I see everything is much the same in the lane," Gabrielle notes.

We pedal out of Aronovitz Lane, swing left on Angela, then turn left on Duval Street. Duval is a procession of casually dressed souls, Christmas Duval-crawlers, some wearing Santa hats or antlers, no Michelin Man or Lake Michigan Man here, although some rascal is wearing what appears to be a faux stuffed turkey on his head. Why not? Let's celebrate! If you can't be a little colorful (read: weird) in Key West, where can you be?

Speaking of, well, weird, just to our left is a snake wrangler dude with a big snake draped around his neck. Now he's draping it around two co-eds' necks. They titter and shriek, and somehow find this appealing and funny. It appears the snake does not share their enthusiasm.

Now Snake Wrangler Dude takes a photo of them and they pay him, what I would think could have been put toward the purchase of alcohol. But who am I to judge? If a deadly constricting reptile coiling itself around your throat floats your boat, then go for it.

We pedal on, and in front of us, motoring along, is one of the Old Town Trolleys. It, too, is decorated for Christmas with Christmas ribbons and garlands and bright-colored lights around the roof.

We carry on all the way down Duval till we hit Caroline. Most businesses on Duval have Christmas decorations, even the Israeli camera store, and we don't think we've ever seen such a glorious display anywhere. We hang a right on Caroline. To our left is the Curry Mansion. Families out with their broods, have de-biked here and are taking Christmas long-stick selfies with the Curry Mansion and its dazzling display of gingerbread men and lollipops in the background.

At the corner of Caroline and Elizabeth, we now catch up to the Conch Tour Train. It has a full load of yuletide revelers. Christmas music is spilling out and the revelers are knocking back eggnog with commendable commitment. The Conch Tour Train would not be a bad alternative for those of you who drove down to our 1-mile-by-4-mile island in your gas-guzzling, diesel, polluting Hummers, or such.

Caroline Street, Simonton, Elizabeth, Peacon Lane, William, Margaret, Grinnell, Francis, Fleming, Eaton, Southard, even Solares Hill, we pedal up and down them all, working the grid like Santa would if he moonlighted for *Miami CSI*, gazing at all the palm trees sporting hundreds of white lights and all the conch homes absolutely aglow with the best

Kmart has to offer.

Then we head over to the Conch Republic Seafood Company and stroll along the harbor walk, walking our bikes, all the way over to Turtle Kraals and the Half Shell Raw Bar, and we look at all the boats that have been decorated with Christmas lights, as well. And may I be the first to tell you, the boats, yachts, sail-and-power are awesome!

We spy one boat, a Hatteras 65-footer, by the looks of it, that is veritably dripping in twinkly blue-and-white lights from the top of the flying bridge down to near the waterline, covering the transom and the swim platform. Does Al Subarsky have a boat we didn't know about?

We spy another boat. This one is covered in lights, as well, and they form a massive shark wearing a Santa hat. So cool.

Then there's a boat that looks like a fire engine, and another that looks like a choo-choo train. From this distance, you don't see the boat, only the fire engine and train. So very well done.

Next year, we'll be sure to take in the Christmas Boat Parade, which we missed this year as it traditionally takes place a few weeks' earlier.

"Deck the hulls…" Gabrielle sings.

"Hulls…ha-ha, funny!" I say and we both laugh.

Now filled with the glow that we all used to enjoy at Christmas as children, Gabrielle and I pedal back over to Aronovitz Lane, to find, hug and cuddle our beloved Mr. Leroy, but he's not out on his favorite seat on the front porch; however, there is a light on deep within the conch cottage.

"Mrs. Grace probably has him up on her lap…"

"Or he's sprawled in the middle of her bed like he used to do at our dump, Villa Alberto."

"We'll come by tomorrow morning when everyone's up and got the yawning out of the way."

* * *

We're at the Bull now. You knew we'd somehow end up here, didn't you? And, no, we didn't chain our bikes to that offending pole. We stuck them in the shed over by the Conch Seafood Farm where Popcorn Joe keeps his PRETTY GOOD POPCORN cart.

Our favorite seat by the window was taken, so we're sitting in the back corner, over there where the door leads out onto Caroline.

Up on stage, the band has just returned from their smoke-a-joint break, and giddily kick off their next set with the Key West classic: "I'D RATHER BE HERE, DRINKING A BEER, THAN FREEZING MY ASS IN THE NORTH."

And, yes, Popcorn Joe is here with us. Popcorn Joe is fleshing out a bit more background about Johnny-Johnny.

"Johnny-Johnny is British, but from Northern Ireland."

"What's his surname?"

"His last name? That would be Goodchild."

"Goodchild," Gabrielle said. "That was the name given to an illegitimate child born in a convent or a monastery."

"That's a new one on me," Popcorn Joe said. "Anyway, Johnny-Johnny joined the French Foreign Legion when he was seventeen…became a desert rat."

"Thought you had to be older than that?"

"The French Foreign Legion was not big on detail back then. They wanted warm bodies and they wanted you young when you could be molded, or older and with issues, so you could be broken and rebuilt.

"Johnny-Johnny had to make his way to France from Northern Ireland down to Aubagne near Marseilles at his own expense. He went down there and simply knocked on the door. That's the only way you can join, knock on the door, show your passport, ask to join. See if they let you in."

"Did he speak any French?" Gabrielle asked.

"Not a word."

"Then, how did he learn?"

"They beat it into you through immersion classes and intimidation. Motivation comes in the form of 30 push-ups and being punched."

"So they'd take anyone?" I asked.

"They're not about to take you on if you've murdered someone or have drug trafficking offenses. Truth be told, the type of people they get are not big on offering too much about themselves. Nobody who presents themselves at Aubagne is going to be an angel. Half of them will be from eastern Europe where, frankly, nobody keeps a record of anything anyway..."

Gabrielle leaned forward toward Popcorn Joe and whispered: "Giuseppe, some guy's been standing in the doorway for the last five minutes watching us and listening to everything we say."

Popcorn Joe jumped up. We thought he was going to get in the guy's face, but he didn't, rather he shook his hand.

"Let me introduce you to Johnny-Johnny," he said.

"You look completely different," Gabrielle noted.

"That's the idea, *Madame*."

Johnny-Johnny did not have his Santa Hat, or the long black hair underneath, indeed, his head was shaven clean and shiny.

"What happened to the long, black hair?" Gabrielle said.

"Wig," Johnny-Johnny answered in that same baritone voice.

I think Gabrielle and I just sat there with our mouths hanging open, partly on account of how different Johnny-Johnny looked, and partly on account of his black T-shirt, which said in white lettering: STEP ASIDE COFFEE, THIS IS A JOB FOR ALCOHOL.

No, shit! I was thinking.

"My shout, Johnny..." I said.

"It's Johnny-Johnny."

"Okay, my shout, Johnny-Johnny. *Qu'est-ce que tu veux boire?*" I asked.

"*Donne-moi un Pernot, s'il te plaît.*"

As I rose and aimed for the bar, I turned and gave Gabrielle a wide-eyed look.

I returned with Johnny-Johnny's pastis.

"Can I ask you a question, Johnny-Johnny?" Gabrielle said.

"Indeed, *Madame*."

"Why Johnny-Johnny?"

"*Mon Dieu, Madame*, no one's ever asked me that before! "In the Legion, the name 'Johnny' is sort of 'Pal' or 'Bud' or like 'Jimmy' in Glasgow. I never responded quickly because my French was not so very good, so they had to repeat. 'Johnny!' became 'Johnny!'…'Johnny!' And that became 'Johnny-Johnny' as you would expect. In reality, I have superior hearing."

"Were the qualifications tough?"

"For me, no, *Madame*. Just the teeth…"

"Teeth?"

"You can't have more than 4 to 6 teeth missing…"

"Four to six?"

"It depends on the quality of the teeth."

(Well, Dear Reader, may I just utter "Holy shit!" here? We had never come across anyone like Johnny-Johnny in our life—although we have met many folk in Key West with more than *four to six* teeth missing.

This is one of the HUGE draws to Key West, I would say: Key West is a melting pot, in many ways a dumping ground. And you will meet some of the most colorful people you've ever run across in your life here. You will NEVER be bored in Key West if you take the time to engage others, *not judge*, just engage, listen, enjoy…even learn.)

"That bloke who stole your bikes. Stuff like that really blows wind up my arse. FUCKING BASTARD, SHOULD'VE RIPPED HIS FACE OFF WHEN I HAD THE CHANCE!"

Johnny-Johnny stopped. Looked over at us. Gabrielle and I had slid our chairs back a few feet. Popcorn Joe was enjoying the outburst.

"*Pardon, Madame*, for the language, and *un autre pardon* for the outburst."

"Johnny-Johnny doesn't need anger management," Popcorn Joe mused. "He just needs people to stop pissing him off."

CHAPTER FOUR

The next morning, we awoke a bit late. No, not the alcohol from the night before, thanks for asking, just unbridled, unrepentant, sloth-like laziness. Popcorn Joe had gone off to the gym, so Gabrielle and I showered...no, not together, but thanks for asking, and then we pedaled over to the waterfront to the Cuban Coffee Queen for a cup of thunder and some Cuban bread.

A small runt of a dog was nearby, chasing its tail. I observed the pooch, enjoying his antics. "Dogs are easily amused," I surmised.

"You've been watching a dog chase its tail," Gabrielle said.

I went up to the counter and ordered. When I returned, Gabrielle was laughing hysterically.

"What?" I said.

"We have a big problem. I just received a text from my brother in Scotland. Remember when my mum was here the last time?"

"Yes."

"And I showed her a text from a friend back home?"

"Yes."

"And she wanted to know what 'WTF' meant?"

"Yes, and you were embarrassed and told her it meant **Wow That's Fantastic!**"

"That's the problem, she's been texting my brother, all her friends, and the rest of the family saying WTF? ... WTF? ... WTF?"

We finished our cup of thunder and, now wired like the national grid, hopped on our bikes and cruised over to Aronovitz Lane. We biked past the Green Parrot and, no, we didn't go in (thought about it though), then turned into the lane. On the left was Mrs. Grace's one-story conch cottage. Still no Mr. Leroy snoozing on the front porch.

"Where is the little fellow?" I said to Gabrielle.

"I'm going to go ring the doorbell. Not liking this…"

Gabrielle de-biked and walked up the steps to the front porch.

"Look," she said, pointing at a range of flower pots on the porch. "All of Mrs. Grace's flowers are dead."

Gabrielle rang the doorbell.

Nothing.

She rang the doorbell again.

Still nothing.

Gabrielle turned to walk away, when the front door opened. Standing there was a woman in her thirties, dressed like a nurse.

"Whatever you're selling, I'm not buying!" said in a not so neighborly manner.

"We're looking for Mrs. Grace."

"Who?"

"Mrs. Grace, she lives here."

"I would have to disagree with that. I live here and I'm not Mrs. Grace." On this, a dead ringer for "Pauli" in the *Rocky* movies appeared behind Nurse Ratched. He was unshaven, paunchy, and in a stained, sleeveless undershirt. Looked as if he'd been up all night getting the meth lab up and running.

"She's dead," Pauli said. "We live here now."

"Mrs. Grace passed away?"

"That's what I just said…"

Oh, boy.

Gabrielle and I were in shock. Mrs. Grace was the

quintessential neighbor. An all-around class act.

"When did she pass away?"

"Dunno, last year…"

"Where's Mr. Leroy?"

"Who?"

"The cat. The cat that lived here."

"Don't know nothing about a cat…"

And on that, Pauli pulled Nurse Ratched back inside, presumably to fire up the meth lab, and then he shut the door. We heard two locks and a chain go. Then, the A/C shunt on…or it could have been an industrial-strength vibrator.

They sound about the same.

I'm told.

Gabrielle walked back down the steps and came over to me.

"A nurse who doesn't look after her plants…"

And then no words were said.

Mrs. Grace was no more.

Mr. Leroy had crossed over the Rainbow Bridge.

We were gutted.

CHAPTER FIVE

Gabrielle and I spent the rest of the day looking for an apartment. If the loss of Mrs. Grace and Mr. Leroy weren't enough of a burden to bear, the hunt for an apartment was.

We were in a decidedly somber mood. Somewhat uncharacteristic.

Perhaps, those of you who have read my original Key West book remember us hunting doggedly for a place to call home when we'd first arrived on the island? Well, doing it all over again, where we know a little about how it all works, and we know the layout of the island, was still not helping.

Prices have gone up.

A lot.

And possible digs (read: *cheap dumps*), such as our aforementioned Villa Alberto (a place that we could afford, and fix up a bit, because, well, it was a dump), just don't exist anymore, thanks to gentrification, and owners turning the apartments into holiday rentals to gouge and make the big bucks during high season. This is one of the reasons Key West is now #3 on the list of popular Florida destinations after Walt Disney World and Miami/Miami Beach.

Now, we will not only have to put in the legwork to find comfortable accommodation, we will have to get *creative*.

The first time around, we had been led by ignorant bliss and the glow that had come from jumping off the hamster wheel of life and having a go at a dream. At least now, we have experience under our Tommy Bahama belts. Did I just say Tommy Bahama belts? We would never lay out good beer money for a Tommy Bahama belt. Perhaps a Ron Jon belt or a tie-dye belt or an old rope or NO BELT AT ALL.

So where do you begin to look for a place to stay in Key West? Well, if you only have a bicycle, how about Key West! Not Geiger Key, not Big Coppitt, not Sugarloaf, not Cudjoe, or Summerland, not Ramrod, and certainly not Big Pine. Nothing wrong with these other Keys, they're all unfathomably picturesque, but we only have bicycles, remember?

If there's ever been a place where you have to turn over every rock, and coconut, Key West is it. But, first things first. This is not for the faint of heart, this apartment hunting. You need to bring CAFFEINE INTO THE EQUATION.

We popped my laptop in my backpack, climbed on our bikes and pedaled over to the Cuban Coffee Queen on Margaret. We ordered *dos* buccis and *dos* Pan Cubanos and sat in the sun. Total $6, the sun was free, as it is daily in Key West.

We sipped and gnawed. I pulled my Hewlett Packard laptop (with the annoying keyboard and temperamental comma key) out of my backpack, and fired the little blighter up. Then we moved into the shade. Couldn't see anything on the screen in the streaming sun.

"We're sitting here at the end of December, in shorts," Gabrielle said. "Last week we were in Wisconsin, freezing our bahookies off."

"I checked the temperature up north just before we came out," I said. "They're having a heat wave for this time of year…"

"A heat wave?"

"Yes, 36 degrees and raining."

We sipped and chomped.

I was approaching caffeine lift-off, so I Googled FURNISHED APARTMENTS FOR RENT, KEY WEST, and the first place that came up, oddly, was in Aronovitz Lane where we used to live!

"It's a sign," Gabrielle said. "I loved everything about living in Aronovitz Lane, except for the hurricane and our troglodyte of a landlord."

"What about Pig Man, he lived in the lane?"

"Oh, yeah, I forgot about Pig Man. He was okay, his pot-belly pig stank, though."

"What about our neighbor Snake?"

"Snake was cool."

"So, do you really think this is a sign?"

"I do."

And guess what? It *was* a sign, and the sign had letters that "would soar a thousand feet high," just like Lulu sang, only this sign read: DON'T EVEN THINK ABOUT IT!

Here's why: **Cozy and comfortable 2BR/2BA home located close to Duval Street. New stainless steel French style refrigerator, gas range, dishwasher, garbage disposal and microwave. 786 square feet of living space with very efficient layout, recently painted. Rent fee is $3,000 per month with a 12-month lease – first month's rent, two months' security deposit, credit and background checks will be required. Maximum 2 occupants; a small pet can be considered with appropriate deposit. Tenant responsible for all utilities.**

Oh, wow, oh, gee. That's only $42,000 (not counting utilities) that you would have to fork out for the first year…if you *don't* want a small pet, then it's even more.

"Who can afford that?" Gabrielle said. "That is a glaring example of sky-rocketing property taxes driving the rent."

A sign, indeed.

Next, we found this:

2-bedroom, 2-bath apartment over by the airport, only $2400 per month. Unfurnished. First, last and security deposit. No drugs, no pets, no wasters. Available March 1st. Beautiful condo, close to everything, great neighborhood.

First of all, this does us no good, as we need a place yesterday, already, and second of all, this place is NOT close to everything if you don't work at the airport, the DMV, or that oriental restaurant where they dice and slice everything with menacing sabres, mid-air, right in front of your very nose.

Also not close to *everything* if you don't have a car.

Next possibility: **KEY WEST, 1-bedroom, 410 square feet, near all the bars, no drugs, no drunks. First, last and security deposit required with good references. $1950/mo.** Okay, what's wrong with this picture other than the size of the unit and the extortionate price? *Near all the bars…no drugs, no drunks.* Pul-lease.

We move on:

Studio apartment for rent off of Flagler Ave. $1400 + 200 for utilities. No parking, laundry on site, utilities included. First, last and security, due at signing. No pets, no drugs, no drama queens. (**NOT making this up!)

Who writes these? Is the employee taking the Ad, just as mental as the person calling it in? Utilities $200 per month…*utilities included!!!* No *drama queens*, that would rule out not only the pick of the Key West litter, but most of the litter itself.

We searched for the next hour, every Classified, every single possibility that we could come up with online, and guess what? We couldn't afford anything unless we rented a spare room or did a house share, something like: **OWN ROOM, SHARED TOILET, SHARED BATH, PETS OK, CRACKHEADS AND FOOT-PROSTITUTES CONSIDERED. $200/week.** Okay, perhaps we misread that one, but that was the subtext we were getting from the Ad.

Now, as we were caffeine rich and higher than a kite, we went to Craigslist to come down, as we all know how reliable (and safe) Craigslist is:

Downtown Condo—Going away from Key West. Will rent for 6 months. Good deal for you…good deal for me. **1 bed, 1 bath, balcony, kitchen…bar, restaurant and band downstairs. Enough room for couple (or four close friends). Queen bed. Sit on the balcony and watch and listen to the band on the dance floor down below. Maybe you will just go downstairs and join in on the festivities for the true, authentic Key West experience. Seconds**

away from Mallory Square and pier, a beach is three blocks away, Duval is just a few feet away, museums and all the attractions nearby. All new tile and fresh paint. Chromecast anything onto the 42" flat screen TV. All furnished. Full Kitchen, and eat and/or use anything in the fridge or in any of the cabinets if not spoiled. Must feed the cat ("Higgins").

Smoking on Balcony only, please (Fresh Paint). If you like the nightlife, this is for you... No taxi cabs, no late night travel problems. Crawl off Duval and up the stairs to crash in your very own Duval Street pad. If you go to sleep before 1am bring earplugs and a blindfold. LOL. This place rocks all day and night. $3000 per month, first, last, security. I will leave money for cat food.

Well, this is just too good to pass up, what with it coming with a built-in cat. And we don't have to worry about the *no drunks* part, because with a rent of $3000 per month there will be no beer money left over.

But wait! There's one more Ad. In any other part of the world, a mobile home might not make it to the top of your list, but Key West is not any other place in the world. Plus, many mobile homes in the Keys are right on a canal or small beach, and they are wonderful places to live. So there!

MOBILE HOME, 1 bed, one bath, Big Pine Key, first, last, security. $1200/mo.

Hmmm, Big Pine Key, that's almost 30 miles away from Key West. A bit of a commute, even with an F-14. Plus, there was no thumbnail picture, just the symbol of a great big marijuana leaf.

Okay, time to move on.

But wait! Check this out. It's perfect for those who aren't afraid of drinking all night long in the Duval Street bars and then taking command of a steering wheel attached to a dinghy: **Large boat for long rent, 60-footer, can sleep in different cabins up to 8 people. All utilities (110 v power from big solar panel, 4G internet, etc.). Vessel stays on dead 1500lb** anchor near KW downtown: 10-15 minutes on brand new motor dinghy and you are at the center of the summer paradise. Free fish, daily swimming and marvelous sunsets would be totally yours!

Just so you know, which you probably already do, a boat is not so very large once you have eight people sleeping on it, unless it's the *Queen Mary*.

And 10-15 minutes by motor dinghy. Where is this LARGE boat exactly? Would you take command of a motor dinghy with seven other fucked-up souls on a pitch-black, blowy night?

Would you be the designated driver?

Didn't you come to Key West to be the designated *drinker*?

Those 10-15 minutes could have you starring in your very own *Poseidon Adventure*.

* * *

"You know what?" Gabrielle said.

"What?"

"Why don't we just ride around the Old Town later and see if we come across any For Rent signs. That way, at least we're on the right island where we want to live."

"Well, you *have vision*...just like Butch Cassidy."

Gabrielle said: "Glad they have a place like the Cuban Coffee Queen. How did Starbucks ever get a stranglehold on the island, anyway?"

"Y'know, if we lived up on the mainland or somewhere in the Great White North, or back in the UK, we might go to a Starbucks..."

"For the Chocolate Chunk Muffin..."

"Exactly, but if there was a little mom & pop café, we would patronize them to give them the custom, instead."

"There's three Starbucks in Key West now..."

"Three!"

"And are you ready? There are over 13,000 in the US of A, and remember what they say about London?"

"What's that?"

"In London, you are never more than 20 feet from a rat, and never more than 50 feet from a Caramel Macchiato. There are 246 Starbucks just in London."

"And you know all this…because?"

"Because I read."

"Is that what you do when I go to bed before you?"

"No, then I eat chocolate…"

Okay, Dear Reader, let me ask you this: How did a chain ever get its sticky little fingers into Key West? Isn't part of Key West's charm all that represents originality, home-grown and independent and, well, mom & pop establishments? Or, as is the case in Key West, pop & pop establishments. Remember Fast Buck Freddie's?

In Key West, we want places like Eden House and the Pineapple Apartments and Blue Heaven and Pepe's and B.O.'s and the Half Shell Raw Bar and Better Than Sex and Turtle Kraals and not the big chains. I could go on. No, I mean I could really go on. When we visit the Keys, especially Key West, WE WANT DIFFERENT. We want unique. We want quirky. One-of-a-kind.

Perhaps we even want a hint of backwater, foreign intrigue and (whispered) *danger*. That's why we hang out at the Bull & Whistle and Rick's and Two Friends, and all the neat places that you may know, but I'm forgetting to list right now. If you are wondering where the "danger" is here, then walk the back streets, late. Or pay a visit to the Gent's in a few of the Duval Street bars.

We want bacchanal, funky Key West and a step backward in time, not a step into the future in the form of Disney World, or the Pokémon GO Frappuccino at your local Starbucks.

* * *

Okay, we're still at the Cuban Coffee Queen. Popcorn Joe has come over on his rollerblades and now the three of us are sitting in the sun, Gabrielle and me, legs outstretched, wearing our flip-flops, getting the all important flippies' or sandals' tan with the two white chevrons, Popcorn Joe, legs outstretched, still wearing his rollerblades. We've treated Popcorn Joe to a bucci and ordered two more for ourselves.

Popcorn Joe tells us: "Been asking around if anyone knows any apartments. Come by 'Sunset' tonight and maybe I'll have some news."

We tell Popcorn Joe that we will do just that: pop by the pier tonight, then he rises, and says: "Going to Fausto's to get cat food and kitty litter. Later!" and he rollerblades up in the direction of Fleming.

Gabrielle and I look at each other. We've each had two, count them, two buccis, our eyes are dilated like Marty Feldman's, and we are ready to lift off like the Space Shuttle. Fortified, and I mean *fortified*, we spring back on our bikes and hit the streets.

"Let's go up and down the streets like we did on Christmas Day," Gabrielle suggests.

So that's what we do. We jump on our bikes and start to pedal like hell.

Over by the library, we spot our first FOR RENT sign. It's outside a two-story conch house with no paint, but lots of Dade County pine. We study the house and like what we see, then we read the sign and like what we see even more: **One bedroom, $800/mo., pets okay, no smokers, no drugs. First, last, security.**

Gabrielle and I look at each other again. Our eyes are even wider now, like an owl on bath salts. "Wow," I say, as I have quite the way with words.

"Guess it pays to just bike around. Some people like to keep it simple."

"Simple," I say.

"Let's go knock on the door," Gabrielle says.

KNOCK. KNOCK. KNOCK.

We wait. No answer. We wait some more.

"Maybe no one's home."

"Maybe they're home, but they're deaf."

We knock again, but no one answers.

"Maybe they're home, but they're tied up?"

"You mean as in a home invasion or kinky sex?"

"No! Tied up, as in *busy.*"

So we wait, and lo and behold the door opens and standing there is the love child of Truman Capote and the Church Lady (and I mean that in the nicest way). Short, rounded, cherubic, flushed, beaming, dressed in a rather flamboyant kaftan, and barefoot with hairy toes. And those glasses.

"Good day," Love Child chirps. "Are you here about the puppies?"

"No," Gabrielle says, "We're here about the one bedroom."

"The one bedroom!" Love Child absolutely gushes. "*Allez!* Come in *mes amis.* Come. Come. Come. May I offer you each a bucci?"

French Canadian, I'm thinking, that French accent and patois that Parisians can't quite grasp.

"We're f-f-f-fine," I stutter, on the verge of levitating.

Our future landlord is certifiable, but we've had worse in Key West (that prick Mr. Tosser, for one) and are not put off.

Love Child leads us into the depths of the house. It's dark and stuffy. I glance over at Gabrielle. Our eyes are so dilated from the buccis, we can see in the dark, and we like what we see. The place is a bit like the apartment in *La Cage aux Folles.*

Love Child gives us a thorough tour of his house. "This is the kitchen and this is the dining room and this is the bathroom and this is the laundry room…"

Love Child has a distinctive theatrical accent, sort of mid-Atlantic sandwiched between a splash of West End and dash of Broadway, and he smells faintly of gin…a good gin I would have to say if I knew about those things, which I don't.

Love Child smiles and I think I can just make out—in a stab of mote-filled sunshine streaming through louvered-shuttered windows—perfect teeth, but not his own. *Veneers or implants,* I'm thinking.

Now, we have come to a narrow wooden stairway leading

up to the next level. "Up here," LC purrs, and he leads the way, one hand holding a large key, both arms outstretched like Boris Karloff.

And we climb.

The stairs CREAK, then CREAK again, and again, and again, and I can't get a certain scene from a Hitchcock movie out of my mind. I glance at Gabrielle and I know we're both thinking the same thing: *Glad we've already showered.*

Twelve steps up we come to a landing with a heavy wooden door. LC enters the key in the lock and swings the door open.

"Et voilà!" he enthuses, now sounding like Dominique the Catman.

Inside we see light flooding the room from a Velux window. In the corner, an A/C unit protrudes from the wall as if it's trying to gain further access and get out of the scorching sun.

"Your new *domain*," LC says, as a sommelier presenting a fine wine might do at one of Key West's fine-dining restaurants, say, El Siboney or Café Marquesa. And yes, yes, yes, and *oui, oui, oui*, these places don't have a sommelier, but I never get to use the word and, well, I just had to put it in…

Gabrielle and I enter what we hope will be our new home, after all, the price is right, it's on the right island, in the Old Town *and* near the library. Our new landlord might be a colorful character slash whacko, but colorful characters made Key West what it is today, a flaming cuckoo's nest, and we're damn proud to be part of that nest.

Love Child flips a switch with a theatrical gesture and the room fills with inset ceiling lights. In the middle of the room is a king-size bed, not a UK king-size, which in reality is an American queen, but a proper king, the size of a heliport.

About now, it's dawning on Gabrielle and me that it is somewhat strange to enter the front door of an apartment right into the bedroom, but then that's Key West for you. Many apartments and flats in Key West have been created out of thin air in attics or out-buildings, even stairwells. You may remember when Gabrielle and I lived at the Pineapple Apartments, we lived up in the attic, and the commode was in the middle of the living room, I'm not talking about the bathroom being in the middle, I'm talking about the porcelain bus.

Love Child points with an index finger. The finger is long and boney, something that E.T. would be proud to call his own, or, at the least, phone home about. Gabrielle and I turn. Off to one side is another door. This must lead to the rest of the apartment, we reckon: the ensuite, the kitchen, the living room, perhaps even an over-the-rooftops' view.

"What's through there?" I so cleverly ask.

Love Child goes to the door, tosses his head back and throws open the door the way a magician displays the scantily clad assistant he has just cut in half.

And we're party to another *"Et voilà!"*

Through the door we can make out—nothing.

"It's a closet!" I blurt out.

"Bingo!" Love Child spouts.

"It's a nice closet," I say.

"So where's the kitchen?" Gabrielle asks.

"Downstairs," Love Child says. "Same place as it was before."

"And the bathroom?"

"Next to the kitchen…"

"And the living room?"

"That's down there too. We share!"

"Thought you were renting a one-bedroom apartment?" Gabrielle says.

"Did I say that? I don't remember saying that?"

"But the sign…" I say, not wanting to be left out.

"The sign says ONE BEDROOM, does it not?"

I look at Gabrielle and Gabrielle looks at me. Now not knowing what to say, I say the only thing I can think of.

"Can we see the puppies?"

CHAPTER SIX

We are down at Mallory Square now.

The sun is setting, it's warm and balmy, and the entire waterside is a throbbing crush of holiday revelers showing too much sin, I mean skin, and carrying open containers of firewater. Fish Man is working the fringes, and families with small children are fleeing Fishman and crossing the footbridge to enjoy Dominique and his Flying Cats. Thank goodness for the Catman because apart from his show, and a few bags of popcorn from Popcorn Joe, there isn't so much for small children to do in Party Central, except to educate them and show them living-breathing examples of how they will end up on the wrong side of adulthood if they don't study, behave and help with the dishes.

"Freddy! Put down your iPad and look over there. That's a waster."

"What's a waster, mommy?"

"It's someone who didn't buckle down in school and now does not give a shit."

"Where do they live, mommy?"

"They live on eBay."

"Amy! Stop texting. See that slinky woman with too much blush and the fishnet stockings standing on the corner? That's a fuck-for-cash."

"What's a fuck-for-cash, mommy?"

"It's someone who skipped school and has dedicated their life to faking orgasms. That alone makes people think they're not getting screwed, even while they're doing it."

"Where do they live, mommy?"

"They live in state capitals and Washington, D.C."

"What about Hollywood, mommy?"

"Yes, they live there, too, darling."

"See, Freddy, look over there. That's what we call a transvestite."

"What's a transvestite, mommy?"

"A transvestite is someone with slim hips and good fashion sense."

"Where do they live, mommy?"

"They live among us."

"And Amy, do you remember that white conch house on upper Duval with the cerise shutters?"

"The one with the little firecracker blonde sitting on the front porch?"

"That's the one, snuggums, that's called a brothel."

"What's a brothel, mommy?"

"It's where ugly men with poor hygiene go to suck on a woman's toes."

"Where are they located, mommy?"

"They're located near airports, on the main roads leading to theme parks and, of course, here. So, children, isn't this better than the Space Center, a ride on the Hogwarts Express, or the old Shamu and the Splash Zone?"

* * *

Popcorn Joe is laughing and handing two bags of fluffy kernels to a handsome couple. Popcorn Joe watches them toddle off in the direction of Will Soto and his tightrope (as it's almost time to moon the schooner *Wolf,* or one of the other sunset cruises, and one mustn't tarry).

Popcorn Joe turns to us: "A good-looking couple, huh? They should be in the movies…"

"Isn't that Chris and Natalie from Boise?" Gabrielle asks.

"Chris and Natalie, yeah, that's them," Popcorn Joe says. "They're 'Conchs-If-I-Could.'"

"They're what?"

"They weren't born here, so they can't be Conchs…they

haven't lived here for seven years, so they can't be fresh water Conchs...but, if they could, they would, so I call them CONCHS-IF-I-COULD..."

"I can see that," I say.

"We ran into them on Duval the other night," Gabrielle says.

"Did you hear what happened to them?" I say. "Talk about movies, they starred in their own horror film."

"I'm all ears," Popcorn Joe says.

"They come to Key West whenever they get the chance. The last time they were here they wanted to celebrate the final night on the island and make it special, so they got all gussied up..."

"Gussied up?" Gabrielle says.

"Yes," I say, "gussied up. They wanted to go out for a proper dinner and drinks and splash out, instead of the usual grab a piece of street pizza and a beer."

"I'm not seeing how this can go south," Popcorn Joe says.

"Problems began when they dressed to the nines," I say. "Natalie got all sexy and slinky in an extremely revealing dress, even by Key West standards. For sure a bit more risqué than what she could get away with back home..."

"Which is part of the appeal of Key West," Popcorn Joe says. "Come down here and be someone else for a week or two, or even come down here and be who you really are."

"And Chris?" Gabrielle asks.

"He went upmarket, as well: slacks and a light long-sleeve button-up shirt instead of the standard Keys attire of shorts, T-shirt, and flip-flops. You can imagine those two clean up pretty well, so everywhere they went, they were drawing attention."

"I'm starting to see the problem," Popcorn Joe says.

After dinner at Mangoes over at 700 Duval, they hit Sloppy Joe's for a few adult beverages and to listen to Electric Circus. The place was sardine-city, but they found a spot at the bar in the corner where they could enjoy the music, tip a few, and people watch. About now, a very tanned couple at a table up by the stage, also well-dressed, started turning around and looking in their direction. No surprise here as everyone had been staring at Natalie all night long."

Popcorn Joe got a customer. He worked his magic, handing over a bulging bag, then quickly turned back to me. "Go on! Go on! Continue! I'm dying to know what happened."

"The couple kept glancing back at them, then they started to whisper and it was pretty obvious that they were talking about Chris and Natalie. Eventually, Chris mentioned this to Natalie, and then Chris and Natalie started staring back and whispering about the couple up by the stage…"

"Oh, oh," Gabrielle said.

"Chris needed to pay a visit to the Men's, but was afraid to leave Natalie alone, but Natalie said 'Just go! What could happen?' So Chris went. When he returned, he noticed right off that Natalie had a somewhat horrified look on her face.

"Natalie told Chris that the minute he left, the gentleman from the staring couple approached and asked if they were interested in *playing around*."

"Oh shit," Popcorn Joe says.

"Chris shot a quick glance over at the other couple, and they just were staring back both with shit-eating grins now.

"Natalie went on saying 'I was so taken aback, I didn't know what to say so I just said…well…maybe…'

"'You just kind of agreed to maybe meet up with swingers,' Chris said.

"Natalie was so flustered she went off to the ladies' to splash some water on her face and recover her composure.

"While Chris was waiting for Natalie to return, the gentleman then got up and approached Chris and said: 'So are you interested in playing around?'

"Chris made it very clear that they were flattered, but that *swinging* wasn't their scene.

"But the man wouldn't let it rest. He kept pushing. And Chris was getting irritated. Finally, the man pulled out a business card, and said, 'If you change your mind,' and he

58

handed over the card. The card actually had a nice glossy photo of the couple, contact info, and the room number of the hotel where they were staying."

"Well, shit on me," Popcorn Joe says.

"Chris and Natalie were afraid to stay and afraid to leave. The couple were still staring and smiling. Eventually the couple turned their attention to new prey that had just entered and Chris and Natalie bolted."

"What else did Chris and Natalie tell you?" Popcorn Joe asks.

"They said next time they're sticking with the T-shirts, shorts and flip-flops."

* * *

Suddenly Popcorn Joe got more custom, a whole family, actually. They were Scottish and they had only been in Key West for two days and were already completely fried medium-rare. The sun's strong rays don't mix so very well with ginger hair and residents of a part of the world that only gets the sun for about an hour, in a bumper year. Okay, that's an exaggeration, the mother was more blonde than ginger.

Popcorn Joe finished serving his new guests, then turned to us: "What's the haps on the apartment front?"

"We have leveled off at zero," Gabrielle says.

"I thought I had a bite," Popcorn Joe tells us, "but they ended up taking an offer on it this afternoon."

"They *sold* it instead of renting it?"

"Someone made them a ridiculous offer."

"What was it?"

"A two-bedroom out by the salt ponds," Popcorn Joe said.

"Did they get the big bucks for it?"

"They got $518,000 for it."

"For a two-bedroom by the salt ponds!"

"I know," Popcorn Joe said, "part of the problem. If someone buys a unit to get rental income, they have to ask for the moon just to pay the mortgage and taxes."

"Do you think the market will tank some day?"

"That," Popcorn Joe said, "is the $518,000 question."

About now, another patron slipped from the thongs…I mean from the throngs. Without blinking, Popcorn Joe plowed his scoop into the mound of fresh popcorn, exhumed a prodigious amount, flapped open a bag and let the entire amount slide on in. Popcorn Joe is a man who knows how to put on a show. It must have the same effect as chumming, because almost immediately he had another queue.

"This one's on the house," Popcorn Joe said.

"*Merci!*" the man said.

Gabrielle and I did a double-take, it was Johnny-Johnny.

"Didn't recognize you again!" Gabrielle said. "You are a chameleon."

"*Madame*, I will take that as a compliment." And on that Johnny-Johnny let go with an explosive sneeze. "*Je m'excuse.* If I had had false teeth, they would have gone."

"But you don't have false teeth," Gabrielle said. "You have all your own, minus four to six."

"You have a memory like a steel trap, *Madame*."

"Thank you."

Johnny-Johnny extracted a few kernels of Pretty Good Popcorn and, ah, popped them in his mouth.

"I've been asking around about a place for you," he said, "it's like trying to find a town in the UK that doesn't have litter. It's a tough room, this Key West."

"No luck then?" I said.

"Oh, there's possibilities if you're willing to pay up the arse for a sandbox. Excuse my, ah, French, *Madame*. I found an illegal dwelling behind a Victorian house on Francis. There was no A/C, no ceiling fans, not even anywhere to keep your bikes and they wanted $2000 a month for it."

I looked at Gabrielle. Could this get any worse?

"At least Key West is not New York City. The average rent there is almost $4,500 a month, highest in the nation."

"I feel a lot better now," Gabrielle said.

"You won't for long," Popcorn Joe said, not rudely, more

perhaps not even believing it himself. "Becky and the kids are coming down early...for New Year's Eve...and I'm going to have to turf you out earlier than expected."

So it not only *could* get worse, it just did.

CHAPTER SEVEN

The next morning, we moved out of Popcorn Joe's. We were saved at the crack of the disastrous twelfth hour by Tina and Patty, our friends who live up on Geiger Key.

Tina was going to drive down and pick us up in the "Pig." The Pig is Tina's *reliably* unreliable 1987, vomit-green Shitmobile. A lonely bumper sticker on the back accurately states: HONK IF SOMETHING FALLS OFF. This was not a statement, rather a call to action.

Unfortunately…or fortunately, depending on your view, the Pig gave up the ghost before Tina could make a U-turn and exit her street, so she's borrowed Patty's black Nissan truck and picked us up, our bikes, and our possessions, such as they were.

As we crossed over the Cow Creek Channel Bridge heading north, I prayed we weren't seeing the last of Key West, and we could find a way to reinvent our dream.

We had the windows down and we could smell the salt in the air as we drove 10 miles up the Overseas Highway to Old Boca Chica Road, and swung right at the Circle K.

Tina had Radio A1A on the truck's radio, and we were listening to Harry Teaford kicking out some awesome Trop Rock.

The sun was shining and the temperature had already climbed to 72 degrees.

But our moods were overcast.

We motored over to Mars Lane, turned right again and skidded gently to a halt in the pea rock drive of an adorable cottage, "Patty and Tina's Castle."

The trip should have taken us 17 minutes, but there was sphincter-puckering construction on North Roosevelt Blvd., and it took nearly an hour. Good thing we hadn't conveyed in the Pig. The Pig overheated at a long red light, or a drive-thru restaurant, or when you switched the ignition off and it continued running. Perhaps not the ideal set of wheels for the Florida Keys. Even the creative mechanics in Havana who can carve mechanical masterpieces out of million-mile wrecks would say *"Qué pesadilla!"*

Patty and dog "Sasha" helped us unload our bikes, wheel them around the side of the Castle and moor them to a palm tree by the canal out back where they would be watched over by the mother-of-all iguanas, that made that drooling, grumpy creature in *Alien* look warm, cuddly and somewhat approachable.

FYI: Iguanas continue to be an issue in Key West, that's if you look at it from our perspective (humans). If you look at it from the iguanas' perspective, they would counter that we humans have become the problem, as, *they*, the iguanas, have no intention of leaving. Part of the problem is that the feral iguanas, the *green* iguanas, can get quite big—five feet long—and they can be quite something to behold, especially if you weren't planning on seeing one when you came strolling around that palm tree, or just happen to notice one swimming in that canal out back of your, ah, cottage, just when you were hoping for a quick dip.

How did the little blighters get here? I hear you ask. Some were pets who managed to make a run for it, some came over on freighters bearing fruit from South America, other most likely were simply given the boot by an irresponsible former owner.

AN IGUANA IS NOT JUST FOR CHRISTMAS.

Iguanas are on the shit-list of environmentalists, as they love to devour plants on the endangered species list. They are even harming the habitat of the burrowing barn owl.

This is a BIG problem as barn owls are cute.

Iguanas are also losing favor among many Keys' residents as they have a voracious appetite for all those fruit and

63

flowering plants you just purchased at the Big Pine flea market and have promptly festooned your garden with. They just love to eat mangos, tomatoes, orchids, shrubs, and trees and, are you ready, cat food and dog food. In fact, they will pretty much eat anything that doesn't eat them first, and that's the problem in the Keys, they have no predators, other than you and me and bubba. All this, plus they just love to defecate near water (your swimming pool, hot tub, waterside wooden deck, children's play pool).

Some disenchanted locals have taken to culling them by using the garden-destroyers as bait in their stone-crab traps. Other locals, especially Cubans eat the *pollo del árbol*, because, yes, you've guessed it: THEY TASTE LIKE CHICKEN. (I've been in some ass-end parts of the world where the chicken didn't even taste like chicken.)

You may choose to live *with* them, but don't try to eradicate them, they're here for the long run and aren't going anywhere, anytime soon. The term "colonize" is now being used to refer to the omnipresence and that should give us all the willies.

BTW, if you see one, don't try to scare it off by chasing it. He/she will be more than happy to turn the tables and chase your ass, instead.

The only hope we poor humans have is that iguanas not only hate the cold (like many snowbirds), they will perish if the temperature drops too low as they are cold-blooded. During the BIG CHILL of 2015, it was literally raining iguanas as they dropped by the hundreds out of palm trees having succumbed when the temperature dropped down into the baltic forties.

Yikes.

Creeps.

Shivers.

* * *

While I'm banging on here about iguanas, and how creepy they can be, let me ruin your day even more with this Burmese python update: They have python-sniffing dogs now.

Yes, python-sniffing dogs.

I didn't even know there was such a thing.

The dogs are very good at what they do, *sniff*. They were brought in and deployed at an old abandoned Nike missile site, and right off the dogs hit on "python presence," but they couldn't hone in on what their superior sense of smell was telling them.

They knew there were pythons on the missile site, but not exactly where.

Soooo, and here is where this gets really good, two snake experts from India were brought in by the federal and state wildlife folks to see if they could do any better.

When our dynamic duo from the Irula tribe in India heard about the abandoned cement missile site, their toes curled. They knew what this meant. It meant an ideal habitat for Burmese pythons.

The abandoned missile base was located within the Crocodile Lake National Wildlife Refuge in Key Largo.

Yes, Key Largo, population 10,433, with roughly 15% being small children.

At the old missile site, these two brave men actually got down on hands and knees and crawled into dark, narrow, claustrophobic earthen shafts filled with ooze and muck, in search of a constricting machine.

And guess what?

Our heroes captured four. One was 16-feet long. A female. Two were 8-foot long males. The fourth python was found in another of the three earthen bunkers, about all that remains of the Cold War installation.

If that's not enough to give you the heebie-jeebies, bite on this: Officials reckon that there are now 150,000 invasive Burmese pythons (minus four) pillaging and decimating the mammal population in the Everglades.

When I say "mammals," I'm talking raccoons, opossums, bobcats, rabbits, foxes, even the endangered woodrat.

Burmese pythons can grow to be 26 feet long and weigh more than 200 pounds, and they have been known to

65

swallow pets and animals as large as alligators.

The pythons thrive in the warm, humid El Dorado that is the Everglades.

It was feared that they could swim to the upper Keys.

And now they are here.

If they are already in the upper Keys, that means relocation down the island chain is next. *Think Big Pine...and think Key Deer.*

Many of these pythons were released by irresponsible owners, others, it is theorized, escaped from pet shops when businesses and homes were destroyed by Hurricane Andrew, in 1992—and they have been making babies ever since.

Researchers found staggering declines in Everglades' mammalian wildlife: a drop of 99.3 percent among raccoons, 98.9 percent for opossums, 94.1 percent for white-tailed deer and 87.5 percent for bobcats.

Rabbits and foxes, which were everywhere in 1996 and 1997, are nowhere to be seen.

In a related horror story, a dead 9-foot python was found on Card Sound Road. Thought I should just mention that, if you're planning on driving down to Key West and have a hankering to stop at Alabama Jack's for some conch fritters, sweet-potato fries, and a cool one.

CHAPTER EIGHT

It's New Year's Eve!

And Gabrielle and I are spending it out on the water with Patty and Tina and Sasha. This was a pleasant surprise as we didn't know Patty had a Mako 21 named the *Patty Wagon* tied up in a canal a few streets away.

Tina is English, so she whipped up some fetching cucumber sandwiches. Patty is American, so she put together an impressive potato salad and some conch fritters. As an overture, we took along bags, and I mean bags, of spicy hot Blue Tortilla Chips we had purchased at Fausto's.

And we took along two bulging bags of Peanut M&Ms, as that's part of the fayre at the Castle.

Patty fired up the *Patty Wagon* and we cleaved the glassy waters of the canal passing a party-hearty group of green iguanas displaying their topiary talents on a once bountiful privet hedge, as we slipped silently along Boundary Lane and out into Hawk Channel. It was still daylight, but we were taking no prisoners with the spicy-hot Blue Tortilla Chips and were already deep into bag #1.

Tina's from Newquay, on the north coast of Cornwall (that's southwestern England). She first came to the Keys twenty-five years ago, when her parents purchased a holiday home in Key Largo. Tina eventually worked her way down the island chain and fell in love with Key West. Tina had always been a bit salty. She sailed from Southampton, England, down to the Canary Islands, first port-o-call being Las Palmas in Gran Canaria, then hopped over to the island of La Palma, then back to the northwest to Madeira, and across the Atlantic.

This was done in a 50-foot Island Trader ketch, with Ray Marine electronics. A fifty-footer may seem robust to you and me, but Tina said when you're out in the middle of the Atlantic, it was like a cork. Nevertheless, crossing the Atlantic takes a sense of adventure, seafaring knowledge—and *cojones*. She was so smitten with sailing, she returned to the UK and went to the famous Hamble School of Yachting in Southampton, England, and earned her Captain's License.

Patty came to the Keys 30-plus years ago, from Maryland, went to high school in Key West, and couldn't even fathom that anywhere was so picturesque (and warm year round). After she finished school, Patty started working with the Navy and now lives just around the corner from her parents and her brother and sister-in-law who all had long ago flocked south.

Sasha is four.

She's local.

* * *

Okay, not much longer than it took for you to read that last bit of background info on Patty and Tina, is how long it took to cruise over to the White Street Pier.

And the sun is just setting.

Patty let the *Patty Wagon* glide to a gentle stop just astern of an old wooden schooner, and we dropped the anchor in shallow, aquamarine waters. We squinted through our sunglasses as the sun squatted on the horizon and then slipped over the back side of the earth.

And everyone applauded: on the pier, on Rest Beach, on Higgs Beach, on the vast flotilla of boats that were anchored off the pier eagerly waiting for the festivities to begin.

Soon we were surrounded by other pleasure craft, both sail and power. There were even a few intrepid souls out here on paddleboards. It was a fetching, exciting environment and, as I've mentioned before, being out on the water—seeing Key West from the water—was a glorious experience.

Many locals were still flocking to the beach, kids and coolers in tow. And many tourists were still making their way down, huggies in one hand, blankets in the other.

Higgs beach was a tapestry of happy families who had come early and had spent the day playing volleyball, snorkeling, swimming and picnicking.

The fireworks began promptly at 9pm, large ones, small ones, cascading ones, some shaped like a heart, then there were the major-league boomers. The obligatory OOOHS and AHHHS emanated from the throngs and echoed across the water.

Even Sasha found some of it exciting.

Some of it.

We think we heard a loud WOOHOO from a gaggle of drunks in a nearby speedboat, and the pyrotechnics went on and on and on, in reality it was probably only about twenty minutes.

Once the concussive blasts ceased rocking the night air, everyone cheered and the boats hooted and honked, and we sat there at anchor. Nobody was speaking, we were just enjoying the evening, being with friends and the fact that it was 70 degrees with a light, balmy breeze out of Havana.

"It doesn't get any better than this," Patty eventually said.

"No, no it doesn't," Gabrielle said.

"Let's motor back to the Geiger Key Marina. See what's for dessert," Tina said.

We motored back in the direction of the Geiger Key Marina. Off to our left, we caught glimpses of the Overseas Highway and we could make out cars leaving Key West and heading back up the Keys. Traffic was crawling.

"If anyone's heading to Geiger Key, we'll easily beat them there."

To punctuate that statement, Patty pulled back on the throttle and the Yamaha 200 thrust us in a foamy leap forward.

The distance from the White Street Fishing Pier to the Geiger Key Marina is about 12 miles and should take you about 20 minutes going up the Overseas Highway by car. Tonight it was taking cars nearly an hour.

We did it in 18 minutes.

Patty skillfully brought the *Patty Wagon* close to the dock at the Geiger Key Marina, I put out the fenders on the port side and we glided abreast, kissed the dock and stuck the landing. We stepped out of the boat, walked two feet and sat at a picnic table facing the stage. Easy to do as the restaurant has no walls.

THIS IS THE WAY TO LIVE!

If you want to find old Key West, look no further, you just found it in the guise of the Geiger Key Marina Restaurant and Tiki Bar.

And, it's pet friendly.

Just ask Sasha.

Greg Burroughs and Chris Rogers were up on the stage, singing and playing the guitar. We ordered the homemade Key lime pie, as one should, and chatted and listened to the music. Tina and Patty were tanned black, and they both looked so healthy and happy in shorts, and sweatshirts against the cool evening (68F now), poor us!

Gabrielle and I hadn't been back in the Keys long enough to forge good tans, but we had done justice to our sunburns. We, too, were in shorts and sweatshirts.

Shorts and sweatshirts on New Year's Eve.

In the distance, way out to the south, direction Havana, we saw a flash of lightning, not so typical for this time of the year, but dramatic and eerily beautiful. Pyrotechnics of the gods. There'd be much more of that when summer came bringing with it the obligatory shards of lightning and concussive thunder-boomers.

Our Key lime pie arrived and we fell silent as we dived in to the tart and aromatic delicacy. Can I say it once more? Shorts and Key lime pie, it doesn't get much better than this. After we knocked off our Key lime pie, we had a nightcap: four coffees and bowl of fresh water for Sasha.

These are the kind of nights that we will never forget.

And that's why I've just written about it here.

**AUTHOR'S CULINARY HISTORICAL NOTE:
A few theories abound on how Key lime pie came about: One

theory is that it originated in William Curry's very own kitchen, created by his cook "Aunt Sally." This is William Curry of the Curry Mansion on Caroline, I'm talking about.

Perhaps more plausible is that Key lime pie originated from the needs of the sponge fishermen. Key West's sponge fishing fleet numbered 350 vessels at one time and the fishermen stayed out at the reef or in Florida Bay for days on end with the smaller boats, or, with the larger craft, far out in the Gulf of Mexico for a month's toiling at the reefs off of Cedar Key or the mouth of Tampa Bay.

Staples were needed that didn't decompose or spoil and could be prepared onboard. One glorious favorite of the sponge fishermen was Key lime pie. Sweetened condensed milk had already been developed by Gail Borden (do you remember growing up with Borden's? I do).

Eggs were aplenty in Key West (think: chickens), the condensed milk was shipped down to William Curry who sold it to ship captains, and the true Key limes (not those imposters the Persian limes found elsewhere "up in America") were readily available.

Now, get this: when Key lime pie is made, the sweetened condensed milk is mixed with the acidic Key lime juice, and it generates a "chemical reaction" of sorts and essentially cooks itself which gives Key lime pie its authentic consistency. Owing to the "chemical reaction," baking was not required on the sponge boats. Remember, this is how it went back then, now there are strict health laws in place, so baking is mandatory.

OTHER RIVETING MUST KNOWS:

**This you probably knew, I didn't: Condensed milk will last for years without refrigeration, if not opened.

**What about cans? I'm glad you asked: the world's first canning factory was established in London in 1813. By 1820, the can was being used in Great Britain and France. It didn't make it big time in the US of A, until 1822. Who knew?

**Now…if you will indulge me for a moment, I just have to tell you this, even though it has nothing to do with Key lime pie. It's just so darn interesting. In "Sponges and Spongers of the Florida Reef," *Scribner's Magazine*, V12, Issue 5, 1892, it said this: "Most of the larger sponge boats go into the Bay (author's note: this refers to the Gulf of Mexico), to reach which they must traverse several hundred miles of open sea, exposed to the fury of Gulf gales. There is however little danger to be apprehended even here; for the coming storm is always heralded by unmistakable signs, and the innumerable reefs and islands of the coast offer a wide choice of snug harbors. Besides these there are in the Gulf, miles from land, SEVERAL VAST SPRINGS OF FRESH WATER, that boil up from the bottom of the sea with an appearance and effect similar to that of a light oil. In these fresh water areas, seas do not break, and the great salt water combers are robbed of their terror, so that within their limits a vessel provided with good anchors and stout cables may ride out the severest gale in safety."

Now, I don't know about you, Dear Reader, but that is a WOW! moment for me.

CHAPTER NINE

We awoke January 1st to a new day, a new year, wall-to-wall sunshine, low humidity, and a sense of wellbeing and good things to come.

We helped Patty and Tina wash down the *Patty Wagon* and get the salt off, and rid her of the remnants of two bags of Spicy Hot Blue Tortilla Chips.

"How'd you get the boat back in here last night in the dark?" Gabrielle asked Patty.

"Radar," Patty said, pointing toward her head. "Come in here often enough at night."

Gabrielle and I looked up and down the canal. Somehow Patty had negotiated the narrow canal, then docked between Tina's runabout and an old beaten-up sailboat.

"Check the spring-lines," Tina said.

"I'm checking the spring-lines," I said.

"Check the fenders," Patty said.

"I'm checking the fenders," Gabrielle said.

How lucky were Tina and Patty, living out their dream in the Florida Keys, spending lazy days on the water with Sasha, fishing, paddleboarding or just cruising about after they returned home from work or on their days off.

"We're taking the two of you to breakfast," Gabrielle said. "A big thanks for putting us up."

"We're happy to have you," Patty said. "You stay as long as you want…"

On that, Sasha bounded over and nuzzled Gabrielle's hand, as if to second that.

We felt very welcome, indeed.

But the clock was still ticking. We had to find our own place. I snore like a buffalo with a deviated septum, and it would only be a matter of time before Patty and Tina twigged. Plus, I'm notorious for paying a visit to the bog in the middle of the night and one day we were bound to meet at the most inopportune time, when, well, time was of the essence.

* * *

We took Patty and Tina to breakfast at Pepe's down in Key West's Old Town. Pepe's has been around since 1909, so they know how to do it, and get it right. This is the perfect place to go after visiting the Geiger Key Marina. It really gives you a feeling for what old Key West was back, well, way back then.

Patty and Tina had the short stack of pancakes, Gabrielle had the French toast, and I had Shit-on-a-Shingle. We consumed enough of their famous Pepe's blend coffee to launch into orbit. We asked everyone in the place if they knew of any cheap apartments for rent (the answer was a resounding NO, and only a few of the patrons laughed at us). And the bill came to just over $30, which we felt was a monumentally good deal in return for our friends putting us up and schlepping us all over the place.

And, yes, we did tip our server.

Now fired, wired and primed, Tina and Patty turned us loose in the Old Town to continue our quest for our new home. Understand, when I say "new home," I'm not talking a house, a villa or an estate, I'm talking a hovel that we could afford, and afforded us the luxury of, say, screens on the windows. I'm talking Home Sweet Shack.

When we'd first landed on this tropical rock and had resided upstairs at Popcorn Joe's in the attic, we'd lived in a daily furnace with only A/C in the bedroom. The furnace/attic was looking pretty good at the moment. At least it had had a view if you stood on your tiptoes and peered out through the hatch in the tin roof. From there, we could see the masts on the sailboats over at the Bight and that had brought us great joy.

"Give us a call later when you've lost the will to live and I'll come back down and pick you up," Tina said. Then she and Patty drove off in the mechanically repaired Pig, direction Geiger Key, leaving us to our own devices.

The first thing Gabrielle and I did was go right to the top of the food chain by hunting down Popcorn Joe. We looked for him in Truman Annex. We looked for him at B.O.'s Fishwagon. We finally found him just coming down Caroline on his rollerblades, leaving a gentle cloud of coral dust in his wake.

Popcorn Joe spun in a little circle and came to a stop. He was one wet noodle. Albeit a noodle with serious muscles. His T-shirt read: **I WOKE UP LIKE THIS**.

"Once around the island," he said with a big smile on his face.

Popcorn Joe was super human.

"Been asking around for you," he said. "There's a small efficiency for rent on the edge of the meadows. They're asking two-thousand a month for it. No A/C, no place to leave your bikes, and it comes with the neighbor from hell."

"Such a deal," Gabrielle said. "Anything else?"

"*Nada* at the moment, but I'll keep asking around. I'm hoping to get wind of a place before it's advertised in the Mullet Wrap."

* * *

Gabrielle and I spent the rest of the day looking.

Then we spent the next ten days looking.

It was soul destroying.

Life sucking.

Toilet swirling.

But we weren't quitters, we were *staying* in Key West if it meant showering at old dirtbag beach and sleeping on porches. Although, having said that, we hoped like hell it wouldn't come down to that. But…then having just said that, if you are going to be homeless and sleep under the stars, best to pick a tropical isle.

We *did* find one place that was affordable, but it was off Key West on Big Coppitt Key, and we didn't move to paradise, so we could buy a rust-bucket, pay up the wazoo for extortionate insurance premiums, get to have a fingernail-pulling-out day trip over to the DMV out on South Roosevelt Boulevard to secure Florida Driving Licenses—for the joy of *commuting* and the nightmare that is the pursuit of parking in the Old Town. Wasn't living in Key West about being able to walk or ride your bike anywhere you wanted or needed to go?

Were we in fact doomed?

Doomed by a part of the world that had become too expensive for us to live in.

CHAPTER TEN

And then one day, everything changed.

Tina was in the kitchen, sipping coffee, and writing something out on a piece of paper when Gabrielle and I toddled in.

"Morning, Tinski. Where's Patty?" I asked.

"At work, already. Been up since the crack of five…"

Tina scribbled some more, erased, scribbled. "Gotta place an Ad in the Mullet Wrap. Selling my boat…"

"Whaaat? I thought you loved *THE WET ONE*…?" Gabrielle said.

"I do. Not selling *THE WET ONE*, selling the *RESTLESS.*"

"The *RESTLESS*?"

"Right. That old sailboat tied up over by Patty's Mako 21."

"That's yours?"

"Yup."

"How much are you selling it for?" Gabrielle asked, giving me a look.

"I would like to get twenty-thousand," Tina said.

"Oh," I said, suddenly having the rug pulled out.

"Sure…that's what I'd like," Tina said, laughing. "But I won't…"

"What will you take?"

"I will take whatever I can get for it. Probably only get a thousand…"

"A *thousand*?" I repeated, looking wide-eyed over at

Gabrielle.

"Yeah," Tina said, "it wants a lot of TLC. Can't ask much more than that. Probably needs a weed-whacker taken to a sub-waterline jungle of algae…or taken to the sloop junkyard."

CHAPTER ELEVEN

Later that evening, after Patty got home from work, we all rode our bikes over to take a look at the sailboat. It was larger than we'd thought. Perhaps a 30-footer. And it needed work...A LOT of work.

But it was afloat.

Gabrielle and I removed our flippies and climbed down and onboard the *RESTLESS*. We slid back the main hatch and went in. It was an inferno and smelled musty and there was a fair bit of angry looking mold. We opened a few hatches and a few windows hoping the heat would get the hint and start to dissipate.

There was a small galley, lounge/table to hangout, read, write. A narrow beam-me-up head, and two bunks in the bow. We had a pretty serious snoop around. Eventually we emerged back out into the streaming sunshine, shading our eyes with a hand.

"What are you two up to?" Patty asked. "You've got weird subtext going..."

"Let's go over to the Geiger Key Marina for dinner," Gabrielle said. "Our treat. We've got a bunch of questions."

"We're all ears," Patty said.

"I could eat a cow," Tina said, displaying her hale devotion to the exquisite fayre on offer at the marina.

The Geiger Key Marina and Smokehouse, as I mentioned above, is a step backwards in time. It's old Florida. It's the Keys of days gone by. It is *the* place to be, but don't tell too many people.

Again, we sat at one of the picnic tables with the Atlantic

just a few feet to our right. The sun had just set, but it was still warm. It felt more like spring than the dead of the winter, even for the Florida Keys.

We ordered drinks: Patty a diet coke, Gabrielle a glass of red, Tina and me a Michelob Ultra each.

And we ordered dinner: Patty opted for the Killer *Patty* Melt, Tina the Hogfish and Chips, and Gabrielle and I shared the Macho Nacho Mega Platter. And we chatted and we noshed and we supped, and then...

"We want to buy your sailboat," Gabrielle said.

"And the reason would be???" Tina asked.

"We want to become live-aboards. It will solve all our problems."

"Where will you shower?" Tina asked.

"We'll use the hose."

"What hose?"

"There's no hose?"

"Oh, there's a hose alright, just nowhere to connect it."

"Hadn't thought about that."

"Anyway, what would you use as a toilet?"

"The head," I said, demonstrating that I was completely au fait with nautical terms.

"And where would you pump it out?"

"The canal?" Gabrielle said.

"Not allowed," Patty said.

"The ocean," I said.

"Not allowed," Tina said, "Florida statute bars you from three miles in the Gulf and nine miles in the Atlantic. Plus, the boat's engine is buggered..."

"It doesn't work?"

"Never has since we docked it in the canal, that's why we don't take it out."

"Oh, shit," Gabrielle and I said in unison.

Well, the sailboat might still have been afloat, but we were sinking fast.

"I'd thought we'd cracked it," Gabrielle said.

"I did, too."

* * *

The next day, Tina loaded us into the Pig and conveyed us back into the Old Town to resume our desperate, enervating hunt for accommodation. Tina pulled up at the library, let us out and then saw us staring at the Pig.

"Number one," Tina said, "the Pig is *not* for sale, and number two, the backseat of a beater might be considered affordable housing in Key West, but it does not solve your problem of where to shower and where to, ah, *pump it out.*" (Tina said *pump it out,* like Dana Carvey used to say "Pump it up!" with an Arnold Schwarzenegger accent.)

* * *

Later that afternoon, after pounding the heck out of the pavement to zero avail, we met Popcorn Joe at the Bull. The house hunt was turning us to alcohol, and the Bull seemed the best place to deal with that joyous dilemma.

"Still asking around for you," Giuseppe said. "Same old same old, too much rent, or up the Keys, or winter let only, yada, yada, yada."

Popcorn Joe went into deep thought for a moment. When he re-surfaced, he said these pearls: "Ever think of living on a boat?"

Well, Dear Reader, you can see where this is going, can't you?

"We'd thought about that," Gabrielle said, "Tina has a sailboat for sale, cheap…but there's no place to shower and there's nowhere to pump out the head."

"Pump it out!" I said.

As always, Popcorn Joe was the guy you could turn to when trouble erupted. "Not a problem," he said, "You rent a slip at the Bight. I know the folks down there. They provide showers and pumping out and electricity and trash disposals and laundry facilities, and you will then have a home in the Old Town where you can sit out, catch some rays and have a great view."

81

"Can we afford that?"

"How many feet is the sailboat?"

"She's thirty feet."

"Perfect, not too long. Absolutely you can afford it. Wonder why I hadn't thought of it earlier…"

Popcorn Joe and I quaffed our beers and Gabrielle lapped at her mojito. A ceiling fan circled overhead. Up near the stage, Sallie was tickling the ivories and singing "My Girl."

Outside, Duval was alive with a wave of sweaty flesh. It was the middle of January, nearly 70 degrees, and we had just landed on our tanned feet. We were going to be able to stay in Key West, live in Key West, have a life in Key West.

A glow settled over us.

'Where's this boat of Tina's?" Popcorn Joe asked.

"Up on Geiger Key," Gabrielle said.

"Well, Tina's got her Captain's License," Joe said. "I'll help you rent the slip, then she can motor it down here and you'll be in business."

"The engine doesn't work."

"Then she'll sail it down here. It's how I came to Key West over 30 years ago. Nothing like seeing Key West from the water when you arrive for the first time."

I looked over at Gabrielle and I knew what she was thinking: We'd be SEEING KEY WEST FROM THE WATER FROM NOW ON IN…

CHAPTER TWELVE

To say we were excited when we saw the Pig careen around the corner of Duval and Caroline does not begin to capture our buzzing emotions at that moment. Tina klunked to a stop in front of the Lost Weekend Liquor Store, we piled in and we drove out along Smathers Beach and the airport. Just before the bend in the road, Gabrielle yelled: "Look!"

Rollerblading and pushing two pugs in a stroller was none other than the love child of Truman Capote and the Church Lady! Love Child was wearing skimpy red bottoms, possibly Speedos, and an international orange tank top. Kaleidoscopic.

We drove on just enjoying the view then Gabrielle said: "Tell Tina..."

"No, you tell her."

"Tell me what?" Tina said.

"We would like to buy your sailboat," Gabrielle said. "We're going to lease a slip at the Bight."

"Really? Well, that pleases me to no end. My old skipper Elmer, the bloke I sailed across the Atlantic with, bought me that sailboat and it has always been anchored in a special place in my heart."

Gabrielle and I were over the moon.

"Sorry I can't give you a sea trial," Tinksi said.

"Doesn't matter," Gabrielle said. "We only need a *sleep* trial."

"A what?"

"A sleep trial."

"When?"

"Tonight."

So that's what we did.

That night, Tina and Patty and Sasha sorted us out with sleeping bags and towels, and pointed to the side of the boat in case the dreaded urge overcame me in the middle of the night (which it always did). Then we bid them goodnight, did some rudimentary cleaning, and killed the mold and mildew with a bit of bleach and vinegar. Boat interiors are fertile breeding grounds for mold, so we knew it wouldn't be long before we would get enough practice trying to find out what would kill off pesky mold the best.

(**Later we would learn that ventilation and air flow are critical in a tropical climate like Key West...AND we found plants—like English Ivy—that thrive on mold. Yes, you heard right, mold-consuming plants. Also, mold is attracted to salt, so we had to keep saltwater soaked *anything*, from getting down in the living area of our boat such as bathing suits, towels, flippers, masks and snorkles.)

When the interior looked and smelled a bit better, we thought about going to bed, but we couldn't. We were too excited to sleep, so we just hung out on the deck, watching for shooting stars. Eventually our eyelids started to droop and we hit the sack.

And we slept like rocks.

Was it because our feverish brows had been dabbed clean, and the lack of stress and worry and downright fear of having to leave Key West had been removed?

I believe so.

The next morning we woke up early, just after sunrise, and sat out on the narrow, teak afterdeck of our soon-to-be new home and watched an iguana in a palm tree across the canal eyeballing us with just the one eye. It was a cool morning, but warming up fast as the first rays of the morning pierced the canal, which we just loved, as did the iguana.

At low tide this morning, the canal where we were docked appeared to be about five or six feet deep, so our keel was just clearing (Did I just say *our* keel?) and the water was clear and we could see swarms of fish having a briny nosh. We even saw an octopus tiptoeing along the bottom as a ballerina might do across the stage at the "*Nutcracker* Key West"—albeit a ballerina with eight legs and four pairs of ballet slippers.

About now, Tina and Sasha-the-dog came out, all smiles. Tina to bring us fresh coffees, Sasha just to hang out and look adorable. Sasha could take first prize in the Dog With the Wagging Tail Contest

"So…how'd you sleep?" Tina asked.

"The best in weeks. What do we have to do to become the new owners of the *RESTLESS*?"

"We need to transfer the title, get the boat registered, and all that palaver. I'll write you up a Bill of Sale and drive you over to the DMV. Boat's not worth much, so no need to insure it unless the marina requires liability…"

CHAPTER THIRTEEN

An hour later, we received a text from Popcorn Joe.

It read: GOOD TO GO. YOU NOW LIVE IN THE OLD TOWN!

Patty was off work today, so she towed the *Restless* with us onboard out of the canal behind the *Patty Wagon* and took us out into the shallows of Hawk Channel, then she cut us loose and went back to the Castle to dock her boat and fetch Sasha.

Tina was our skipper for the day, so under her command, we raised the main and the jib and we cleaved the near-shore waters of Hawk Channel at an impressive 2 knots. We were being owned by a breathless gentle offshore breeze and we weren't going anywhere in a hurry.

"At least we have the aid of the current here in Hawk Channel," Tina informed us. "It flows from Biscayne National Park all the way to Key West. If we were outside the reef, the current is the Gulf Stream. It's much stronger, and it flows in the opposite direction, north, up the east coast of America and over toward Europe."

"Doesn't it pass Scotland?" Gabrielle said.

"Indeed, it splits and goes north of Ireland and the UK, and also goes south along western Europe down toward the Canary Islands…"

Tina went on: "Back in 1582, Ponce de León already knew about the Gulf Stream and that ships could sail much more quickly back to Spain from the Caribbean, than coming this direction. When Elmer and the rest of the crew and I sailed across the Atlantic, we had many days with little wind and we were actually going backwards. That was an eye-opener."

FY-nautical-**I:** The Gulf Stream runs, *más o menos*, 62 miles wide and 2,600 feet to 3,900 feet deep. The current is the strongest/fastest near the surface speeding along at a zippy 5.6 mph one of the reasons the *balseros* (Cuban rafters) have had such a struggle reaching the Keys. On occasion they've aimed for Key West been swept north, and ended up in Ft. Lauderdale.

It took us nearly four hours to get even with Fort Zach and, now using the most nautical of terms, we hung a right around the breakwater and entered the main channel.

Tina texted Popcorn Joe that we were on final, and we crawled over to just outside the entrance to the Bight, where he was waiting for us in his skiff. We threw a line to Popcorn Joe, he secured it to a cleat on the stern and he fired up his little outboard and expertly towed us (even more slowly) in to our new berth at the Historic Seaport Key West Bight.

For once, Popcorn Joe's outboard behaved and didn't melt down.

Waiting on the dock with all smiles was our welcoming party of two: Patty and pooch Sasha, who had driven down in Patty's pickup and had easily beaten us there to join in the homecoming festivities.

We got the fenders out, boat secured, tied up, and then yelling "We owe you!" the three of them jumped in the truck and headed back up the Overseas Highway to most likely run about the Castle with their hands in the air, resting assured that me wandering into their bedroom by mistake in the middle of the night was no longer a viable threat.

Back on the *RESTLESS*, Popcorn Joe and a fellow in a blue boiler suit who worked at the Bight helped us get connected to water, electricity, then showed us around the marina, where the laundry facilities, toilets and showers were located.

Where to get ice.

Where to dump trash.

How to receive WiFi.

Then Boiler-Suit Man showed us our very own dock box!

FYI: "All marina tenants are allowed one (1) white fiberglass or molded plastic dock box not to exceed 6' 2" long, 27 inches deep and 30 inches high. The dock master will request in writing that the slip owner remove any non-conforming dock boxes. In the event the owner does not remove non-conforming dock boxes within 7 days of written notice, staff will remove the non-conforming dock box. Dock boxes must be bolted to the dock with the approval of marina staff. Hazardous materials of any nature may not be stored in dock boxes. In the event of a storm tenant agrees to remove anything stored in the dock box that may be harmful to people, the marina, sea life, or water quality."

Well, there you have it.

To show our sincere appreciation, we treated Giuseppe to an early dinner at B.O's Fish Wagon—distance from our new home, one block.

After dinner, Popcorn Joe reminded us: "Don't forget to keep an eye on the bilge." Then we bid him good evening, and Gabrielle and I walked the length of the historic port's boardwalk from the Half Shell to the Conch Republic Seafood Company—twice. We just strolled along, holding hands. In the distance, heat lightning split the sky with jagged shards, and we talked about how lucky we were that everything had turned out alright.

When it was finally time to repair to our new home, we did just the opposite and went to the Bull for a nightcap. Now we had a three-block walk home.

Didn't have to drive.

Didn't have to take a taxi.

Or a bus.

Or the subway.

Not even a pedicab.

"This is the way life should be," Gabrielle said. "Now all we have to do is find jobs."

"Shouldn't be too hard," I added. "There's so much turnover in Key West…"

"Folk go back up north," Gabrielle said.

"Get fired," I said.

"Get arrested," Gabrielle said.

CHAPTER FOURTEEN

We awoke the next morning in a blissful glow. The blissful glow that comes from finally having a roof over your head—or as in our case—a deck over our head, and landing on your two bare feet after swimming hopelessly against the current of life. And what, pray tell, was our life-saving flotation device? *Not giving up* was what had saved us.

Not giving up in the ugly face of diversity in the form of gentrification.

I yawned, blinked a few times and squinted up at the hatch that was just above our V-bunk in the bow. The hatch was open for ventilation. I could hear someone up on the deck above us, moving slowly, very quietly, albeit flatfooted.

WTF?

I glanced over at Gabrielle. She was still sleeping happily away and looking all cuddly—and VERY tanned against the white sheets that Tina and Patty had so kindly loaned us.

I slipped out of bunk (not bed), pulled on a pair of shorts, padded through the lounge/dining/galley area and snuck up the steps and into the cockpit. Up on the bow, staring back at me was—a pelican.

"And good morning to you, Mr. Pelican!" I said.

"How do you know it's a *mister*?" came the reply. It was Gabrielle, forehead and two eyes just peeping out the forward hatch. "Perhaps it's Mrs. Pelican or Miss Pelican or Ms. Pelican?"

Minutes later, Gabrielle, wearing a large black T-shirt with COLETIVO COFFEE in white letters, emerged from below with two steaming cups of coffee. In the east, the sky was pink. No breeze. Harbor glassy.

"I think it's a miss," Gabrielle said.

"What's a miss?"

"*Her.* The pelican."

"And you know this how?"

"She has style...good bearing...nice ankles...cute feet. Must be a girl. Let's call her 'Helen'."

Helen the Pelican.

We sipped our coffee and watched as Helen the Pelican took to the sky, did one lap around the marina, then folded her wings and became a feathery smart missile hitting the glassy waters with instinctive precision. Helen popped buoyantly up, drained water from her throat pouch, then threw her head back twice, and GULP, SWALLOW. Success!

We finished our coffee, changed into our cossies, had a cockpit shower, toweled off, and I can't even begin to tell you how good we felt.

On so many levels.

"In case you're wondering," I said to Gabrielle. "Sunset in Wisconsin is 4.30 this afternoon. Down here it's 7.15pm."

"That's 2 hours and 45 minutes more daylight," Gabrielle said, being quick with the numbers.

"With sun..."

"Indeed, with sun."

"Just had a thought," Gabrielle said.

"Does it have anything to do with food?"

"No, it has to do with clothes."

"Clothes?"

"We only have northern clothes. Don't need them down here. Plus, they take up too much room on our boat."

"And your plan is?"

"New Town. Salvation Army."

"Let's bike up Duval and pick up a few *beignets* at Croissant de France, then we'll aim for the New Town. Afterwards, we'll come back here and give the boat a good cleaning."

We packed up our northern clothes in two bulging bags, secured them in our bikes' baskets with bungee cords, then just before setting off, Gabrielle pulled her cell phone out of her back pocket.

"Let's take a pic of our new home and send it to John Rubin back in the UK. He said he would come visit later in the autumn."

Gabrielle took a few different angles of our boat, then hit "send."

We hopped on our bikes and pedaled up to Caroline and turned right. Coming toward us on his rollerblades, hell-bent, was Popcorn Joe.

Joe stopped and we pulled up just in front of him.

"How'd you sleep?"

"Gloriously," Gabrielle said. "Thanks for saving us yet again from peril."

"My pleasure. Where ya headed?"

"Salvation Army."

"Unloading northern clothes?" Popcorn Joe said.

"You're clairvoyant."

"No, just eyeballing those bags there," Popcorn Joe said. "See youse at sunset?"

"We'll be there."

Popcorn Joe started to rollerblade off then screeched to a halt and turned toward us: "You'll be needing some shorts and T-shirts. Got tons back in Truman Annex. Stop by before I go to Sunset, and if any of it fits, it's yours. Later!"

And he was off down Caroline.

"Good friends are hard to come by," Gabrielle said.

"Indeed," I said. "Indeed, they are."

* * *

There was an early morning queue at Croissants de France, but better to queue in the streaming sun of the Florida Keys than on an icy patch of wintry pavement.

Gabrielle queued. I stayed with the bikes and the bags to prevent them from becoming dirt-bag booty. As I was waiting for Gabrielle, I noticed a young man about twenty-years old. He was sitting on a fold-up chair right there on the sidewalk, and he had a white handkerchief stretched across his knees. He was very pale and he wore sunglasses. A sign at his feet read: "I AM BLIND. I NEED MONEY TO GET BACK HOME TO GERMANY. PLEASE HELP." The young man had hair like Squiggy on *Laverne & Shirley*. I guess if you're blind you don't spend a lot of time in front of a mirror.

I observed. He just sat there motionless. He seemed very sad. A wave of kindness swept over me and I dropped a dollar on his cloth. He must have sensed it somehow for he snatched it away and said in funny English: "Zank you."

Soon Gabrielle returned. She had spied the young blind man as well, and she had brought him out a coffee in a take-away container.

"Zank you."

Feeling decidedly good, we loaded two piping hot *beignets* and an impressive two-foot long *baguette* into Gabrielle's basket. "Breakfast and lunch!" she beamed.

Okay, amigos, chew on this: If you've read my behind-the-guidebook-pages travel essay *NAKED EUROPE*, look away now. If not, carry on reading: "Napoleon had instructions issued to the bakers of France to bake breads of a peculiar shape so that his soldiers could more easily carry the coveted staple rolled up in a ground cloth atop a backpack, or even up a trouser leg. The result? A lengthy, slim loaf called—*la baguette.*"

And...*le beignet*, check it out: *Beignets* are traditionally served with powdered sugar on top. They are best when eaten fresh and hot. You can find the real deal in French Canada, New Orleans, and, yes, right here in Key West.

BTW, *beignets* are the official state doughnut of Louisiana. Who knew?

And the 2nd of June is National Donut Day! Who knew?

* * *

It takes about 10 minutes to get to the Salvation Army store from Croissants de France if you put the pedal to the, well, the pedal. Twenty minutes if you take the back tropical lanes and stop to smell the frangipani. And 30 minutes if you pedal past Bayview Park and stop to watch Will Soto doing Tai Chi.

"He and Amy teach Tai Chi, as well, over at the MCC Fellowship Hall."

"Is that over on Petronia?"

"Yeah, Petronia, between White Street and Georgia."

"Will's seriously fit," Gabrielle noted.

"He used to be a gymnast, so he knows how to take care of his body. A lesson to us all."

"Did you ever see that photo of him snorkeling out by the mangroves?"

"The one where his dog is riding on his back with his paws curled over Will's head as he snorkels?"

"That's the one. So cute!"

"He and Amy are living the dream, aren't they?"

"They are, indeed," Gabrielle said, then laughed

"What?" I said.

"I'm just thinking about Will reading your first Key West book. Do you remember what he did after he'd finished reading it?"

"No, what?"

"He was so inspired by your spirited portrayal of him, he went down to Mallory that night, did his tightrope act and mooned two sunset cruises, not one, *two*. Said he did it as a tribute."

Now I was laughing.

"Key West would not be the same without Will Soto."

"Indeed, it wouldn't…"

CHAPTER FIFTEEN

We donated our two bundles of northern clothes to the Salvation Army on Flagler, then pedaled up Flagler to 12th Street, hung a left and hit up Kmart on North Roosevelt Blvd. Distance, 1.3 miles. Time, about 5 minutes. There wasn't a cloud in the sky and we both felt as if we had been in a microwave for the last 5 minutes.

Gabrielle and I made life-changing purchases in the form of new flip-flops, then aimed for the sunblock aisle.

For sunscreen, I selected Coppertone because when I was a little boy I liked the original Ad of the Boykin Spaniel puppy and the little girl in pigtails that was so oft used on billboards in Miami in the 60s. Of course innocence is now lost and the Ad is no longer politically correct.

FY-sunning-**I**: In 1965, a three-year-old toddler made her acting debut as the Coppertone little girl on TV. The little girl must have had seriously innate acting skills as she became an Academy Award winner. Her name was Jodie Foster.

"I'm buying SPF 30," I said to Gabrielle.

"Do you know what SPF stands for?" Gabrielle asked.

"Absolutely, Sun Protection Factor," I said, with perhaps just a bit of brio.

"But, *esposo lindo*, do you know how it works?"

"Absolutely not," I said, being brought back down to earth.

"Let me enlighten you: The SPF refers to the length of time you can be in the sun without getting burned. An SPF 30 for example, would allow you to stay in the sun for 15 times longer than if you went out unprotected. All that, plus, you need to apply it 15 to 30 minutes before you go out into the sun to allow the active ingredients to bond to your skin."

"Well, live and learn," I said.

"And," Gabrielle went on, "do you know why your skin gets red when you are out in the sun?"

"I'm guessing the redness is caused by the, ah, burn?"

"Wrong, hubby, when the skin is cooked, blood rushes to the surface of the skin in all those little capillaries. That's why if you press on sunburned skin, it will turn white, and then return to red as the capillaries refill."

Well, I'll be...

After selecting the Coppertone (and aren't there a lot of different brands to choose from?), we moved into a different aisle and I selected some Tums. As I've grown older, I seem more susceptible to acid reflux. I had an endoscopy once, and I will now do everything on this earth possible to keep from having to do that again.

BTW: An endoscopy was not on my bucket list. I would rather poke my own eyes out with a fork.

Anyway, this is how my conversation went with the girl at the counter when I was procuring my lonely jar of Tums:

Me: "Hi."

Her: *grunt.*

Me: "How goes it?"

Her: "I will be better at 14 weeks when my morning sickness stops..."

Me: "Okay...what are you at now?"

Her: "Three weeks. He doesn't like Coco Puffs."

Me: "Who?"

Her: "Archie."

Me: "Who's Archie?"

Her: "My baby."

Me: "What does, ah, Archie like?"

Her: "TV."

Me: "No, I mean what does Archie like to eat...for you to eat?"

Her: "How should I know, he's not born yet."

The young clerk and I had a silent stare down, wrestling with our eyes, then I selected my Tums and Gabrielle and I fled over to the Clothing Section.

* * *

In the clothing section, I had a thought—something that is not a frequent occurrence for me: Why do people who go on vacation in Key West, buy their holiday clothes in the Great White North? Or the Bible Belt? Or anywhere north of I-10, really? You may recall that I've addressed this disconcerting conundrum before.

Remember?

Is it coming back to you now?

A light flickering somewhere in the dark, beer-polluted recesses of your once gray matter?

Well, for those who don't know what I'm on about, might I just lay it all out before you again: Would you shop for that dream jaunt to Hawaii in, say, Aspen? Would you shop for a drug-fueled dirty weekend in Little Havana, in, say, International Falls? Would you shop for that Pensacola right-of-passage herpes-contracting Spring Break in, say, Ottawa?

Or would you wait until you arrived on the rock?

I'm thinking rock.

Sooo, why not come on down to the end of the world with an empty soft bag or one of those cool Trunki suitcases that the kids can ride like a pony (even though it looks like a cow), purchase some colorful tropical hot numbers, and be the talk of Buffalo or Sheboygan or the entire province of Saskatchewan?

Alright?

For those of you ladies absolutely rolling in it (or have married above your station), we have Lilly Pulitzer, Local Color and Fresh Produce...for you men (same parameters, so as not to be a sexist slug), if you feel the need to be a Hemingway lookalike and drink Sloppy's dry, you can hit the Bass Pro Shop as you drive your 200-dollar-a-day rental convertible through Islamorada, then there's Evolution or

97

Assortment in Key West if you want to splash a bit and impress your Friends on Facebook…or that slut you brought down on the QT.

BTW, everyone back home knows about your perverted tryst with that little vixen 25 years your junior, because you just couldn't keep your mouth shut, could you? You had to boast conspiratorially to every male you came in contact with how you were taking a twenty-something Bow Bunny to Key West, even though your randy *amour* is the poster child for breast enhancement gone too far and wouldn't know the stern of a boat from the transom of a bar.

Now…if dressing for suck-cess is not quite so impotent to you, I mean *important* to you, and you just HAVE TO LOOK LIKE A LOCAL, then purchase your tropical T-shirts and sweatshirts from the artists down at Mallory Square at the Sunset Celebration. They will be most appreciative and they will show you how to bung your hair into a ponytail when it finally lengthens to a quarter-inch long.

After our foray in the clothing section, Gabrielle and I purchased a whole bunch of cleaning supplies and fled Kmart. Much to our horror, we found Archie's mom outside, on her break, *smoking!*

Me: "Hi."

Her: *Long vacuous stare.*

Me, pointing: "From inside the store…Tums."

Her: *Puff puff, drag drag.*

Me: "You're smoking…and you're pregnant."

Her: "I'm trying to cut down…"

Me: "Just cut down? Not stop completely?"

Her: *Long stare, no emotion.*

Me: "You're endangering your unborn baby, Archie."

Gabrielle was now tugging on my elbow. This was a losing cause here. Really sad as nothing gets under my skin more than a pregnant teenager smoking.

Me: "You should put Archie first?"

Her: "What, and you're my father now?"

Gabrielle whisked me away to the sanctuary of our bikes.

I was fuming.
Really upset.
And I had to have a Tums.

* * *

Gabrielle and I are back onboard our boat now and life is once again good. There's a serenity here in the marina, a feeling of being away from all that pisses you off in the world.

Now I have a question for you:

Have you ever cleaned a boat? Any ideas? Tips? A boat that hasn't been cleaned in, well, forever?

"I don't even know where to start," I said.

"We'll start in the head. Let's get that sorted first. Then we'll attack the galley."

As you probably already know, the head on a boat is not so very big. At least on our boat. Hardly room for one in there and then you need to be a contortionist. You know how teensy those lavatories are on a plane? Well, those are cavernous compared to our head.

As always, being the great protector (and wanting to get fed later), I volunteered to go in first.

FY-nautical-**I**: It's called the "head" because back in the days of the great sailing ships, the toilet was all the way forward on either side of the bowsprit, right where the figure*head* was fastened. Get it?

Anyhoo, I'm in here now and it's stuffy and hotter than Hades.

I bleached.
I scrubbed.
Even scraped.
Yuk.

There was a tiny sink, the size of that salad bowl you use when you have the outlaws, I mean the in-laws over. The sink was set in mahogany. There was a miniature mirror above the sink. You'd only be able to brush one tooth at a time. The mirror was old and losing its silver backing around the edges.

I cleaned, and I mean *cleaned* the commode first. That way

99

I was able to sit on it while I cleaned the sink.

You would have been well impressed. We might not have had the most modern head in the marina, but now, and I can assure you, we had the cleanest.

By the time I did the walls, the floor, even the small ceiling, I was dripping in sweat.

Some heads have a shower in there, so you can shower and clean the commode all in a oner. Ours didn't. We were just thankful we had the salad bowl.

When I had finished the head, I staggered out and Gabrielle was well on her way to winning in the galley.

And, she, too, was ringing with perspiration.

"If we had a shower, we could shower," I said.

"I'm putting my bikini on," Gabrielle said. "Go throw on your cowabunga jams. We'll have a cockpit shower, then we'll finish the galley."

I'm not keen on speculation. That means, I won't tell you how hot it was "down below." All I know is when we emerged from our cabin and stepped up in to the cockpit, it felt cool. The temperature on a little thermometer that we had up in the cockpit read 82.

And it was in the shade.

We had our cockpit showers, then still wet, went back below to finish the galley.

Okay, I'm going to need your help here, please.

Stand up. Yes, you.

Right in front of you is our galley. Reach out about a foot. *That* is our kitchen sink. Not much bigger than a salad bowl here, too, wouldn't you say?

Now, see just behind the sink? There are two skinny shelves on the back wall/hull. This is where we store small items like coffee and tea and salt and pepper and other condiments. And marmite. I'm joking about the marmite.

And, on that skinny little shelf just above? That's where we store coffee cups and a few wine glasses and two cans of *condensed milk.*

Below the sink, see those two cabinet doors? Go ahead,

open them up. See in there? That's where we keep sponges, rubber gloves, bleach, the world's smallest waste bin, and a few other cleaning items. Notice the two kitchen towels, one hanging on each door.

Okay, you're doing fine, don't leave me now, I know it's hot down here. Now reach down to your right. You don't have to move your feet as there's really no place to go. Anyway, down there to your right is our half fridge. You can open it and have a peek in there if you wish, but we haven't cleaned it yet, so you might be jeopardizing your olfactory senses and getting a whiff of ugly.

See that flat area just above the fridge and to the right of the sink? That, dear friend, is the luxury of *counter space*.

To the right of the counter space (you still don't have to move your feet) is the two-ring gas stove. We're talking serious luxury, wouldn't you agree?

I can boil water here.

I can make coffee.

I can make tea.

Perhaps even *cook* something.

The world is my oyster.

Oh, I almost forgot, lying on its side under the left cabinet door, right on the floor, by your left foot is our fire extinguisher. Don't worry if you kick it. It needs to be updated and recharged as nothing's been done since the millennium. Fairly important I would think as we don't want to burn the boat down to the waterline.

Now, I will say thank you for staying the course.

You are excused.

You may go up above for a cockpit shower.

* * *

Gabrielle and I cleaned the rest of the interior of the boat. We worked until it got dark. There's so much more work our new home needs, such as painting the entire boat, varnishing all that is mahogany, sanding and varnishing the boom, sanding

101

and varnishing the mast, even possibly bleaching a bit of teak in the cockpit, if in fact it is indeed teak.

But it's a start.

CHAPTER SIXTEEN

The next morning I rose early, before Gabrielle, and I stealthily slipped up into the cockpit. I waved at an elderly early-bird across the marina, then turned toward our dock. Next to where we tap into the electricity supply was a gecko. He was watching me, doing that thing where they stick their colorful throat skin out…and he was doing "pushups." Geckos do that you know, these head bobs, these pushups.

This brutish display meant that this gecko was a male. They do this to establish territory.

And impress the ladies.

Was this a challenge? I took the challenge. I did seven pushups. He only managed four. Feeling pretty pleased with myself, I went back down below to wake Gabrielle.

We sat out in the cockpit and enjoyed a glorious sunrise. Did I just say *sunrise*? Can't say we've seen a lot of sunrises in our lives before this boat adventure. They're gorgeous, those sunrises. Who knew?

We have never arisen this early in our lives. Is it the salt air? One of the perks of being a live-aboard?

Stay tuned.

The sun was bathing the harbor in a golden glow, the humidity already cranking up, so we showered at the marina, then hightailed it over to the Cuban Coffee Queen for rocket fuel (It took us 1 minute).

When we returned to our boat Gabrielle announced: "You are going up the mast."

"I'm going where?"

"Up the mast."

"How?"

"In our bosun's chair."

"We have a bosun's chair?"

"I found it up by the anchor."

"We have an anchor?"

"Here," Gabrielle said, "I'll show you how it all works."

"And what, pray tell, will I be doing when I get up the mast?"

"You will sand."

"Afraid you were going to say that."

Gabrielle fetched the bosuns chair which, personally, I thought looked like a big canvas diaper.

"What are you going to do with that?"

"I'm going to attach it to the spinnaker halyard…"

"We have that?"

"Watch and see."

I was pleasantly surprised how salty Gabrielle was. She affixed the bosuns chair to the halyard by cleverly crafting a bowline (I was seriously impressed, and she didn't even have to say: "Up through the rabbit hole, round the big tree, down through the rabbit hole and off goes he.")

"I'm punching above my weight," I said to Gabrielle.

"What did you say?"

"I said 'I'm punching above my weight.'"

"Which means?"

"I'm really lucky to have married you."

"Awww, that is so romantic!" Gabrielle said, pushing the bosuns chair my way.

Gabrielle got me squeezed into the bosuns chair, handed me some 120 sandpaper and some 320 sandpaper, and slowly, jerkily, I pulled and she hoisted, and soon I was above the spreader. I knew it was called a spreader, because Gabrielle just taught me.

"Sand!" she commanded.

"Aye, aye," I said.

"Let me know when you need to be lowered for a

bathroom break."

"You are too kind…"

* * *

Two hours later I needed lowering. I was shattered.

"Let's go to the beach," Gabrielle said. "It's getting too hot to sand, plus I've got something up my sleeve."

"What?"

"Tell you later."

We pedaled our bikes over to Fort Zachary Taylor Historic State Park. A curly-headed ranger greeted us, we paid the modest entrance fee and aimed for the beach.

Ft. Zach or "Elizabeth Taylor" as some theatrical locals love to call it, is Florida's southernmost state park. With the amenable opening hours, you can get there really early and work on your sunburn. You can stay all day if you so wish, snack at the café, fall sleep in the shade of the Australian Pines, or even take a tour of the fort. The Civil War-era fort closes at 5pm. The park at sunset.

Here's a list of the entry fees to save you the trouble of having to Google it all on your own…or arriving at the park in just your bikini and cowabunga baggies with insufficient spare change, as we did our first time.

Entry:

--$6 per vehicle, limit 8 per vehicle, so that means no articulated semis with the entire Stanford band. Or loading up the trunk of your Chevy like you used to do at the Drive-In Movie out there by the State Fair Park.

--$2 for pedestrians, bicyclists, extra passengers (articulated lorry) and passengers in said vehicle with a bonafide holder of the coveted Annual Individual Entrance Pass.

--$4 for the driver of a single-occupant vehicle or motorcycle.

PLUS, 50 cent per person for the cheeky, sneaky Monroe County surcharge.

We parked our bikes in the shade of two palm trees,

chained them together (the bikes, not the palm trees), then laid out towels down by the water's edge, with the rocks just to the left and the breakwater off there to the right, where the fishing is good and abundant. Today the sea was gin-clear (Tanqueray), glassy and calm. Good thing we brought along the masks and snorkels that came as accessories with our Home Sweet Sailboat.

The beach is made up of sand and pebbles and is a good place to spend some quality time beachcombing or hanging out with your newfound tropical fishy friends in the guise of snapper, jacks, even tarpon, grouper and barracuda.

It's also a peaceful and serene venue to work on that hangover from last night's pillaging of Duval. If you are gay, then you will want to lay down your beach towels over in the somewhat seclusion of the breakwater. Peek over the breakwater and you will be witness to the main shipping channel, and possibly a same-sex couple canoodling.

If you haven't just purchased an old sailboat that comes with the snorkels and fins, then get yourself back over to the park's Cayo Hueso Café where the owner operates a small concession stand. Just over there near the showers. They will gladly rent you snorkels, even towels. Leave your driver's license or student ID as a "deposit," that way you won't find it missing from your meager belongings when you return from your first dip/drip of the day.

Whaaat!

Yes, you heard right. Scum-level petty thieves actually pay the entry fee to Ft. Zach so they can hit us folk up who somehow feel safer because WE PAID.

So as not to be the voice of doom, might I just mention that here, yes *here* at Ft. Zach, this is a great place to get married. Hire Bongo D Scott to play the steel drum during the ceremony, and you will have a day that you will never forget. Which is the whole idea, isn't it?

* * *

106

We tippy-toed into the ocean, which was an exceedingly pleasant 71 degrees! We snorkeled for about half an hour, one eye under the water watching all the schools of tropical fish, one eye on our towels. From time to time rising out of the water like a mob of meerkats do when they "stand up" to see if there's a threat in the general vicinity of their multiple burrows.

We dripped out of the ocean, feet on warm sand, stood in the sun and dried off. It was quiet here today: an older Cuban fisherman over on the rocks to our right, a few gays over that way, as well. All and all, pretty quiet for this time of the year.

We watched as a rather curvaceous lassie (nooo, not the canine) walked across the sand and spread out her beach towel not far from ours. Her beach towel was all sorts of colors and it had writing in big block letters. We tried reading it upside down. When that failed, we positioned ourselves for a better angle and increased legibility. It read: JUST BECAUSE WE HAD SEX LAST NIGHT, DOESN'T MEAN I'LL SNORKLE WITH YOU THIS MORNING.

"Fair enough," Gabrielle said, then she pointed toward the horizon…a cruise ship moving from our left, aiming for the main channel, most likely on its way to block the sun for Popcorn Joe and the rest of the vendors at Mallory Square at the Sunset Celebration later this afternoon.

Alright, I have to whisper this next bit so as not to piss off a *whole industry,* but, when the larger cruise ships arrive and depart, they stir up the shallow bottom and create a growing menace called "siltation." The short story: this kills off the reef and the protected marine sanctuary. Do you see where I'm going with this? If you and I were stirring up the delicate, endangered bottom in our sailboat, or our putt-putt, we would be "hanged, drawn and quartered," and have to face harsh state and federal penalties.

Nuff said.

No, actually, I don't think *nuff said*, I think I'll rage on a bit more, if you don't mind. If you are ever flying into Key West as a large cruise ship is coming in or leaving, you can see the horrifying "silt plume" that is trailing as its "prop wash" blows sediment into the coastal pristine waters. Siltation is a major contributor to coral reef decay. Simply said, corals, sea grass and marine plant and animal life depend on sunlight for photosynthesis. If the sunlight is blocked by cloudy, silty water, they croak.

And don't even get me going how this is reducing the tarpon population. You know how much fun it is to go down to the boardwalk by the A&B Lobster House, or the Ocean Key House and watch the feeding of the "harbor sharks"? Well, it won't be forever.

Why isn't the cruise-ship industry being made to pay? Or controlled?

We all know the answer to that.

And it's not just Key West that's getting thrown under the oceanic bus by big money, it's also Charleston, SC, and, are you ready, Venice, Italy.

As the cruise ship turned and came closer, Gabrielle noted: "That's the *Disney Magic*, it has propellers the size of a bus, God help the reef."

* * *

FOR YOUR BUM-CLENCHING ENJOYMENT: To be **"hanged, drawn and quartered"** was a brutally extreme punishment doled out in England beginning in 1351 for those evil souls found guilty of seriously unsavory deeds.

The offending crim was dragged (drawn) by the mother of all horses to a public area where hundreds of rubberneckers had turned up to gawped and revel in the execution and the festive atmosphere that surrounded all executions. Now, just when you may have thought that *that* was fairly tough punishment, I have to tell you that there were TWO interpretations of the word "drawn." Are you sitting down? Do you have a bucket at the ready in case you blow your cookies? The other interpretation was the removal of the inner organs. Yes, disembowelment. Sometimes the hanging part took place first, but the local authorities would only hang the prisoner by the neck for a short time (*I'm thinking anytime is not short enough*), until almost dead…then he was removed from the gallows, placed on a table (still on public display) and he was cut open at the abdomen and had his sex organs and intestines removed (drawn). This, of course performed while the poor sod was still alive. A public execution is not so very entertaining if there's not a lot of screaming, squirming and squirting of blood. The organs, which were removed, were burned in a small bonfire right next to the prisoner (as if that made much difference to him at that point).

Then, for the climax of the event, in front of a baying crowd, the individual was decapitated and the headless body hacked into four parts (quartered).

Traditionally, the five body parts (e.g., the four quarters of the body and the head) would be put on public display in different parts of the city.

Drawing and quartering wasn't removed from English criminal law until 1870. Scottish warrior William Wallace (portrayed by Mel Gibson in the movie *Braveheart*) was one such victim of the above. And we wonder why there is no love lost between the Scots and the English.

* * *

Back in paradise now, harangue over, we showered the salt off at the beach (great feeling), dried off in the sun (great feeling), then hopped on our bikes and slipped on over to Blue Heaven for brunch (great eating). Out front of Blue Heaven was a bicycle parking lot. I thought you might want to know, so I counted for you. The total 31. Ours made it 33.

Blue Heaven: "Serving heaven on a fork and sin in a glass."

We slipped in the side door, which was open for once, and stopped.

"It's been over a year since we were last here," Gabrielle said. "How can a year go by so fast and yet so slowly?"

We took a quick, refresher turn around the courtyard, under the canopy of tropical foliage, past the "shower" with the sign, which reads: **SHOWERS $1.oo, TO WATCH $2.00**.

We both laughed. "Forgot about that," I said.

We eventually took seats over near the bathtub. We ordered two cappuccinos and two Banana Heavens. It was in the upper seventies already, with two-shirt humidity. The fragrances of fresh roast coffee and jasmine wafted our way. A few peeps pecked at nothing in particular a few feet away.

We felt we were the luckiest people in the world.

CHAPTER SEVENTEEN

There were even more bicycles parked outside when we exited Blue Heaven. Plus, two trikes. Owing to the vintage state of these push-bikes, in any other part of the Western world, it would have been a bike graveyard or junkyard, but not down here on the rock. These were coveted beauties in all their multiple-layers of black-paint-and-rusted glory.

We exhumed our bikes by prying them away from two pink conch cruisers that appeared to be embracing each other, and pedaled off down Petronia, past the Rooster Gallery and the Turtle Gallery. We turned left on Whitehead and pedaled in the direction of the Green Parrot. Just as we approached Aronovitz Lane, Gabrielle swung right. "Shortcut!" she yelled.

But we didn't carry on down the lane, we stopped in front of where we used to live. Still couldn't believe that they built such beautiful cottages where rundown Villa Alberto had blighted the landscape along with the other dumps.

We didn't speak. Just reflected.

Gabrielle broke the reverie: "Did you hear that?"

"That what?"

"That cry."

"No."

We went silent.

"There! There it is again!"

"You have hearing like a bat."

Gabrielle gave me a look. "Do bats have good hearing?"

"They must do, they can't see."

"There!"

"Where?"

"There, over where Villa Alberto used to be!"

And then I heard it, clear and distinct: *Meow!*

And crawling out from under a plumeria bush/tree was a black cat with a white moustache and white spats.

"It's Mr. Leroy!" Gabrielle yelled it out.

We both jumped off our bikes and knelt down. Slowly Mr. Leroy came over to us. He was limping.

"He's in bad shape," Gabrielle said. "His fur is matted and look at all these bald patches."

Gabrielle held out her hand. Mr. Leroy approached, cautiously, then stopped and had a good long protracted scratch under his chin.

"Do cats remember?" Gabrielle asked.

Mr. Leroy sidled up to Gabrielle, dipped his head and then sort of head butted her hand.

"I believe they do."

"He's a mess," Gabrielle said. "He's got that limp, and I think he's got the mange."

In rough shape or not, we both petted Mr. Leroy's head and he kept his head down, enjoying each and every affectionate stroke.

"We'd better get him to the vet," Gabrielle said. "See if you can find a box."

While Gabrielle stayed with Mr. Leroy, I hurried over to the Green Parrot and secured a box that said LandShark Lager on the side.

When I returned, Gabrielle said: "He never liked boxes, remember?"

"I do, indeed, he became the cat from hell when we tried to put him in a box the last time. The *only* time."

"Look," Gabrielle said, as she lifted Mr. Leroy and gently set him in the box. "Cats sense it when the highlight of their day will be taken to the vet and have a thermometer stuck up their back passage. But today Mr. Leroy's too weak to fight it."

* * *

We placed the box with Mr. Leroy in it, in Gabrielle's basket and then we rode very carefully to the vet and Mr. Leroy behaved the entire way.

At the vet's, we checked in and soon thereafter a female vet who looked as if Bette Midler had had a career change stepped out from an interior door, and smiling, beaming actually, announced "Mr. Leroy!"

Proud parents that we were, we jumped to it.

The vet peered in the box and poor, woeful Mr. Leroy just stared forlornly back.

"I can see how he got the name *Mr. Leroy*," she said good-naturedly.

Vet Midler led us to an examining room that smelled oddly of wet fur and gingerly lifted Mr. Leroy out of the box and placed him on a white table in the middle of the small examining room. She gently petted him to calm him. Then, she turned to us, pointed at a nearby sink and said: "Better go wash your hands. Use hot water and soap."

We did as instructed, then we told the vet how Mr. Leroy used to work the tables at the old Mobster Lobster, and that nothing fazed him (except cardboard boxes).

"How old is he?" she asked, as she gently began her examination.

"We don't know..." Then we gave her the rest of Mr. Leroy's history, about how he was a dyed-in-the-wool alley cat, until he adopted us. He gave up a life of hanging out in Duval Street fish restaurants, begging at the tables, and in charge of mice control in the kitchens. He retired and came to live with us in Aronovitz Lane.

The vet listened patiently, then said these words. "He has the mange and appears to be malnourished. Think we'd better do a few X-rays and see what's causing him to limp. Might be a bit of arthritis, but he doesn't seem to be in much pain. Won't know until we take some pictures. We'll need to keep him in overnight."

Gabrielle shot me a look.

"Mr. Leroy will be fine," the vet said, reading the concern

on our faces. "I'll take special care of him. He reminds me of the cat I had as a little girl."

"What was your cat's name?"

"Spats," the vet said. "No surprise there, huh?"

The vet beckoned an assistant over and she whisked Mr. Leroy away.

Then she thoroughly washed *her* hands.

We thanked Bette Midler the vet for her bedside manner, bid her farewell, and stepped out of the air-conditioned office into unseasonable humidity and unchained our bikes from a telephone pole.

We were overjoyed and depressed all at the same time.

Upper downer.

One of the main reasons we didn't drink Red Bull with vodka.

CHAPTER EIGHTEEN

We headed down to Mallory Square just before sunset and told Popcorn Joe all about finding Mr. Leroy and taking him to the vet. Popcorn Joe was thrilled and happy for us.

"Get him back to being fighting fit, then he can live with you on the boat."

"But the lane is his home," Gabrielle said.

"He needs to be with the two of you now," Giuseppe said. "Catch him a small snapper and give it to him the first few mornings. He's going to love being a live-aboard."

Popcorn Joe got slammed with a large, multigenerational family from the Great White North (easily distinguishable by northern clothes purchased in Door County), so Gabrielle and I, now feeling markedly more upbeat, strolled through the sweaty, ripped, drugged, fucked-up crush of open-container, gawking humanity that is the Mallory pier at sunset. Of course I'm exaggerating here. It wasn't like that at all, there were two sober souls.

Our destination was "Will's Hill," at the southern end of the pier, which meant Will Soto and his tightrope act.

FYI: This is going to be one of those "if you've been here, then you will know it…if you haven't been here, then I will tell you." WILL SOTO ROCKS!

Before the Sunset Celebration (or just "Sunset" as it's known to locals), there was simply a gathering of folk of hippie ilk or alternative lifestyle or even suspect mental health who would worship/enjoy/ogle the setting sun each evening and pass around a bottle of Thunderbird, some really good shit, and just about everything else under the, ah, sun. Someone would play the guitar, someone might sing, someone might juggle. Folk went skinny dipping. This was in the '60s.

In the '70s and '80s, this evening ritual became quite infectious, especially with tourists from all walks of life who realized there was more to life than sitting in a rush-hour commute on the Pennsylvania Turnpike, the Eisenhower Expressway, Lincoln Memorial Drive in Milwaukee, or pretty much every freeway in and around Houston.

Soon, fledgling entrepreneurs began showing up at sunset to flog their wares. Performers found "Sunset" a safe and practical venue to hone their skills.

And Sunset exploded in popularity.

The city wanted to shut it down. Some say pressure came from *certain* Duval- and Front-Street merchants who claimed to be legitimate merchants. *Certain* merchants felt the vendors down at Mallory were cutting into their piece of the Key lime pie. Everyone on the rock knew that *certain* merchants were full of shit as they were patently corrupt, but then they had big bucks and the backing of City Hall, so when they cried foul, a lot of folk listened, as money speaks with a loud voice.

An annoying loud voice.

I've mention this before, but it bears repeating: Led by tightrope walker Will Soto, the artisans and street entertainers down at Mallory formed a kickass nonprofit organization called the Key West Cultural Preservation Society—and they've had clout on their side ever since. Extremely difficult to push out Key West's biggest tourist attractions no matter how much money you burn.

Eventually, the city and *certain* merchants had a coconut drop on their heads, came to their senses, such as they were, and threw their support behind Will and the beloved Cultural Preservation Society.

And that was in 1984.

Still going strong.

Sunset.

And Will Soto.

We found Will Soto just starting his show. He climbed up onto his tightrope and deftly swung himself upside down and up. The man is an animal!

Suddenly, Will thrust a hand down the back of his tights and moaned comically at the crowd which surrounded him: "Not easy to start the show after giving yourself a wedgie!"

The crowd roared.

I won't describe in detail any more of what we saw, so that you may enjoy it afresh when you tell your boss to go BLEEP himself and then take a spontaneous cheeky trip down here, but I will give you a splash of back story:

Will Soto ended up in Key West by chance. He was a sculptor, working a show up in Coconut Grove. When the show was all over, an artist friend asked Will if he wanted to come down to Key West to hang out for the winter. Will Soto said he preferred to go back to New Orleans. The friend said: "Well, then let's have one last drink together." They did, but the drink was rum and the elixir worked it magical wonders and before Will Soto knew it, he was in the back of a truck "passing over many, many bridges." He ended up in Key West, liked what he saw down at Mallory and now is a revered icon down here and a true Key West original. Will Soto embodies all that Key West was, and now is, excluding gentrification, the rape of paradise, the destruction of the reef, the toxic misuse of the marine sanctuary, the rising rents, lack of affordability of housing, on and on. And on.

FYI: When Gabrielle and I first moved to Key West (the first book in my series, where we sold our Key West sunset photography at Mallory Square), Will Soto was one of the first locals to come up to us, introduce himself, offer his hand and a smile—and we will never forget that.

CHAPTER NINETEEN

Have you ever been so excited that you didn't sleep so very well?

Have you?

Big event upcoming?

Wedding?

Graduation?

Holiday?

Chance at getting laid? (**You've heard the joke, haven't you? There's a convention in town. The convention's topic is: "LET'S TALK ABOUT SEX".

Makes you want to go sign up, doesn't it?

Anyhoo, back to the joke. At the end of a very enlightening week, the Lead Speaker pipes up with "Here's a question for the assembled: Who here has sex more than once a day?"

One male raises his hand (the assembled are sincerely impressed AND rightly envious but, owing to the ugly mug on said person, wonder if the sex involves another human being). Then the Lead Speaker asks: "Who has sex more than once a week?" A few more hands go up.

Then: "Who has sex more than once a month?" A whole lot of hands are raised.

Then he asks: "Is there anyone in here who only has sex once a year?"

"It's me! It's me! Oh, yes, it's me! I'm the one who only has sex once a year!" comes a plaintive voice.

In the back row a man is waving frantically.

Everyone in the auditorium turns to face him.

The moderator asks: "Why the declaration! Why such joy?"

The man in the back row throws his hands in the air like Rocky Balboa and shrieks at the top of his lungs: "Because tonight's the night! Tonight's the night!"

Got that image?

That's me.

Except it's not about sex, and it's not nighttime, it's the crack of dawn, and we're standing outside the vets.

We are here to pickup Mr. Leroy.

We hear dogs barking, they're up early, as well, hoping that they get to go home today. Hoping that a loved one will come by and hug them and pet them and reassure them that they are indeed getting to go back and live with their human family, back in that warm and cozy human house (or air-conditioned house). Hoping that their family hasn't *abandoned* them.

Not that it crossed their mind.

ABANDONED!

Now the dogs are going nuts. We think someone has opened a back door and salvation for our wee Mr. Leroy is not far off.

Is he afraid?

Wondering if we will come back?

Is all that barking frightening him?

"He's tough," Gabrielle tells me, reading my mind and my concern.

A light flickers on inside the vets, then another, then the barking temporarily stops.

Why?

We are suddenly all ears, just like the furry little ones inside.

We hear the sound of clogs on tile, then a key is inserted in the lock: *Someone is opening the front door!*

The door swings open and we are led in by a sleepy albeit friendly assistant type woman in clinically blue orderly kit. The friendly assistant smells faintly of hand sanitizer.

The BARKING resumes with a vengeance now. If I could read doggie subtext, I would say it means:

WE ARE SAVED!

SOMEONE IS COMING FOR US TODAY!

WE ARE LOVED!

And most importantly: I GET TO GO BACK HOME AND SLEEP AND EAT WHERE ALL THE SMELLS ARE FAMILIAR!

Yay! Bark!

Yay! Bark!

Yay! *Meow.*

Gabrielle and I exchange looks.

A door which leads to the back where the cages are kept opens, and out steps Dr. Vet Midler...carrying a new, fresh, specially designed cat carrier box!

Vet Midler places the box on the floor in front of us. She opens it. Staring back at us is Mr. Leroy. Once again, if I could read subtext—feline subtext, now—I would have to say that Mr. Leroy's subtext reads: ABOUT TIME! LET'S BLOW THIS POPSICLE STAND!

Gabrielle lifts Mr. Leroy out of the box and hugs him close and tight, never wanting to let go. "He got a haircut," Gabrielle notes.

"Yes," Vet Midler says. "We cut Mr. Leroy's fur short to treat the mange. We did a skin scraping and took a look at the sample under the microscope. The mange in cats is not as common as in dogs because cats bathe themselves frequently, but Mr. Leroy was sleeping rough..."

Gabrielle and I are all ears, peaked and twitching.

"There are several types of the mange," Vet Midler goes on. "Mr. Leroy has what's called Notoedric mange. Also referred to as feline scabies..."

"Scabies," I sort of blurt it out.

"Yes," Vet Midler says. "It's caused by mites. The disease is similar to sarcoptic mange in dogs. It's highly contagious."

"To humans, as well?" Gabrielle asks.

"Yes. Killing mites isn't a one-step process as you can imagine. Mr. Leroy will need extended treatment for the next four weeks to clear out the infection and to kill the remaining mites and eggs. Be prepared not to see positive results for at least a week or so. Skin...fur, they both need time to heal."

"What about the problem with the back legs?" Gabrielle asked.

"That..." she says, her brow wrinkling a bit. "Mr. Leroy limps and gets unsteady on the back legs because of nerve damage. I believe someone hit him or threw a rock at him..."

Bastards!

"Is it permanent?" I ask.

"I'm afraid so. I've been wrong in the past though, so hope springs eternal."

Vet Midler went on to advise us about how to deal with and treat the mange and what to do with bedding and how we should protect ourselves and wash our hands again and wash our clothes when we get back home.

"Can Mr. Leroy sleep with us?" Gabrielle asked.

"Soon," came the reply.

My head was spinning as I went up to the receptionist and paid $450. Worth every single penny, I must say. *How lucky were we to find Mr. Leroy all over again?*

Or did he find us?

What life would Mr. Leroy have had without us?

How much time would he have had left if we hadn't intervened?

CHAPTER TWENTY

Gabrielle and I got up early the next morning and strolled over to Fausto's to load up on cat food, cat treats, all the cat toys we could carry, and a replacement can of tuna, as Mr. Leroy had dined heartily the previous evening.

Fishing was not allowed in the Bite, so catching a small snapper for Mr. Leroy would have to wait until we had time to slip over to the rocks at Ft. Zach.

After shopping, we walked down the shady side of Duval. As we approached the Fat Tuesday/Hard Rock corner.

We stopped.

And observed.

There's a new "act" in town.

It's a formerly busty, presently droopy woman, a bit rough around the edges, a bottle-blonde with impressive roots, somewhere between good-looking and a bit too heavy on the crystal meth.

Thus the acne and the leathery skin. And the scabby fingernails.

She's twirling two balls, each on the end of a nylon cord about two-and-a-half feet long, one in each hand. This apparently is called "poi." I know this because I asked her.

If she screws up and, ah, drops the ball, she can't start up until there's no foot traffic or she'll accidentally garrote someone. This lag of "Showtime" in not being able to start back up is asking a lot of Duval Street. She's twirling for tips. Haven't seen this one before. Location is everything, and Duval Street is that.

Oops, Miss Poi is having a wardrobe malfunction. A breast is making a cheeky run for freedom. Miss Poi would stop to adjust, but stopping is just not an option.

Eventually gravity wins and she makes a cock-up of her twirling and she is forced to cease and desist. She adjusts the offending breast by forcing it in the general direction of her knees.

At her feet, on a ratty ol' blanket, is the obligatory dog. The dog looks like it wants to eat your face. This can't be good for custom.

Now she's looking right and left, like a small child does before crossing the street, but she still can't start up on account of the parade of tourists heading toward Sloppy's and Two Friends and all points Mallory.

Now she blows her nose by putting a thumb against the side of, ah, her nose. This won't help business, either, I'm thinking. At what stop on the mental-health train to nowhere do you feel that this is acceptable public behavior?

Wait! Someone has given her a tip. I think the tip was "Give up show business!"

No, I'm wrong, it is of actual monetary value, possibly a fiver!

Well, this act of kindness has given her renewed motivation and she avails of a ten-foot opening in the people stream and she's back twirling.

And she gets yet another tip!

Location, location, location.

Perhaps we should give her more credit; she's endeavoring to make a living, endeavoring to feed her drug habit by doing an honest day's work. She's not hooking, not thieving, not ripping anyone off.

She has standards.

BTW: Poi refers to both the performance and those quirky little balls. As you've sussed, poi involves swinging tethered weights through a variety of rhythmical and geometric patterns. Poi artists may also sing or dance while swinging their poi. Poi can be made from various materials with different handles, weights, and effects (such as fire).

Poi originated with the aboriginal Maoris of New Zealand and is still performed there today.

Who knew?

Gabrielle and I left Poi Woman behind and headed further down Duval. Down around Rick's, I stopped and pointed. Across the street was my blind student-type with the Squiggy-hair, wearing sunglasses, trying to raise funds to get back to Germany. He was sitting on his familiar fold-up chair, only now he was deeply tanned and his Squiggy-hair was bleached.

"Remember him?" I said to Gabrielle.

"Something's wrong with this picture," Gabrielle said. "I'm going to go try something."

Gabrielle crossed the street and I followed. When she approached the blind fellow, she dropped two quarters KLINK in his lap which was covered with that same cloth, then she walked on. The blind fellow did as he always did, he said "Zank you," and stared straight ahead, then after a few moments, he turned and watched Gabrielle walk off down the street.

What was that all about?

Later in the summer we would see him dressed in nice clothing window shopping in the New Town.

Key West brings out the entrepreneur in us all.

For better or worse.

CHAPTER TWENTY-ONE

March Madness is over.

Baseball season has started.

NBA playoffs are well underway.

The NFL draft is done and gone.

Okemo Ski Resort in Vermont just had a fresh snowfall.

And down here on the rock it's 82F, wall-to-wall sunshine, and the wind is a gentle breeze out of the southwest.

It's spring.

Springtime in Key West.

Spring is a glorious time to be in Key West.

The ocean is already up to 78F.

The plumeria are in full glorious bloom, pure white, yellow, pink, rose, orange, scarlet, and cerise.

And the island is the temporal domain of creepy nasties that have come out of hibernation: scorpions, palmetto bugs, mosquitoes. To make our lives just that much more exciting than we really need them to be.

If you want to look at the good side of scorpions, which is not always so very easy to do, they just love the Florida cockroach or palmetto bug. I don't mean that as besties or an inamorata—I mean as a meal.

Scorpions like to hang out under boards, rubbish, and other crap in your backyard or under your house. This provides them with shelter and protection. You may want to make a note for that drunken walk home, scorpions are active at night (like yours truly), and they do their share to reduce pests in and around the home.

Scorpions, palmetto bugs, mozzies…they're part of the deal and now, finally, we've settled into our new life living onboard a boat in Key West, FL, not quite the USA.

As has Mr. Leroy.

Mr. Leroy loves living on a boat. Everything smells so fishy. And there's always something moving down there in the water to keep his attention. A bad day at sea is better than a good day at the office (or at the pound).

Mr. Leroy is thriving and he's never looked healthier. He sleeps with us at night in our forward bunk, up by our heads, his feet always touching the top of Gabrielle's head or the top of mine.

He likes that.

We like that.

During the day, he climbs up on the boom and uses our furled sail as a hammock. And snoozes. He understands what the siesta is all about.

Mr. Leroy's debilitating mange is long gone, but he still has nagging problems with his back legs. The vet had told us that incontinence could eventually be an issue, but by the grace of God, that has not materialized.

Issues or not, he purrs a lot and that brings all of us great joy.

* * *

Johnny-Johnny has stopped by our boat.

And he's asked if we would do a favor for him.

Are you thinking what I'm thinking?

This can't be good. In reality, we owe him one.

As our minds swirl, Johnny-Johnny's cell rings.

"Excuse me, *Madame, monsieur.*" And Johnny-Johnny steps off our boat and goes up and sits on our dock box. He's just close enough for us to hear, but not close enough for us to make out the conversation. The odd words waft our way: "dealt with," "I'm not waiting around for it," "Money's not a problem," "I've got two friends who'll take care of it."

126

Gabrielle and I are on the verge of upping anchor and setting sail.

"What do you think he wants?" Gabrielle asks.

"It can't be good, can it?" I say. "He probably wants us to torture someone with a blow torch or drive the getaway car."

"And what does all that mean? 'Dealt with.' 'Money's not a problem.'"

Johnny-Johnny finishes his call and then just sits there, staring at us.

"Oh, oh," I utter under my breath. "Here he comes."

Johnny-Johnny boards our boat takes a seat on a cushion in the cockpit. Gabrielle and I are about to shit our shorts, when Mr. Leroy comes down from his nap up on the boom. Mr. Leroy walks right up to Johnny-Johnny and puts his paws up in the air as a child would who wants to be picked up.

Johnny-Johnny obliges and picks up Mr. Leroy.

Mr. Leroy likes Johnny-Johnny.

"Don't know how to ask this," Johnny-Johnny says. "But it's about that favor. I can't do it without the two of you."

I shoot a look at Gabrielle.

"What—is—it—you—want—us—to—do?" I squeak.

"I want you to take care of something for me."

Oh shit, here it comes.

"I have a kitten and I need to go out of town for a few days. Could you feed her for me? I know it's a lot to ask, but…"

Gabrielle and I almost burst into tears.

"Of course we'd do that for you, Johnny-Johnny," Gabrielle says. "Happy to do it."

"What's her name?" I ask.

"Manxsie," Johnny-Johnny says. "She's a wee, little Manx from the Isle of Man. A rescue cat."

127

CHAPTER TWENTY-TWO

We didn't know where Johnny-Johnny lived.

"Do you think he lives rough?" I asked Gabrielle.

"He said he'd stop by and take us over there."

"I hope he's not sleeping under a house in some back tropical lane like our old friend Captain Jerry? Remember, he resided in the crawl space under Don and Shirley's house?"

"Or what about Eddie, the transient who spent all his time at the library reading, but then at night he would sleep on different porches in the Old Town?" Gabrielle said.

"Oh, yeah, I forgot about him. Remember, he rolled over one night and a scorpion stung him in the face?"

"That was awful. He looked horrible."

"What about 'Feather'? Remember him? He slept in the bushes over at the Porter House and then just didn't wake up one morning."

"God rest his soul."

"Look! Here comes Johnny-Johnny now."

Johnny-Johnny pedaled up on an old conch cruiser.

"*Madame, monsieur*, follow me!"

Gabrielle and I jumped on our bikes and took off after Johnny-Johnny. We caught up to him at the corner of Caroline, and then all three of us pedaled lazily along.

"I'll be gone about three days. Have to run up to the mainland for a favor."

As we approached Simonton, we had to overtake the Conch Tour Train because one of the passengers had tried to take a selfie, using a selfie stick, and had whacked a transient on a bicycle on the back of his head, as the train passed by.

The transient was yelling that he had whiplash and was going to sue, and the passenger, some corpulent woman was still videoing it all with her cell, yelling back: "You can't get whiplash from a selfie stick. It won't hold up in court!"

"No?" the transient said, suddenly deflated. "Then I'll settle for some spare change."

We almost fell off our bikes laughing.

A sense of humor in Key West is an important asset.

Johnny-Johnny led us across Simonton, then across Duval, past my office, the Bull, and we turned left on Whitehead, by Kelly's and the sign that marks the "Birthplace of Pan Am."

We pedaled up to Southard trying to keep up with Johnny-Johnny and we turned right into Truman Annex. Johnny-Johnny stopped his bike by the gatehouse, took a key out of his pocket and opened the door.

"He lives in the gatehouse?" I whispered to Gabrielle.

We got off our bikes and peered in the door.

"Where's Manxsie?" I said.

"Over at my flat."

"You don't live here?"

"Who could live in this gatehouse, it's so small? Was just dropping off something the guard wanted for the weekend."

Hmmm.

We climbed back on our bikes, biked back down Whitehead, then turned right on Fleming. Just before we reached Duval, and right across from La Concha and, ah, Starbucks, we de-biked and chained our bikes to the bike-stand just in front of the glass doors on the side of the old Kress building.

Johnny-Johnny inserted a key in the lock, then we climbed through three muggy floors to the top.

"Didn't know there was another floor up here," I said.

"No one does, they think the penthouse is the top, but my wee corner actually reaches higher. I'm above the old parole board."

Johnny-Johnny slipped a key into a nondescript door and we stepped in to the smallest flat I've ever seen.

"I know what you're thinking, you're thinking it's not much larger than the gatehouse, but look here."

Johnny-Johnny opened another door and behind it was a large room with a high ceiling, similar to the one Tom Hank's character lived in, in the movie *BIG*, except with a skylight rather than large windows. Instead of a trampoline and a Pepsi machine and a pinball machine and skateboards and an inflatable palm tree and dinosaur, the place was a maze of cat toys, scratching posts, and a round yellow plastic pad with a motorized revolving mouse tail.

An adorable, little Manx kitten trotted up to Gabrielle.

"Well, that's a good sign," Johnny-Johnny said. "Meet my Manxsie!"

Gabrielle got down on the floor and pulled Manxsie up in her lap. A bond already forming.

Johnny-Johnny smiled like a proud parent would, then showed us where he kept the cat food and the kitty litter. He looked around his quirky place with pride: "Cool, huh? I don't need much. I do some security in exchange for rent. It's a symbiotic relationship."

CHAPTER TWENTY-THREE

Early the next morning, we rode our bicycles back to the old Kress Building to feed Manxsie.

As before, we chained our bikes to the bike-stand out front, inserted the key in the door, and started our climb through the dimly lit furnace that was the stairwell up to Johnny-Johnny's flat. Halfway up, a door opened and a Cuban maid smiled at us as she swept up in front of the door.

We climbed one flight higher and it was even hotter and stuffier up here. We approached Johnny-Johnny's nondescript door.

"I'm going to open the door," Gabrielle said. "You stand guard in case Manxsie tries to make a bid for freedom."

"Of all the people on this earth, I think Johnny-Johnny is the last one I want to upset."

Gabrielle pulled the set of keys that Johnny-Johnny had given us out of her short's pocket and inserted it in the door. It didn't fit. Neither did the next two.

"Why does Johnny-Johnny need so many keys?" Gabrielle asked.

"Perhaps that part of a gofer's armory."

Gabrielle tried the last key (it's always the last key, isn't it?). The key fit and we heard the lock go. But the door still wouldn't push open. That's when we realized there was another lock, a deadbolt, down near the floor.

Such security against cat-toy theft!

Gabrielle opened the door a crack to peer cautiously in and a lightning bolt of fur exploded past me and hightailed it (or, in Manxsie's case No-tailed it) down the stairs.

"She's doing a runner!" Gabrielle screamed.

Have you ever tried to herd a cat? Not so very easy, is it? It's somewhere between fright, flight, and a big game for them. In Manxsie's case, I think it was a big game.

"Get her!" Gabrielle yelled.

I chased Manxsie down the steps. I was bent over, knees splayed, like I had a stick up my ass, arms wide, trying to corral the speedy little critter. I was afraid she was going to run all the way to the ground floor and escape if someone just happened to open the front door at that moment.

Sod's Law.

Murphy's Law.

Manxsie's Law.

But I didn't have to worry about all that. Not in the slightest, you see, Manxsie stopped on the next landing below, and I swear on my mother's grave (although she was cremated and had her ashes scattered on the golf course) gave me a catch-me-if-you-can look and darted into the apartment just as the Cuban maid was closing the door.

And locking it.

Twice.

Gabrielle came thundering down the stairs.

"What took you so long?"

"I had to lock Johnny-Johnny's door, both locks…"

"The cow's out of the barn!" I think I might have raised my voice here, as I was starting to lose it, what with my life passing before my eyes.

"Ring the doorbell!" Gabrielle said.

But ringing the doorbell would do no good, for at that precise moment, we heard the vacuum cleaner start up. And it must have been a Dyson, because it sounded like a 747 just lifting off the runway.

"Jeez. What a racket," I said. "Guess she must've emptied the bag…"

"Shut up and pound on the door!"

I pounded on the door.

132

No answer.

"She's deaf!"

"Pound louder!"

I pounded louder, not Sheldon-esque with three timid knocks, more concussive blows with the side of my fist...and the vacuuming stopped.

"Ring the doorbell now!"

I rang the doorbell.

And we heard CLICK...and then another CLICK.

And the door opened a crack.

Two beady eyes, about five feet off the ground, peered up at us. "*Sí?*"

"Oh, shit, she doesn't speak English."

"Our cat," Gabrielle said. "*Gato...*"

"*No tengo un gato,*" the beady eyes said. And she closed the door.

"Nooo!"

CLICK...CLICK.

"Ring the doorbell again before she starts to hoover!"

I looked at Gabrielle. "In the time it took you to tell me that, you could have rung the doorbell yourself!"

"RING IT!!!"

I rang.

We heard two locks go.

Then the door opened up a crack again.

And there were the two beady eyes, two pissholes in the snow, searching for confirmation of anything.

"*Tenemos un gato. Nosotros, no usted. Ella corrió en su apartamento Ella está adentro ahora mismo. Por favor, abra la puerta y déjenos entrar.*"

Now, not only are the beady eyes staring at my wife, *I'm* staring at my wife. "Since when did you become a polyglot?"

"It just suddenly came to me," Gabrielle said. "I guess from when we used to study Spanish."

The Cuban maid opened the door wide, smiled as if we were now family and said: "*Pasale!*"

We entered and gasped. We had just entered a palace, a

temple of books and art to some rich person's life. The place *reeked of* wealth and opulence.

And, of course, the carpets looked freshly vacuumed.

"Nuestro gato es, de hecho, un gatito. Probablemente tímido."

The Cuban maid got it all figured out that the cat was, in fact, just a kitten and probably frightened, and the three of us formed a search party and started looking for cheeky little Manxsie.

"Cats don't like vacuum cleaners," I hissed at Gabrielle. "He's probably stuck to the ceiling somewhere."

The three of us searched for nearly half an hour, under the king-size beds, on top of the fridge, behind the piano, next to the harp (yes, a harp!), and no Manxsie.

How was that possible?

"I don't think she's in here," Gabrielle said. "Are you sure you saw her go in?"

"Pretty sure, the landing was so dark, and my eyes hadn't adjusted from being out in the bright sun."

"We'd better take another look out in the stairwell."

Gabrielle explained our agenda in Spanish to the Cuban maid, then the three of us crossed to the front door as if we were attached at the hip, opened it gently and peered out.

No Manxsie.

Then, all three of us stepped outside onto the landing and looked out there. Over the railing, on top of the fire extinguisher.

No, Manxsie.

Where could she have gone?

The three of us gave up, went back inside.

Sitting in the middle of the recently vacuumed carpet, looking smug and looking at us like we were the Three Stooges, was Manxsie.

Cats pull that kind of shit on humans.

CHAPTER TWENTY-FOUR

We've decided to change the name of the boat. Name it something that has more meaning to us.

But...can it be done?

Are there legal considerations?

Nautical ramifications?

Is it bad luck?

We spoke to some of the boat owners and skippers around the marina and received hearty responses such as: "Don't do it!" "It's bad luck!" "You'll regret it!" "Can't be done!"

Yet having received those replies, it became glaringly obvious that nobody really knew if it were possible or not. These were uneducated, without experience, emotional responses.

Where is Ed Robinson when you need him? He must have done it with *Leap of Faith*, wouldn't you have thought, and look at the great life he and Kim are enjoying.

Eventually, we went out to Stock Island and spoke to some of the old shrimpers. And one old, crotchety sumbitch said: "Just paint a new name over the old one."

Okay, perhaps this wasn't going to be such a big deal, after all. I could sand most of it off and then we would go over to chandlery and ask if they knew anybody who painted boat names.

Now, cue the music from your favorite horror film, we went to the library over on Fleming and started to read about how it all worked.

And we read this:

"According to ancient mythology, it was widely believed that a king of the sea, Neptune, and a Greek ruler of the sea, Poseidon, lived on the floor of the ocean in palaces. These gods of the sea would assure safe passage over the Seven Seas to all sailors that followed their doctrine and respected their protocols.

"Neptune and Poseidon are said to maintain a 'Ledger of the Deep' that records the name of every seagoing vessel by name. Changing the name of a boat is thus said to be disrespectful to the sea gods."

Oh, shit! Neptune you do not want to piss off...and Poseidon, well, we saw the movie.

And then we read: "You can and are able to rename your boat, but if you do not properly rename it, you are doomed to a lifetime of bad luck. Before you rename a boat at a christening ceremony, you must remove or destroy ALL references, traces and proof of the boat's old identity. It is critical that the old name is completely removed before you even say the new name out loud, or bring anything on the boat with a new name inscribed on it. Be clinically thorough. If you christen your boat and then unearth any trace of the old name, you will need to re-christen it."

Now we're getting somewhere.

We rang Tina and asked her if she minded if we changed the boat's name.

She said *no problem.*

Then, we asked her if she knew whether Elmer's boat had ever had another name.

"I'll go through his old papers that he had in a safety deposit box and let you know," Tina said.

We rang off and went back to the library.

We then read that if you purchase a boat and properly change the name as instructed, the old Bill of Sale will not reflect the changed name. This could be a big problem if we ever wanted to sell it.

"So let's never sell it," Gabrielle said. And that was that

solved, and that hoop jumped through.

Then, we read: "Remove the old name on the boat itself. Removing the exterior paint or lettering is obvious, but you also need to check if the boat has ever been repainted. If so, you need to get down to previous layers and literally scrape off the old name. It is not enough to just paint over the old name.

"The same applies for the interior of the boat. Make sure any fixtures: badges, engravings, upholstery, or decorations with the old name are obliterated or removed.

"You must get rid of any accessories with the old boat name. Common accessories are floatation devices, life rings, brass bells, clothing, coffee mugs, floating key chains, license plate frames."

Tina rang us back and said that the *RESTLESS* was the only name the boat had ever had.

Then we came to this slightly daunting bit: "The tricky part is what to do with all the paperwork like cruising journals, maintenance logs, and receipts. It is ok to keep the paperwork, but you must cover the old name with White Out every time it is written."

So we rang Tina again. She said she would hunt up all paperwork, journals, logs and the like and motor down in the Pig. We said we'd have coffee ready.

Tina arrived, but not in the Pig, rather a cool Jeep Wrangler with soft top.

"What happened to the Pig?" Gabrielle asked.

"The Pig ate it," Tina said. "If B.O. needs another heap to display out front of his fish wagon I will gladly donate her..."

"The Pig was a female?"

"Don't ask."

We had coffee, and we examined the paperwork Tina had brought with her. Luckily, there wasn't much and we were able to white out the few references to the old name.

"What did people do before White Out?" Gabrielle asked.

"Led a much more frightening existence," I said.

We kept Popcorn Joe apprised about our adventures and he talked to a few folk that he knew in the Coast Guard, and he got back to us with something that went like this:

"Facebook and digital media have created a real mess of things. Find the boat's digital footprint, if there is one, find any Facebook posts or photos ANYWHERE showing the name. No need to delete all photos of the boat, just make sure the name is not visible."

Once again, luckily, Elmer had not been active on social media and there was no digital footprint. We did find though, an old photo of the boat on the wall of the Geiger Key Marina, but no name was visible in the photograph. So dodged another armor-piercing bullet there and jumped through those hoops.

Then…we read that a boat's christening "should only be done on certain days: Friday is unlucky apparently because Jesus was crucified on this day of the week. If, say, a new Coast Guard boat is finished on a Friday, they always wait until Saturday to christen it.

"Thursday is a bad day to be on the water because it's Thor's big day, and he's the god of thunder and storms." *Don't want to get on Thor's bad side.*

"The first Monday in April is the day Cain slew Abel. It might also be April Fool's Day, which can't be a good thing.

"The second Monday in August is the day the kingdoms of Sodom and Gomorrah were destroyed."

Not sure what bearing this had on the process, but Sodom and Gomorrah, jeez!

Of course what this all boils down to is if new boat owners don't follow these strict guidelines, then all sorts of awful things could happen, such as: Long periods of foul weather (we had that in the UK), fires down below, personal injuries, collisions at sea.

Then we read about some poor soul who didn't pay attention and heed the advice: "Since then, his boat has been struck by lightning, had its engine ruined by the ingress of the sea, been damaged by collision and finally sunk! It pays to be thorough."

Holy shit!

"Don't forget," Popcorn Joe said, "after the christening,

to complete it, you will need to take a maiden voyage."

We wanted our christening to be memorable, so we brought in the big guns in the form of Popcorn Joe, Johnny-Johnny, plus Tina, Patty and Sasha.

We held our ceremony at sunset, on a Saturday, and we welcomed our friends, thanked them for attending, and toasted our new boat/home/life.

Red wine is supposed to be used to christen a boat, not champagne, as red wine represents the blood of a virgin. Virgins used to be sacrificed way back then. There was no way we were going to find the blood of a virgin—let alone a virgin in Key West.

And never during Spring Break.

We didn't want to break a bottle over the bow, as we didn't want glass to go in the water, and we were just a bit afraid that a good striking blow with a bottle might just sink the boat.

If you don't break a bottle over the bow, you are allowed to simply pour the red wine over the bow.

So that's what we did.

Gabrielle had the honors, so she poured some of the red wine on the bow and proclaimed proudly: "By the powers vested in me, I hereby christen thee sailing vessel *MR. LEROY.*" And then with a very regal English accent like the Queen of England would: "God bless her and all who sail in her."

* * *

Slowly, we're settling into our second time around in Key West.

Gabrielle is back painting her Tropical Names at the Ocean Key Resort, and I've been walking up and down the docks and quays of the marina, seeing if I could rustle up any "DAY WORK."

I was asked if I had any experience working on boats, and I said: "Just cleaning, but I will turn up for work on time, and be sober."

And I got my first job, which was simply *cleaning* a very dirty boat, inside and out. "I can do this! I'll start with the head!"

The boat was an old Chris-Craft, 55-footer, flying the Canadian flag. It was caked in salt and covered with gull poop. And it smelled of shrimp. The owners were two elderly gentlemen who lived in Barnstaple, out on Cape Cod, in the summers. They'd been wintering in Ft. Lauderdale, but decided to give Key West a good, hard look. They had just returned from a short trip over to Cuba. One was Canadian and the other Welsh.

Oddly the boat reminded me of our former home in Aronovitz Lane, long and skinny, passing from one room to the next, through a series of doors.

I worked on the boat for a week.

I was paid cash, daily, and…don't ask.

Then I found more work around the marina doing some sanding, doing some varnishing, doing some more cleaning. Someone even asked me if I knew anything about changing the name of a boat!

"Yes," I said. "Yes, I do."

And now we both have jobs, sustainable sources of income.

Life is good.

We are both as brown as berries.

We don't own a car.

Or have a mortgage.

And we don't owe anyone any money.

We don't even have a bar bill.

Gabrielle's commute is along the historic seafront, distance two blocks.

My commute is just over to that sailboat, powerboat or swim-wagon, right over there.

And we are very happy down here at 24 degrees north, 81 degrees west.

CHAPTER TWENTY-FIVE

Are you one of those individuals who wish you could push the Pause Button on weekends?

Are you the type of person who feels the only antidote to Monday mornings is, say, Friday?

It's time you and I had a little talk. Yes, *you*. You're thinking of taking the big plunge, aren't you?

Making the big break?

You're thinking of throwing in the towel, giving up your old life and MOVING TO KEY WEST.

So, what are you waiting for?

Do you really want to spend another winter in the Great White North?

Can't afford to swing it?

Why not come down and do a test drive?

Consider it research and development.

Write it off your taxes.

See how you like it down here.

See if Key West works for you.

If we can make it work, why can't you?

CHAPTER TWENTY-SIX

If you are easily shocked and God-fearing, look away now.

It's Spring Break.

And Spring Breakers are everywhere, drinking, drugging and stripping off.

Girls gone wild.

Boys gone wild.

Skin is being flashed indiscriminately.

And there is much sucking of face.

Spring Breakers have annexed Smathers Beach. It used to be Frisbee and volleyball on the beach, now it's twerking, and dry-humping daisy chains, and petting heavily al fresco in broad daylight!

Not everyone, mind you, but enough to realize things just aren't like they used to be.

Or...have we been living in a cave?

Over on Duval Street, it is only marginally more subdued, there's a river, make that a torrent of girls wearing teeny-weeny bikini tops and skimpy cutoff bottoms, buttons fashionably undone an inch or two or three.

At least past the tan line.

And that's low.

We saw one young lassie prancing down Duval, yes, prancing (*oh, the freedom of it all!*). She was wearing the obligatory cutoffs, which were unbuttoned *and gaping!* That was her bottom half. On the top half, she had only pasties. *Butterfly* pasties. Written in magic marker across her ample breasts was FREE KISSES.

Her parents would have a cow.

Then there were the guys. They were all shirtless, all buff, all oiled and cut. Testosterone was ejaculating right off the charts.

You are probably aware that some popular beach destinations for Spring Breakers are Panama City Beach, South Padre Island, Clearwater Beach and Daytona Beach.

Spring Breakers flock to these towns as it's not so far to drive. Having said that, you might not be able to outrun those March and April cold fronts if you don't head all the way to the bottom of the Keys.

To the rock.

On account of Key West being the most distant, the most difficult to get to (and back home with a positive PCR blood test for genital herpes), you get a different breed of Spring Breaker—you get the professional, the resolutely motivated, the closet-case-everythings. Those willing to go the extra mile, literally, for a chance to not be caught by enquiring eyes, those willing to do and try things that perhaps they've never tried before. Sex, drugs, rock and crack.

Sex with anything warm and in every shape and form.

What Spring Breakers get up to sexually, would scare the bejesus out of mom and dad (parents who still can't get the image of Aruba out of their minds).

Then there are the creepy males who descend on Key West to press up to coeds in short skirts on crowded dance floors to snap up-skirt photos and videos with their cell phones, which will then be later distributed on social media.

Horrifying.

But what befalls the Spring Breakers *drug-wise* is even more disconcerting, you see, there are unscrupulous dealers, both male and female, who come all the way down to Key West, and they are ready to sell illicit drugs to any student who wants to buy it and try it. These male and female dealers make no mention of what could go wrong, what could harm you, what could kill you, what could lead to addiction, their only concern is to make money, lots of it, and not get caught by the police.

143

*But I'm only going to **snort** heroin, that can't be so bad. And I'm only going to try it once.*

These scum dealers often don't even know the purity of the drug they're selling or what it's been cut with. Pure can kill, so can the myriad of shit it's been stepped on with, such as rat poison, Ajax, fentanyl (a powerful pain killer), or carfentanyl (an animal tranquilizer). Fentanyl is 100 times stronger than street heroin, carfentanyl is 10,000 times stronger than street heroin.

YOU MAY REMEMBER: The singer Prince died of a fentanyl overdose.

But my baby is a straight-A student, you say, *she would never do heroin.* Okay, perhaps she wouldn't try heroin, but think Aruba again, and have a squizzy at this:

Some of the legal (*lethal*) highs are Spice and Black Mamba, it will only reduce your child to a trembling, vomiting zombie.

"But, Mom, everyone else is going to Florida on Spring Break, why can't I! I'm an A-student. I've worked hard. I deserve it. I won't do anything I shouldn't."

"Well, if you promise."

Even the purportedly upstanding, newly elected Student Body President of a major Florida university was arrested, so wasted beyond clinical belief, he blindly endeavored to steal a moped so he could zip back to his northern campus. Embarrassing, seriously misguided, but what's worse, he was so fucked up, he thought he was in Clearwater (432 miles to the north), not Key West.

Yikes, I utter.

Okay, go take an aspirin and then meet me back here, I've got something else I need to tell you.

Are you back?

Are you ready for this?

Are you sitting down? Again?

One of the latest party games is so thrilling, yet intimidating, that Spring Breakers will only engage in it if they're really, really drunk, or perhaps high.

It's thus: You are given a key to a certain hotel room, you go there, insert the key and enter. All the curtains are drawn, blackout curtains in place. You have to get undressed, and get into bed, naked. Not long after you are tucked up and tittering like a randy sailor's first visit to Hamburg's Reeperbahn, you hear a second key go in the lock, the door opens, someone enters, and the door closes. You can't see shit, but your hearing is suddenly keen. You could hear a pin drop, but you don't, rather you hear clothes being removed, snaps, zippers, underwear dropping on the floor—and then suddenly there is a hot body in bed with you. NO WORDS ARE ALLOWED TO BE SPOKEN. NO EXCHANGE OF PHONE NUMBERS (only bodily fluids). Presumably moans and groans and euphoric oohs and ahhs and squeals *are* allowed. The only rule for this game is that there are no rules. Let your imagination go as far as you dare, for you must do as physically coaxed by touch, as must your bed partner.

YOU MUST OBEY.

CHAPTER TWENTY-SEVEN

On account of Spring Break, we've hung around the marina a bit more, and avoided all Duval Street bars.

And guess what?

Mr. Leroy has a friend.

A manatee.

The manatee comes up and eyes Mr. Leroy and Mr. Leroy returns the mutual admiration and curiosity. It has only happened twice, but we're hoping they're in it for the long haul.

Wait!

Perhaps that is the wrong approach. We can't encourage this. Manatees and marinas don't mix so very well. You've heard the horror stories, haven't you? Manatees are friendly, docile, sociable. Can I even say *naively trusting*? They are a wild animal, but they would rather just hang out with us than scarper to safety. And therein lies the problem, they are getting constantly run over by boats, propellers ripping into their precious hide, snagged by fishing hooks, caught up in litter and monofilament line, even *ridden* by that slut up in Tampa Bay, as I mentioned in *KEY WEST, Part II*.

So perhaps it's not such a good idea. We can't fall for the bedroom eyes and the cute facial hair. If we give in, we'll soon be offering the manatee fresh water from a hose.

And that's a major No-No.

Perhaps Mr. Leroy can befriend a saltwater catfish. They're down here, you know. Fishermen don't like them as they steal bait, but Mr. Leroy is not so sensitive or judgmental.

* * *

We now have full-blown Spring Fever.

We are giddy.

We are delirious.

And we have decided to take the boat out. I know, call the Navy, alert the Coast Guard, every man and woman for themselves and stay onshore, please!

We want to see if we can do it—sail—plus, part of the christening of a new name is to take the ship on a voyage, and we haven't done that.

When I say *voyage*, we won't be doing what Gary Cairns and Cindy Law Cairns did recently, sail down to South America, then hang in Panama, do the Panama Canal, be away for yonks.

There's virtually no wind today, so we reckon we are no threat to anyone, lest ourselves. Popcorn Joe has cleverly rigged a piss-poor hp motor to our stern and we are able to PUTT, PUTT out of the Bight at the speed that mold grows.

No problem with the "idle speed and no wake" rule here.

Since Tina has her Captain's license, she has come along to teach, guide and generally steer us away from disaster.

Tina took the tiller and maneuvered us out of the marina and over into the lee of Christmas Tree Island. Tina idled the outboard, and I hoisted only the main, not the jib. (Notice how I shamelessly pepper the narration with nautical terms now?)

I sucked on an index finger and stuck it in the air to determine wind direction.

"What are you doing?" Tina asked.

"Checking the wind direction."

"First of all, there is no wind as the little breath of a breeze we have today is being blocked by the Australian Pines of Christmas Tree Island. And second of all, you use those." Tina pointed up at a few rags hanging, dead, up on a halyard.

"And those would be?"

"Those are the tell-tales."

"The tell who?"

"The tell-tales. You can look up there and see which direction the wind is coming from…"

"But there is no wind," I said.

"Good observation, sailor-boy, that's why we're going to motor around to the other side of the island."

Wow, there was a lot to learn. I gave Gabrielle a look and she gave me a smile and the good ol' thumbs up.

I looked over at Mr. Leroy for reassurance, and he was so bored he was going down below for a nap on the forward bunk.

Tina positioned the boat on the windward side of Christmas Tree Island and the tell-tales came to life with an almost imperceptible flutter.

"She's all yours," Tina said, handing over command of the vessel to Gabrielle. In a previous life, Gabrielle had lived in Hermosa Beach, CA, and used to sail from Long Beach over to Catalina Island, and back. With this nautical/seafaring experience, this meant I was relegated to third in command. Possibly fourth in command if Mr. Leroy awoke from his nap and made an appearance back up on deck.

A gust of wind played at the tell-tales and Gabrielle set a southerly course on the far side of Sunset Key. The boat rocked gently, almost imperceptibly, then began to silently cleave the aquamarine waters. We tacked south, then east for about a mile. And we stayed out for the rest of the afternoon, barely moving.

Sunning.

Sailing, sort of.

Kicking back.

Even pinching ourselves.

CHAPTER TWENTY-EIGHT

May in Key West.

Royal Poinciana are blooming in vibrant red, scarlet, orange, red-orange, gold and bright yellow.

The highs are around 88F.

The lows around 79F.

The water temperature in the Atlantic is 80F, *más o menos.*

The water temperature in the Gulf is 82F.

(**The water temperature in Lake Michigan is 44F.)

Relative humidity in Cayo Hueso is at a two-shirt-daily 75% to 98%. Yikes.

And I've found some work on a powerboat in the marina. The owner is an older retired dentist, Dr. Schildkraut, who used to live in Milwaukee. He'd purchased a 41-foot Richardson (built in 1955) in Ludington, Michigan, motored it himself the 100-plus miles back across Lake Michigan to the South Shore Yacht Club, just across the Hoan Bridge from downtown Milwaukee. Then he hung up his dental hat and, are you ready?...in early spring, he took the boat down to Chicago, navigated the canals, the Des Plaines, the Illinois River, ended up in the Mississippi and dodged all sorts of debris and barges all the way to New Orleans. He was thrilled when he finally made it to New Orleans and the Gulf of Mexico, until he came face-to-face with an early tropical storm. Thankfully, the tropical storm swung well to the east and he skirted and hugged the coast, all the way through the Gulf, except for Flamingo Bay, where he made a mad dash for the protection of the Keys.

It took him almost two months to reach Key West.

He said he could have done it faster, but then he would have missed a lot of good watering holes on the way down.

He also said he wouldn't do it again. Once was enough.

"Did you want to get as far away as you could from the snow?" I had asked him.

"No, my ex-wife."

He wants the boat sanded and painted. I recount this little tale to demonstrate an example of what can happen if you get your behind down here to Key West, get settled, and start to make some contacts: WORK CAN BE HAD!

So many folk were stuck in dead-end jobs and dead-end lives before they came down here. I've talked before about the fellow who was a stockbroker, but now he sits in the sun all day long at a small parking lot collecting the fee. Before he was a tightly coiled spring and he specialized in road rage. Now he rides a bicycle and he's so laidback, he's almost horizontal.

I know I've been hammering this to death and harping on, but go look in the mirror. We only live once, *amigo*.

* * *

I've begun the work on ol' Dr. Schildkraut's boat. We all know that preparation is critical when it comes to painting, but sanding the entire hull on a 41-footer is not so very easy.

I've begun and I've attacked with great vigor. Only now, I've essentially sanded away my fingerprints, and my fingertips hurt.

And my right shoulder.

I guess I never put in this many hours of straight sanding before.

I told Popcorn Joe this and he said: "Try to sand with your left hand for a few days for the shoulder, and tape your fingertips with masking tape."

Hmm, why hadn't I thought of this?

My fingertips are so sanded away, if you're planning a heist anytime soon, call me.

I'm your man.

My fingertips are screaming at me.

My shoulder muscles are sore.

But I'm working outdoors, not cooped up in an office somewhere with no windows and no ventilation.

CHAPTER TWENTY-NINE

Have you heard of the CoffeeMill? (Yes, that's how it's spelled, together like that.) The CoffeeMill is all about dance and it's where you want to go if you want to do Zumba or Ballet or Tap or Jazz or Modern or Hip Hop, even StreetFunk, and Pilates and Yoga.

Yes, all those.

You can even send your kid there.

They like kids.

There are now TWO new locations, one "The Annex," at 605A Simonton (just across from the new fire station), the other out by the beach "By the Bay" at 3340 North Roosevelt Blvd. #2.

The CoffeeMill is owned by Penny Leto. Remember her? Dark burning good-looks? Yes, that's her. She was one of the original members of the Fabulous Spectrelles, "Toni Spectrelle." Gabrielle and I used to go watch her at the Bull. I'm telling you all this because Gabrielle has just said this to me: "Want to go to an aerobics class with me?"

"You mean accompany you? As in walk you there and back?"

"No, go there and sweat..."

Hmmm, if I go I will make a fool of myself in front of perfect strangers (who aren't all that perfect themselves), and if I don't go, I will not get fed this evening (or worse). You can see my dilemma, can't you?

"I would love to go...with you...and...take a class..."

Well, I went, and guess what? Penny Leto was teaching it and she was so enthusiastic and welcoming and charming. I stood in the back row with another male and actually had fun… although it killed me just a little.

When we got back to the marina, Gabrielle and I showered then sat out and had a strong coffee Americano.

"I wouldn't mind taking another class with Penny," I said. "It's so important to have a user-friendly instructor."

"Indeed," Gabrielle said. "No airs and graces with Penny. She's so down to earth. And she's good."

"Remember that Pilates class you roped me into back in the UK?"

"In Berkshire, near Newbury."

"That's the one. I just didn't bend in all those places and twist in those directions. That, plus the instructor's voice drove me crazy. Perhaps that's a requirement to teach Pilates. Her monotonous, nasal drone and delivery was too much for me. If I had been a judge on *THE VOICE*, and this woman came on, I wouldn't have turned for her."

"Everyone else had fallen under some sort of hypnotic spell. More catatonic, actually."

"I'm sure glad I married you and not her," I said. "I can just hear it: 'Here's your dinner, now take a deep breath, exhale to crocodile, inhale outer thigh and reach back and grab that spoon, exhale to plank and commence eating in cow face. Press your feet down into the floor…tuck your chin in and exhale from behind.'"

Gabrielle laughed.

"You've inspired me," I said. "Think I'll join Popcorn Joe's gym again."

* * *

The next morning, before I start work, I go to the gym with Popcorn Joe. As always, he rollerblades over and I follow distantly behind on my bike, struggling to keep up.

We enter the gym and it's oppressively hot. I read somewhere this is supposed to be good for you, exercising in a sauna, but now I'm not so sure.

A juiced endomorph sitting behind the counter greets us

in soprano tones (not the mob ones, the high-pitched ones). He's leaning back in his chair, hands intertwined behind his head. His biceps are the size of coconuts, and they have tattoos. One bicep says MOM, the other says PATIO AMERICAN BAR AND GRILL, PROVINCETOWN, MASS. 02657, US of A.

All in capitals.

This man is huge!

I'm thinking of getting a tattoo on my biceps now. Perhaps just one letter, as I don't have much space to work with. Or, if I continue to work out religiously and inject steroids, I could get WTF on one bicep, and a question mark on the other.

It's something I'm considering.

Popcorn Joe goes over to the free weights and starts by doing curls with 40 kilos. Jeez, I usually use 7.5 kilos.

In another corner, a 20-something woman is flirting with a bulging hulk by the treadmills. There's a lot of smiling, much innuendo, even some touching. I fear they are using the workout as foreplay. It's all a bit awkward and uncomfortable, for sure, so I go over to the free weights to use the bench press, but before I can get there two linebackers have beaten me to it. Laughing, one linebacker *rolls* the largest, heaviest discs to the other linebacker, not carries them over, *rolls* them over. They do all this very loudly and with much bravado. I do believe they are showing off just a bit.

I go to the elliptical machine and jump on. But…do I pedal forward or backward? I'm not sure. I try to get it going either way, but just can't jumpstart it. Finally, a five-foot-no-inch women of 60 years plus, hops on the one to my right and I follow her lead.

I've been doing the elliptical machine for 20 minutes now and I think I'm about to cave. My legs are rubber and areas of my groin hurt where I didn't know I had groin.

Mrs. Sixty-Plus shows no sign of stopping and is only just starting to break a sweat. As I step off my machine she gives me a withering look, and I think she hisses *"piker!"*

I look over at Popcorn Joe and he's hitting the lat machine now. The man is an animal, super fit, and he knows what he needs to do to maintain his bulk. He's a good example for us all.

Wait!

Look over there!

No, over there, the two linebackers are finished with the bench press and it's now free.

But they've left all the weights on. About a thousand pounds, I reckon. I was planning on using just the bar.

Isn't it gym protocol to *replace your weights*?

I shouldn't have to do it, should I?

Plus, now I've got that tender shoulder.

And a dodgy groin.

What should I do?

What would you do?

I could go ask Popcorn Joe to set them straight on gym protocol, but he's transitioned to the chin-up bar and he's hauling himself up (over grip) with a 40-pound weight hanging from his ankles. Plus, I don't want to involve him.

I'm on my own.

I approach the two linebackers who are now crushing walnuts with their bare hands and eating light bulbs. I could bark at them as barking is probably their lingua franca, but what if they bark back? Or bite?

Wait!

I'm not the sort of guy that lets anyone push him around (remember the gecko?)...so I sort of bleat, beg: "Excuse me gentlemen, could you be so kind and replace your thousand pounds of weight on the bench press. You can even roll them, if you so wish."

They both stop whatever it was that they were doing, and I'm sure they will now crush *my* nuts with their bare hands, but they don't, rather they say: "Sure, sorry, mate, no worries."

They are Australian. And gay.

So...they're not linebackers, they're ruggers. Had I known that, I could have burst into the Haka, and that would have scared them straight.

After the Aussie ruggers remove all the weights from my bar, I set off to accomplish 10 reps. I manage that with ease, probably could have done 11, and am so pumped from my encounter with the Aussies, I add 5 more pounds to each side. You can bet that *I'm* going to replace my weights after I'm finished.

Both of them.

In between sets, I glance around the gym. Many of the women look as if they've *put on* makeup to come here. And everybody on the treadmills is on their cell. If I were the type of person who used a cell phone a lot, I would come to the gym to escape it.

Oh, oh. Look! Right over there by the mirrors. Do you see what I see? Wait! Don't look! Now she's looking our way. Is she looking at us? No, she's looking at *everybody* to see if everybody is looking at *her*.

I position myself near a mirror, in a corner, so I can observe the woman in the reflection. Perhaps she's hit 40. She's all hips, tums and bums, but that's not the frightening part. She's wearing exceedingly heavy makeup, sort of like a St. Pauli whore and that's a little unnerving, but that's not the frightening part. She's got breasts, clearly not hers as they are shaped a bit too uniformly, like she's stuffed a couple *beignets* down there and the cleavage makes me want to run, BUT THAT'S NOT THE FRIGHTENING PART.

Are you ready?

This is the frightening part:

It's the fake camel toe.

Oh, and you're an expert on these, are you? you're thinking.

Nooo...I'm not an expert on these things, thank you for asking, but puh-lease believe me here, it's the way she's (gonna gag here) *flaunting* it.

"They sell underwear in the Orient with a built-in fake camel toe," comes a voice from behind me. It's Popcorn Joe. Popcorn Joe is a man who's been around.

"Does she think that will somehow increase her chances

of getting laid?" I say.

Popcorn Joe is beyond words. When he re-finds his voice, he says: "Sometimes I believe aliens would be wise to give Key West a wide berth."

* * *

When I returned from the gym, Gabrielle had a nice cafetière of strong, dark roast.

But she was decidedly upset.

"What?" I said.

"Someone in the marina has complained about Mr. Leroy."

"For what, being cute?"

"No, they said he was jumping off our boat when we were gone and making a mess…"

"Mistaken identity," I said. "He can barely walk. Geez, it always takes one, doesn't it? Who was the person who complained?"

"Dunno, whoever it was wrote an anonymous letter to the dock master and left a copy on our dock box."

"This pisses me off. I'm going over there."

"Don't lose your temper!"

"I've already lost my temper!"

"DON'T LOSE YOUR TEMPER." *Advice, sentiments,* Gabrielle drove them home and made it very clear how I should respond.

"I will behave myself."

"Promise?"

"I promise."

* * *

I hustled over to the dock master's office, but it was locked.

"Hi, can I help you?" came a voice from behind me. I turned to see a rather corpulent fellow with ginger hair and a Hitler cut.

"I'm looking for the dock master."

"How can I help?" he repeated

I identified myself and told him about Mr. Leroy and how he was nearly immobile and wouldn't, couldn't, go walk-about.

"He never leaves the boat."

The dock master seemed to understand. He listened. He was patient, and understanding.

"Probably nothing to do with you and your cat," he said.

Phew, was I ever glad to hear that.

Then he said something that froze me.

"Perhaps you missed it, but no animals are allowed in the marina."

* * *

Gabrielle could tell by my body language as I walked back along the quay to our boat that things hadn't gone well.

I climbed back onboard.

"Where's Mr. Leroy?" I asked.

"Down below asleep in the sink."

"Animals not allowed in the marina," I said.

"What are we going to do?" Gabrielle asked.

"We're not going to give Mr. Leroy up," I said. "He's family. And we're not going to move."

About now the wind picked up, the skies opened, and we were hit with a torrential rainstorm.

Gabrielle and I scarpered below and hung out with Mr. Leroy and listened to the rain drill the deck and the wind clang through the rigging on all the neighboring sailboats.

"Remember when we lived over in Aronovitz Lane in our shack with the tin roof?"

"It made a heck of a racket. At least here, there's little chance a coconut will fall overhead."

Gabrielle put on the kettle and made us some tea.

I opened a can of tuna and gave Mr. Leroy the tuna juice.

And all three of us sat there in silence.

Then Gabrielle broke the silence: "Remember Jane Tilden?"

"She was our landlady when we lived in Austria."

158

"Let's do what she did."

"But what if we get caught?"

"We can't let it happen."

FYI: Jane Tilden was a famous Austrian actress, in her late eighties, and our landlady when we lived up in the Alps in Kitzbühel, Austria, and worked with the ski school. One night we came home and Jane Tilden beckoned us into her kitchen. She poured out three large globes of red wine and told us a horrifying tale of when she ran a theatre in Vienna.

It was the autumn of 1938, Kristallnacht had been only a few days earlier. Jews feared for their lives. Synagogues and prayer houses in Vienna were ransacked and destroyed. Jewish shops were plundered. Six-thousand Jews were arrested and sent to Dachau and Buchenwald.

One of the actors Jane Tilden worked with was Jewish. Pogroms were on the rise. The actor's days were numbered. Jane Tilden knew there was only one thing to do.

She hid the actor.

Hid him in the theatre until the war was over.

"We will hide Mr. Leroy," Gabrielle said.

CHAPTER THIRTY

It's June 1st.

Do you know what that means?

It means we've been hiding Mr. Leroy for two weeks now. We have not seen the dock master and there have been no more threatening letters.

But we are not allowing ourselves to become complacent.

Mr. Leroy has become the actor in the Viennese theatre.

We only let Mr. Leroy in the cockpit when both of us are present so we can keep an eye on him. He misses being able to crawl up in the furl of our mainsail, but that's when we pull out his guilty pleasure.

His elixir.

The tuna juice.

No matter what Mr. Leroy has on his mind he quickly forgets about everything when he hears the can opener pierce the can of tuna. Mr. Leroy may limp, but there is nothing wrong with his hearing.

The POP! of the can of tuna being opened, has much the same effect as the neutralyser's FLASH in the movie *Men in Black*.

Mr. Leroy forgets what he was doing.

Also, curiously, it's almost as if Mr. Leroy understands his role during these trying times. Perhaps it's the debilitating blanket of heat that has been thrown over the island, but Mr. Leroy is basically lying low during the heat of the day. Oh, sure, he comes and hangs out with us in the evenings when there's a cool breeze and we're sitting out in the cockpit. It's dark then, and it's dark where our boat is docked. There's the odd light shining, but in our case it's blocked by a large palm tree.

Fingers crossed.

* * *

It's June 1st.

Do you know what that means?

Yes, yes, yes, I know I just asked you, but there's a second reason I mention this date.

Hurricane season has started today.

Atlantic hurricane season, I'm talking about.

The Weather Channel tells us this. They make a big announcement. Do a few features.

But no one who lives in Key West needs to be told. We all know it. And it hasn't been keeping us up at night, we have Mr. Leroy to help us with the slumber side of the equation.

BUT WE ALL KNOW WHAT IT MEANS.

Something out there is coming.

No, not today.

Not this week.

Probably not even this month.

But down here at the end of the world, where the highest point on the island is a lofty, nose-bleeding 18 feet, no one's too bothered, right? Well, *yes* and *no*. Conchs have grown up with the scourge of hurricane ghosts of distant past. Locals who have been here a long time, like Will Soto and Popcorn Joe and Sallie Foster and Henry Fuller and Al Subarsky, know what to expect. They know how to prepare. They know how to batten down the hatches.

And they know when to evacuate.

But…it still rattles around in the back of your brain once it hits June 1st.

Have you ever had a dental appointment? I'm not talking an annoying poke-around-the-mouth checkup or brief scrape and clean—I'm talking protracted root canal of the most insidious and painful nature?

161

Or…have you ever had to go into the hospital for some sort of procedure?

Perhaps colonic irrigation?

Endoscopy?

Anal wart removal?

Have any of the above appointments been in the future, say, a month or two or three or more down the road?

Didn't really bother you at the time, did it?

But you knew it was out there.

That it was coming.

Sure, you would go about your everyday duties, enjoying that new hobby, playing with the grandkids, enjoying the game on Sunday, perhaps an adult beverage in the garden on that new back deck, the one with the view of the lake, the one you sealed with Thompson's…

And then suddenly it would hit you BANG! and a silent scream would emanate from your now wide open mouth. And then it would pass and life would be good again. The hobby, the grandkids, the ball game, the deck…

TICK. TICK. TICK.

But it was still out there.

Coming.

No way to avoid it.

Sure, sometimes Key West gets a premature reminder, a wake-up call, a teaser in the form of a tropical depression, tropical wave or even a tropical storm…as we did this year. Forty days *before* the start of the Atlantic hurricane season on 20 April 2017, to be precise…a tropical storm formed. "Arlene" was her name, and she was the first of the season even though the season hadn't officially begun yet.

Arlene was born and then began a crazy track westward, thanks to being ingested by a larger low-pressure gyre building to the west and south. Seas were running at forty-feet high.

Then, on April 21, that same low-pressure gyre cut off the warm, moist air that was feeding Arlene, and that was all she wrote.

Arlene was only the second "April" tropical storm on

record in the satellite era, but fortunately remained far from land in the central Atlantic Ocean.

Nevertheless, Arlene got our attention.

Is this a harbinger of what's to come?

Are we going to get our ass kicked?

Watch this space, because you know I'll report any and all developments and threats right here on these pages. An above average number of named storms are forecast for this season.

And we know they are coming.

Oh, yay!

I guess all I'm trying to say is if you live at the end of the line, last stop on the train to rebirth and a new life, you pay a bit more attention to the weather when summer comes in like a mullet, knowing damn well it could go out as a great white.

* * *

Per usual, Mr. Leroy is dozing in the sink in the galley. It's cool and he likes the contour. Have you ever seen a kitten play in a bathtub? They love it. It's all smooth and feels good, and they just love scooting and sliding all over the place.

Mr. Leroy is long from being a kitten, but we would like to believe that when he was just a kitten someone loved him and let him play in a tub.

And now I need to whisper something to you so Mr. Leroy doesn't twig: Al Subarsky is playing at Two Friends, so we've left a small bowl of tuna juice out for Mr. Leroy, in case he wakes, and we're going to walk over to listen to Alfonse's music.

It's three blocks.

* * *

And just like that, Gabrielle and I are at Two Friends, listening to Al Subarsky. We like coming here. We like Big Al. The setting is appealing, the drinks reasonable and Al Subarsky kicks ass.

And he's amusing.

I MEAN HILARIOUS.

A Jersey boy in the best sense of the term. Dyed in the Red Bank hood. And a mellifluous voice. What more can you want? How about the "meanest of Reuben sandwiches," he does that, as well…it's just not fair, is it?

Right now Big Al is singing Jerry Jeff Walker's "Cowboy Boots and Bathin' Suits."

Gabrielle and I look around the place. This, indeed, would be a good venue to eventually have a hurricane party, having said that, there's a storm-a-brewin' right now.

And it's in here.

Inside.

Indoors.

The atmosphere should be memorable and tropically exotic, romantic even.

But it's not.

It's toxic.

A slutty-rich, stupid-with-drink, middle-aged touron-couple are sitting at the table *directly* in front of Alfonse. I mean right in his grill. The woman is singing along to *every* one of Al Subarsky's songs. But that's not the bad part. The woman is singing along LOUDLY. But that's not the bad part, either. The bad part is, she's singing along in a screechy operatic sort of voice and drowning Big Al out. What is her problem?

She's obviously an attention seeker.

She's so full of herself, she's bloated.

She thinks she's a siren, but she's more of a foghorn.

I bet you anything she's wearing fake camel toe underwear.

Give it a rest, lady! Is what everyone in the place is thinking.

Actually, no, that is incorrect: Everyone in the place is thinking *shut the fuck up!*

Now what? Big Al sends one out to all the folk from the Lone Star state, and is singing George Strait's "All My Ex's Live In Texas:"

And the operatic cow continues to sing over Big Al and now sounds like an animal being slaughtered.

Or drawn and quartered.

In between songs, I slip up to Al and stuff a fiver in his tip jar. While making eye contact with me and "smiling thanks," he hisses: "Prison food might be worth it!"

I guffaw as I return to my seat and tell Gabrielle what Al Subarsky said. Now Gabrielle's laughing. We have a quick squizzy all around the room. Perhaps it's the lighting, or lack of it, but the place looks like it would if there were a lynch mob in there about to make their move.

Rule #27.5 in Key West: DON'T TALK OR SING OVER AN ENTERTAINER.

Always the pro, Alfonse quips: "It is said: There are four ways into Key West—by car, by boat, by plane, or birth canal. I do believe we've just discovered a fifth—by broom…"

Everyone gets it and roars, except Mr. & Mrs. Well-Heeled…because *they just don't get anything*.

Al Subarsky then plays "New Jersey Snow Day Blues." It's a clever original by writer, singer, musician John Sudia…and the foghorn doesn't know the words because the song is so new!

> **"Well I'm sittin' round the house**
> **On another snow day,**
> **Thinkin' to myself**
> **Why the hell should I stay,**
> **Wishing that I was someplace**
> **Sunny and warm…**
> **It's been a long cold winter**
> **And I'm sick of this stuff,**
> **Y'know winters in New Jersey**
> **They really kinda suck…"**

And that shuts her the eff up.

Soon after, flummoxed Foghorn and her foggy hubbie get up and hastily exit stage left.

Life in Two Friends is good again.

Everyone's now finally able to enjoy the venue and the music.

And Al Subarsky won't have to concern himself with prison food.

CHAPTER THIRTY-ONE

The tuna juice is gone.

And Mr. Leroy is out in the cockpit waiting for us when we get back to the boat.

We weren't expecting this.

How did he get out?

Does he have his own key?

"A rat was crawling on your stern line," comes a voice.

Gabrielle and I turn to see an older man with a lost-at-sea beard walking down the dock.

"I went to get some sustenance at the Owl Market...I still call it the Owl..." Sailor Man holds up a brown paper bag with a bottle in it. "The rat was trying to get on your boat and your cat scared him off."

We thank the man for the update and turn toward Mr. Leroy. Mr. Leroy is looking quite pleased with himself and he doesn't seem upset that we left him to his own devices. He doesn't have his arms crossed and he's not stamping a paw.

Gabrielle sweeps Mr. Leroy up in her arms, and the three of us sit there enjoying a warm, tropical breeze.

In the distance we can just make out the PUTT-PUTT of a very ineffectual outboard motor.

"Hear that?" Gabrielle says, "I bet it's Popcorn Joe trying to sneak up on us."

We still can't see Popcorn Joe coming, so we get down low in the cockpit, so we can surprise him.

"Probably coming over for a coffee," I say.

The sound of the outboard is marginally louder now, and

definitely coming our way.

"Stick your head up and tell me what you see," Gabrielle says.

I do as instructed.

"I can't see anything yet. I think he's just a few boats away. Let's scare the shit out of him. I'm going below and surprise him through the forward hatch."

"Do it!"

Stealthily, I slip below, sneak up to our V-bunk and stick my head out the forward hatch.

Gabrielle has followed me, carrying Mr. Leroy. "What do you see?"

I quickly pull my head back in.

"It's not Popcorn Joe. It's the dock master."

CHAPTER THIRTY-TWO

I've heard people say: "I can put up with 3 months of bad weather, so that I can enjoy the 9 months of good."

Guess what?

They're not talking about winter in the Great White North, they're talking about Key West *summers*.

Remember the movie *The Endless Summer*? Move to Key West and you can star in it.

Sure there are hotter places on the planet, but it's not the temperature that drives us into the ocean. It's the humidity. Need I say it again? The HUMIDITY. If dew points and percentage points mean nothing to you, let me put it this way: Remember those scorchers last summer in Boston? Milwaukee? Chicago? Ontario? Red Bank? Boise? Remember the gorgeous evening sitting out at your favorite pub, café, or sidewalk pizza joint? It was balmy and warm and you got to wear that plunging top, the sandals, and the bug repellent?

It was fun at night, wasn't it?

But the next morning, when you had to go to work and sit in rush-hour traffic or in the subway or on the bus or on the train...or even walk, it wasn't so very appealing, was it? And that had nothing to do with the hangover or the five pounds you put on by treating yourself to a large Quattro Stagioni the evening before.

Remember opening the door to your car the next morning and it was so hot in there you thought you had opened your kitchen oven by mistake? Remember it took you nearly a half an hour to drive to work and your A/C only really got cranking about the time you pulled into the parking lot? And then you had to step outside and do the walk on embers to get to the front door of your office and the waiting A/C?

Remember all that?

That suffocating, debilitating, life-sucking heat lasted for 3 days, then the wind changed and came in off the lake or the ocean or swung back around and came in from the north, and you could breathe again, sleep again, and not feel as if you were the proverbial wet noodle.

Yes, dear sufferer, you had to endure 3 days straight of inferno, but if you move down to Key West—unless you "just live for the heat"—you will have to endure not 3 days, not 3 weeks, not even 3 months—you will have to endure oppressive sauna-like heat from *before* the start of hurricane season (think April or May, and pray), to the end of hurricane season (30 November) or later, which will suck the energy from every living form during the middle of the day.

Are you up for it?

Some of you won't be bothered, but some of you will wonder just what in the hell you've gotten yourselves into.

It's something to mull over *if* you are planning the big plunge.

BTW: The high yesterday was 89F, the low was 86F.

The 97% relative humidity didn't help.

* * *

The heat has become unbearable to try to sleep below, in our V-bunk. Even with the hatch open and a few portholes open. So we've opted for sleeping outside. Gabrielle sleeps in the cockpit and I sleep on the deck nearby.

And therein lies the problem.

Mr. Leroy is used to sleeping with *both* of us. With his feet touching our head. Sometimes he sleeps with Gabrielle and sometimes he sleeps with me. Sometimes he changes during the night and we all win.

But if he sleeps with me and morning arrives, he's visible for anyone walking along the dock by our boat. Or anyone on

170

the neighboring boats. We still haven't figured out who complained in the first place. This is putting us on edge.

"What are we going to do?" Gabrielle asked me.

"I have a solution," I said.

"Great. Let's hear it."

"Get Popcorn Joe."

We texted Popcorn Joe and invited him over for coffee. We all sat in the cockpit. Mr. Leroy, too.

Mr. Leroy likes Popcorn Joe. He can probably smell his cat "Fausto" on him. We reckon Mr. Leroy thinks Popcorn Joe is cool with cats.

"We've got months more of heat," Popcorn Joe tells us. "It's only going to get worse. Mr. Leroy misses sleeping up on the boom. He could catch a breath of air up there."

We sat in silence for a few minutes, sipping our café Americanos.

Then, Popcorn Joe spoke: "Got it! We'll get you a portable marine A/C. Don't know why I didn't think of it sooner."

"We won't be able to afford that," I said.

"Sure, you will, we'll get a used one off eBay."

"Will a portable one work?"

"It'll take a while to get all the heat out of the boat, but after that, Mr. Leroy won't want to leave."

* * *

We pulled out my laptop with the annoying keyboard and fired it up. We did a quick search on eBay for "portable A/C for boat." Oddly, it came back with **0** results, then showed about twenty.

Haven't figured that one out yet.

"Look at that one there," Gabrielle said. "What do you think, Giuseppe?"

"I had one similar to that in my bedroom at the Pineapple Apartments until I got a window unit. Let me read all the details."

Popcorn Joe read about the unit. "This would work fine,"

he said. "It's an A/C *and* a heater. Might need it about two days each winter," he laughed. "It has 10,000 BTUs, a built-in water tank for non-stop drainage, and an exhaust hose. We'll stick that out a porthole. It weighs 60 pounds...what else? Oh, look here, it ships from St. Augustine and the seller has a 100% rating."

"Oh, oh," Gabrielle said.

"What?" I said.

"What?" Popcorn Joe said.

"He only takes PayPal. We don't do PayPal."

"I have a PayPal account," Popcorn Joe said. "I'll buy it and then you pay me later."

"Look," Gabrielle said, "see what the seller says?"

This A/C and heating unit was very lightly used in my previous apartment, as I had an additional cooling unit, and should have plenty of life left. I used it to cool and heat my large living room. It works great, and I was very satisfied with it. Only drawback was that it was a little noisy but I put it on a yoga mat and it made a big difference. It both cooled and heated well, and is great for security, as the exhaust hose can be easily removed from the window. It is in perfect working order, but I recently moved to a place with central air so it is no longer needed. I haven't been able to find the instructions, but I will keep trying. Includes exhaust hose and remote control. Please ask me any questions you may have and I will be happy to answer! Thank you for your interest.

"All you need now is a yoga mat," Popcorn Joe said.

* * *

Every day is a scorcher now, and the suffocating humidity lies upon Key West like a fat ol' wet grouper.

Every night is a sauna.

But we don't mind, because we sleep well.

We have A/C.

172

And, sure, it is a bit noisy, but it's white noise and we've adjusted.

My daily routine now is thus:

I awake just as it's getting light, heat up some coffee on our miniature galley gas stove that Gabrielle has prepared the night before (the coffee, I'm talking about). Then, I sit in the galley. If Mr. Leroy wakes up, I feed him and then he sits on the seat next to me. I get the laptop up and running and go online and see what's cooking on the Weather Channel. I check the BBC, and the Mullet Wrap online. Sometimes I check *Das Bild*, as Gabrielle and I used to do that when we lived in Austria. *Das Bild* does not pull punches when it comes to censorship and, the downside is, it's rife with gore and sex. It does have some pretty good videos of animals though.

Then I have a peek at KeysScene.com to see all the goings on around Key West and all the other Keys in the arts, music and about a zillion other things.

And finally I have a squizzy at Facebook to see what all of you are up to. Our cousin Deborah (in Liverpool) says that "Facebook is dangerous."

But some posts are humorous.

Here are three posts I saw on FB in the past year. I just have to share them with you:

"YAAAY! I'm so happy! It's official the puppies are 100% house trained, DRY ALL DAY and now ALL NIGHT!! I'm so pleased as they're now 6mths 4days. It's been hard work, but my astute planning, efforts, commitment and patience have paid off! And on this day 16yrs ago, I had corrective bowel surgery that saved my life so it's a double celebration."

AUTHOR'S NOTE: Yaaay!

And then here's the second posting:

"I'M TRYING TO MAKE FRIENDS OUTSIDE OF FACEBOOK WHILE APPLYING THE SAME PRINCIPALS, THEREFORE EVERYDAY, I WALK DOWN THE STREET AND TELL PASSERSBY WHAT I'VE EATEN, HOW I FEEL AT THE MOMENT, I SHOW THEM PICTURES OF MY DINNER, AND I SHOW

173

THEM PICTURES OF MY SCARS, I TELL PERFECT STRANGERS THAT I'M FAT AND THAT I KNOW THAT I HAVE A WEIGHT PROBLEM, THEN WHEN THEY CALL ME FAT, I HAVE NO PROBLEM PUNCHING THEM. I PONTIFICATE ABOUT THINGS THAT I KNOW NOTHING ABOUT, BUT WHEN OTHERS DO IT, BOY DO I LET THEM HAVE IT!"

AUTHOR'S NOTE: Hmmm...

Oh, crapola, listen to this story I just read on the internet: A women who used a plastic penis to dupe her girlfriend into believing she was actually a man has been jailed as the judge told her "Sometimes truth is stranger than fiction." Gayle NewXXXX cried in the dock as she was sent back to jail yesterday for tricking the woman into believing she was a man by making her wear a blindfold when they met and by using a prosthetic penis during sex.

The 27-year-old created a "disturbingly complex" online persona to achieve her own "bizarre sexual satisfaction" and continued the deception over a two year period.

AUTHOR'S NOTE: WTF?

When I'm finished perusing the news and am visibly shaken by the level of degradation and inhumanity of man, I listen to Harry Teaford on Radio A1A and begin writing, just as I'm doing now with you looking over my shoulder.

A writer is meant to write what he/she knows, so I'm doing that, but you get a vote here, as well. I write what I think might interest you, yes *you*! I know some of you through FB, and I know some of you through correspondence. I know some of you by sitting next to you on a bar stool. And I listen. Many of you make me laugh, and only a couple of you frighten me, so in an odd sort of a way, you are my guide.

My inspiration.

I write until about noon. I used to shoot for 10 pages a day, but now I seem to break that rule an awful lot. What's that you ask? Do I ever get WRITER'S BLOCK? *What's writer's block?* I respond. I don't have that in my vocabulary. I don't acknowledge its puny existence. You see, I have a trick: I write each day, but always leave a bit for the next day. It's so I know where I'm going when I wake up all sleepy and dopey and the caffeine hasn't clicked in yet. It's much like cleaning the bathroom, but leaving the commode until the next day. It gives you a sense of continuity and direction. And motivation.

What's that you ask? Is the inspiration always there? Perhaps not, but I have a trick for that, as well. If I'm totally stumped and have cleaned the commode without saving it for the next day, I go back a chapter or two and REWRITE. And it works a dream because by the time I get to where I was, ah, stumped, I'm on a roll and I just keep right on rolling. This is sort of like watching a favorite video on YouTube about kittens or puppies (you know the ones), or even baby goats ("Babies!"), and suddenly the signal goes wonky and the little ball on the bottom of the screen stops dead...so you move it back 10 seconds or so...get a running start and keep on rolling.

* * *

I've finished writing for today, and now I'm sanding the sides of an old powerboat. This is good for my mental health: using the ol' squash, then switching to the brawn.

The owner of the powerboat is elderly, filthy rich, and quite endearing and kind. I overheard him on his cell: "Yeah, it's sunny again down here, I got the guy (me!) working on the boat, and I'm going to dinner tonight with the boys. Life couldn't be better."

One of the reasons I got the job, *sanding*, is that it's dangerous. Yes, very, very *dangerous*. You see, I'm squatting in a dinghy, which is tethered to two cleats on the yacht, and I'm sanding the hull just above the waterline stripe—with an *electric* sander.

You've spotted the problem here right off, haven't you? Electricity.

Water.

Frizzy hair,

Death by stupidity.

175

I'm dripping in sweat and I don't think that it has anything to do with the temperature being 87 degrees and the relative humidity at a spongy 83%.

Wind out of the south at 7mph.

Chance of precipitation 83%.

Chance of survival 50%.

Before I began this suicidal quest, I had the wherewithal to ask around if there was a better way. The response: "Pull the boat out of the water."

Well, that wasn't going to happen with the owner cozily ensconced living onboard, so I sanded.

And just so you know, when you're in a dinghy sanding just above the waterline shackled to 120 volts, you are extremely and inordinately focused. (*Why are you not using a cordless sander?* You ask. Well, I haven't figured that one out yet, have I?)

But…what everyone failed to mention is, that no matter how tightly or creatively you tied your dinghy to the big bad boat, the dinghy pushes away when you apply the sander to the BBB's hull. Sanding only works if the object to be sanded is stationary. Can't exactly sand a swaying, surging, floating object. The harder I drive the sander into the hull, the farther away I push the dinghy and the risk of me toppling face first in the drink increases exponentially.

"What the fuck are you doing!"

I killed the sander and looked up. Standing on the quay is the dock master.

"No electric sanders allowed in the marina. Don't you people ever read the rules?"

Geez, this guy's got a bad attitude.

"Sorry, didn't know."

"You should. Don't let it happen again."

Prick!

* * *

When I got back to our boat, I told Gabrielle about my run-in with the obstreperous dock master.

"Oh, boy, it always takes one, doesn't it? What's his problem?"

"Miserable, probably. Hates his life, therefore hates the world."

"Then he shouldn't be in that job. Do you think he recognized you?"

"No, I was crouched down in the dinghy and my hair was probably sticking straight up in the air out of fright on account of using an electric sander so close to water."

"Good."

"Owww!" I yelled it out.

"What's wrong?"

"My right shoulder. Must've strained it again."

* * *

When we awoke the next morning, I couldn't move my right shoulder. It seemed almost frozen. I couldn't raise my right arm over my head. I couldn't even put my contact lenses in.

I had this same problem once a few years back, and I knew what it meant.

It meant rotator cuff.

CHAPTER THIRTY-THREE

The 4th of July is here!

Fireworks!

Hotdogs!

Fried chicken!

Beer!

Coleslaw (yuk for me, perhaps not yuk for you).

We're excited, but Mr. Leroy is not, so we're staying put. Fireworks scare him. The pyrotechnics are on the other side of the island over by Higgs Beach and the Casa Marina, but the wind's from the south tonight, so you will still be able to hear them. Plus, there's a lot of private fireworks in the Old Town (illegal) and general throwing of firecrackers around the marina (illegal), and tossing them in the water from passing boats (illegal, and major NO-NO!). Manatees get scared, harbor sharks get spooked. When an adorable manatee comes up to have a peek at us humans and you throw M-80s or Cherry Bombs into the water, that is just not cool.

Al Subarsky has just texted that it's already like a war zone over on Harris Avenue, and Bailey (who is a *she*, and a rescue) is not happy. Cute dogs get scared, too.

The rule in Florida is: IF IT EXPLODES OR FLIES, IT'S ILLEGAL.

Go celebrate the 4th with a fifth, and leave that illegal doodah alone.

The conditions are very dry this year, so you might want to even give sparklers a miss.

THEY START FIRES!

When I was a kid, I picked one up, the wrong end. I only needed to make that mistake once.

I KNOW YOU ARE DYING TO KNOW, SO I WILL TELL YOU: Sparklers burn at a sizzling, face-melting 1200 degrees Fahrenheit. *That's almost the temperature of lava.*

If anyone grabs the wrong end of a sparkler, you are looking at 3rd degree burns.

And a night ruined.

Something else to bear in mind, when you're out on your bike tooling around the back tropical lanes, you will become quickly aware of the density of wooden structures on the rock. This makes Key West a potential tinder box. It's so dry this summer, even the public fireworks display would have been in jeopardy if it weren't for them being displayed over water.

Fireworks may be illegal, but they are being produced faster than fruit flies.

FY-effing-**I:** In 1983, an explosion at a secret and unlicensed fireworks factory in Benton, Tennessee, killed eleven, injured one, and inflicted damage within a radius of several miles. The factory made M-80s. The facility was by far the largest known illegal fireworks operation ever, and the initial blast was heard as far away as fifteen miles.

May I just repeat this for those of you who went out to the fridge and missed that last bit: Your dog doesn't like them, your cat doesn't like them, manatees don't like them, and fish don't like them.

* * *

Okay, so you really, REALLY want to watch the fireworks display with your friends or family or main squeeze (and you promise to behave and not blow up the island). Here are a few possible ways to do it:

NÚMERO UNO: Spend Lots of Money for a Good Cause—"The Fourth of July Picnic benefits the Visiting Nurses Association & Hospice of the Florida Keys (VNA/HFK). As the Keys only non-profit hospice and home-health organization, VNA/HFK provides over $150,000 annually in unfunded and underfunded hospice care for residents and visitors of the Florida Keys. Their mission is to honor life by providing comfort, care and compassion. The Fourth of July Picnic was the organization's first fundraiser after opening their doors in 1984 and for 33 years has been their largest annual fundraiser, enabling them to provide hospice care to those in need *regardless of their ability to pay.* The Casa Marina Resort has partnered with VNA/HFK and has hosted the Picnic for 32 of those years."

Doors open at 5:00PM and the Picnic runs until the end of the Fireworks. (Fireworks provided by The Rotary Club of Key West and sponsored by VNA/HFK).

All tickets to this event include the following:

Live Local Music and Dancing on the Beach.

Family Fun Zone with slides, bounce houses, face painting, picnic games.

Complimentary Popcorn (*don't tell Popcorn Joe*), Watermelon and Pepsi Products. *Woo-hoo!*

Silent Auction (over 300 items including hotel stays, attraction passes, restaurant certificates and fabulous artwork).

Fireworks at 9 p.m.

Best Seats on the Beach - $150 (*pricey, told you, but then you get the free popcorn*)

Reserved seating on the beach with Upscale Picnic Buffet, 2 Drink Tickets, Private Bar, Wait Staff and Picnic Gift Bag *Whoo-hoo!*

Menu: Pulled Pork, Fried Chicken, Assorted Salads, Assorted Vegetables, Assorted Desserts, Hamburgers and Hot Dogs.

All Activities, Silent Auction, Live music and the best view of the fireworks! (*debatable*)

General Admission w/Food (Adult) - $25

All-American Picnic Buffet with paid adult food ticket, all activities, Pepsi Products, Popcorn and Watermelon.

General Admission w/Food (Child 4-12) - $15

All-American Picnic Buffet with paid adult food ticket, all

activities, Pepsi Products, Popcorn and Watermelon.
General Admission w/No Food - $10
3 & Under Free with Adult Admission

* * *

NÚMERO DOS: Spend a Lot Less and Still Get the Pulled Pork—"Since 1976, the Rotary Club of Key West has presented the island's annual fireworks show. Staged from the Edward B. Knight Pier (formerly called White Street Pier) overlooking the Atlantic Ocean where White Street meets Atlantic Avenue, fireworks are to begin at 9 p.m. Attendees can purchase food, drinks, burgers and hot dogs to benefit the Rotary Club's scholarship funds at a booth across from the pier on Atlantic Avenue.

* * *

NÚMERO TRES: Spend No Money and Mooch Off Your Friends—Find a friend or make a friend who has a boat or just about anything that floats. BYOB. *Woo-hoo!*

* * *

NÚMERO CUATRO: Pricey Again But You *Do* Get the Coleslaw—If you don't have access to a boat, or friend, you can go out on one of the "Sunset Cruise" catamarans like the Sebago. It only costs $128 per person. *A bit pricey, as well, I'm thinking, but as mentioned above, you do get the coleslaw and an open (pay) bar, drinks $6 a pop.*

CHAPTER THIRTY-FOUR

Mr. Leroy climbed up in the sink for his afternoon nap, so Gabrielle and I flicked on the A/C for him and locked up the boat, so we wouldn't let out all the "bought air." We needed to pay a quick visit to Fausto's to pick up some avocados, kale (yes, kale), tomatoes, rice crackers and mackerel.

Perhaps, some chocolate chip cookie dough.

Perhaps some Chunky Monkey ice cream.

We parked our bikes in front of Sam's Antiques. You know this place, the one with the sign in the window that says: WE BUY JUNK AND SELL ANTIQUES.

At Fausto's, a frightening thing happened. Gabrielle was down one aisle, I was down another, I must have reached in my pocket to look at the shopping list and pulled out $80 by mistake, which fell on the floor.

And I didn't notice.

I perused the shopping list, moved to a different aisle, eventually found Gabrielle, and it was only then that I reached in my pocket for the $80 and realized it was missing.

"Oh, shit," I said. "I've lost all our money."

"Where?"

"I don't know. I probably did it when I pulled out the shopping list."

"When was that?"

"At least ten minutes' ago, and three aisles back."

"It won't still be there, the place is crawling with tourists, locals, and homeless who've come to dine."

FYI: If the **tourists** find the $80, they won't turn it in, because they've only just realized how expensive well-drinks are in Key West, and they now need the extra cash.

If the **locals** find it, they won't turn it in, as they are already working three jobs and need the extra cash.

If the **homeless** find it, they certainly won't turn it in as it would take them at least two full hours of panhandling on Duval to make this much money.

If by the grace of the big kahuna, some **righteous soul** finds it and does turn it in, then we'll for sure never see it. (That is not meant as any comment on any particular establishment's staff's drug and alcohol problem, or the pittance they are paid in the form of wages.)

Gabrielle and I ran off in different directions in the hunt for the $80. I hit the produce aisle, then the ice cream aisle (where the chocolate chip cookie dough is kept), then the aisle with the crackers…and right there on the un-swept floor right in front of me, sitting nicely scrunched up and possibly tread on once, was the $80.

You've got to be shitting me! I think I must have said this out loud, not just thought it, because Gabrielle suddenly came belting around the corner and into my aisle.

"You found it!"

"I found it, I can't believe it. This just doesn't happen in Key West."

"And not in Fausto's," Gabrielle said. "The place is always heaving."

MIGHT I JUST SAY HERE: If you ever lose something in Key West, in any establishment, in any venue, whether it be your beer money, your rent money, or a close friend, don't EVER expect to see it/them again.

Relieved, we pedaled home with our precious groceries by cutting down Peacon Lane.

Peacon Lane is another one of those back lanes that make you understand how wonderful it was a long time ago, when Key West was nothing more than a charming, exotic, romantic backwater. It's quaint and tropical and mostly old. The lane proudly displays sprawling banyan trees and spreading traveling palms. Go down to the end, where it spills out onto Caroline. Look up to your left, that's the old Pineapple Apartments, where Gabrielle and I first lived when we came to Key West. Look up to that little third floor window under the tin roof. That used to be our bedroom.

When we returned to our boat, we found Johnny-Johnny sitting in the cockpit and he had Mr. Leroy on his lap.

Gabrielle and I almost fell off our bikes.

How did Mr. Leroy get out again?

We chained up our bikes. Johnny-Johnny was sort of laughing to himself. He was up to something. And with him, that meant just about anything.

We climbed onboard, but Mr. Leroy didn't look up. He must have been upset that we would leave him alone and he was playing hard to get.

Gabrielle approached Mr. Leroy and gave him a little scratch under the chin, then she laughed.

"That's not Mr. Leroy!" she said.

Johnny-Johnny handed over the "sleeping cat." It wasn't Mr. Leroy, and it wasn't a real cat, rather one of those life-like furry replica prop toys.

"My gift to you," Johnny-Johnny said. "Leave him out on the deck, let's blow some smoke up the dock master's arse. Beggin' your pardon, *Madame*."

Johnny-Johnny stood up. "Got something else for you." It was a yoga mat.

"Where'd you get that?" Gabrielle asked.

"I have a couple of them."

"You take yoga?" I asked.

"*Mais, oui*, have been for years. Keeps me fit. Keeps me calm. I'm trying to turn my life around. Up until recently, I was going straight to hell and they were holding the door open for me..."

"Where do you take your yoga?"

"Over at the CoffeeMill. You come with sometime?"

"Indeed, I now have a yoga mat," Gabrielle said, smiling.

Suddenly, the wind picked up. Off, over the Gulf, Johnny-

Johnny pointed at a waterspout, and then the heavens opened up.

"It's going to be a frog strangler," I said.

Johnny-Johnny laughed. "Never heard that expression before…"

And the heavens opened, and we were soaked before we even managed to scramble down below.

"Frog strangler…I like that," Johnny-Johnny said. "Back in the UK, I used to say 'It's pissing…or it's chucking it down'…"

"Differences in language can get you in trouble," Gabrielle said.

"You got that right," Johnny-Johnny said. "When I first came to Key West, I worked at a guest house, but I got the sack. We had some woman who was staying with us. She had an early flight the next morning, so I asked her if she wanted me to knock her up. I didn't know what it meant in America."

Gabrielle and I both laughed.

* * *

Mr. Leroy was still curled up in the galley sink and was only mildly interested when Johnny-Johnny placed the fake cat on the counter next to him.

"It doesn't smell like a cat."

"We need to give him a name," Gabrielle said.

"I got it!" Johnny-Johnny said. "Let's call him Johnny Cat!"

And we all had a really good laugh.

And then the sun came back out and the humidity was about a million percent.

And a two-shirt day, became a three-shirt day.

All three of us were still wet from the downpour, so we sat out in the cockpit, drying off. Another perk of Key West. It rains. You get wet. The rain stops. You dry off. Almost a daily occurrence during a normal summer.

"Have you noticed how many people don't wear underwear in summer down here?" Johnny-Johnny said.

185

"Going commando?"

"Just saying. Doesn't seem to be that many people who wear underwear. I'm not talking young things frolicking about forgoing the bra, I'm talking *all* things frolicking about forgoing knickers, underwear, *sous vêtements*."

"You mean the dirty old men at the Garden of Eden Rooftop Bar letting their junk hangout?"

"No, I'm talking about locals and holidaymakers and tourons. Went to the library the other day and a 30-something, rather respectable woman with blond hair was sitting on the steps, very spread-eagle, airing her privates out and I could testify in a court of law that she was a true blonde." Johnny-Johnny shot a look at Gabrielle. "Beggin' your pardon, *Madame*."

Then: "In case you're wondering, I don't bike around the island looking for this sort of thing. *Mais, mon Dieu!* You couldn't miss it."

"Everywhere?" I asked.

"Everywhere," Johnny-Johnny said. "Even if you can only read the top line on the chart at the optometrist, you'll be able to spot it."

"Everywhere?" I repeated.

"Even down at Mallory, check out some of the vendors or the tarot card reader." Johnny-Johnny crossed himself, then he turned to Gabrielle. "Now, *Madame*, may I trouble you for one more coffee. *Un espresso*, with a short glass of water *à côté?*"

* * *

BREAKING NEWS: Patty and Tina just called us. I don't want to use the description FREAKED OUT, but I will say they sounded decidedly unsettled.

Here's what happened: Patty came home from work, unlocked the front door, walked into the living room, turned on the lights and saw blood everywhere. And I mean *everywhere*. It looked like a crime scene out of *KILL BILL*. Right in front of her, lying on the carpet was a headless corpse.

There had been a bloodbath.

186

Patty did a double-take. The headless body was the carcass of a once very robust five-foot long iguana. Off to the side of the living room, looking quite smug, was Sasha. Sasha had attacked the ferocious beast outside, decapitated it, then dragged the blood gushing vermin through the doggie door, leaving an oozing trail behind.

This is *not* your tabby proudly leaving a dead mouse on the doorstep.

This is the stuff legends are made of.

So I guess I need to take back what I said about iguanas not having any predators other than you and me and bubba.

They have another—a Doberman Rottweiler mix—Sasha the dog.

CHEW ON THIS: The head of the iguana was never found.

CHAPTER THIRTY-FIVE

How do Gary and Cindy do it?

How do Ed and Kim do it?

This living on a boat lark, I'm talking about.

You have to be creative, you know, to be a live-aboard, there's not a lot of space, no man cave, no sprawling entertainment center, no ensuite facility, not even much privacy, and very little *storage*.

The storage part is not so much a problem for us as we don't own anything, not even an electric Black & Decker cordless sander. Although I'm thinking of investing in one.

We don't have a lot of clothes, no lavish wardrobe, but we do wear underwear.

Since we possess a limited supply of knickers, it behooves us to wash them out in the galley or hit the Laundromat in the marina—often—but lately the Laundromat at the marina has been much in demand. Lots of visiting, transient boats in the marina now, lots of salty folk seeking "safe harbor." *Safe harbor* we've come to learn is a harbor with access to a washing machine and proximity to a bar.

So we have left Mr. Leroy in charge of the galley sink, positioned Johnny Cat up on the deck, and have hit the road with two bulging bags full of laundry and biked our dirty clothes over to the Hilltop Laundry on the corner of Elizabeth and Eaton.

Distance three blocks.

The Hilltop is about 10 feet above sea level, so hardly a hill, but that is the name, nevertheless. This is where we used to come to do our laundry when we first moved to Key West, before we got our job and accommodation at Popcorn Joe's Pineapple Apartments, cleaning apartments—doing laundry.

One good thing about doing your laundry in Key West in the summer in a coin-operated venue, it's so hot inside you can pretty much strip off and throw your entire wardrobe in.

We parked our bikes outside the Hilltop and chained them to the skinny pole that's right there in front of the sign that says NO LOITERING, where a couple of homeless scalawags were loitering, smoking and gaily greeting passersby.

We entered. *God, it was hot!* Still a furnace, just as before. Nobody hanging about in here in this heat.

"Probably all up at the Duval Street bars," Gabrielle theorized.

We sought out an available washing machine, but they were all in use, tumbling and spinning. We went outside where it was marginally cooler. In front of the Laundromat, just to the left, was a dirty white van. Some cheeky sod had written in the dirt: ALSO AVAILABLE IN WHITE.

Also to the left of the Laundromat is Shea's Pet Grooming. This is where you want to take your beloved little furry one for a big treat. Shea's been a groomer, we're talking pets here, for ten years and word on the pet grapevine is that all pets love her. She has that all important good doggie bedside manner.

We peered in the window, then took a step back as a smiley woman exited with her pug, who had quite a spring in his step, might I add. Good advertising that.

Next to Shea's is Puptown Girl Doggy Boutique ("doggy treats, toys and accessories"), so you can see these are a few wonderful establishments that we all need to know about. If Mr. Leroy wasn't so damn good at grooming himself, we certainly would bring him here.

We returned to the Hilltop Laundry and hung out with the scalawags under the overhang on account of a pesky tropical shower.

Scalawags in Key West have good stories. The older of the

two told us that his name was Oliver. He used to live in Boston, but wanted a less stressful life…plus, one away from family, so he went north, first to Portland, Maine, then Boothbay Harbor, then Bar Harbor. But he found nothing but people trying to impress other people with possessions. "I don't want to impress anyone," he told us. "I just want to be left alone and be happy."

"And are you?" Gabrielle asked.

"Immensely so," he replied. "Once I realized that I was not going to find what I was looking for by going north, I started to head south. I tried Charleston, then Savannah, then Fernandina Beach, then Ft. Licquordale—for about an hour—finally, I found Key West."

"And what makes it so special for you?" I asked.

"Nobody judges you down here. Oh, sure, the rich folk who come for the winter or a vacation will. Even some students down for Spring Break, but the locals don't. Most just let me live. I don't bother anyone and no one bothers me."

KLUNK!

"Hear that?" Gabrielle said. "Final spin!"

"Sounds more like it's about to roll over and die," Oliver said.

Not much later, we heard another KLUNK, the cycle was finished. We entered the furnace again and stood by the now idle machine.

"Someone will magically appear, remove the clothes and throw them in a dryer, then we'll be good to go," I said.

We waited.

No one came.

KLUNK, another machine finished.

We waited.

No one came.

"Should we?" I said.

"No!" Gabrielle said.

"Why not?"

"Remember what happened the last time we removed someone's clothes from the washing machine, the owner of

190

the clothes came in and went ballistic."

"That woman who had underwear the size of a parachute?"

"That one."

"She thought we were stealing them."

"As if they would have fit either of us."

"Perhaps for the three-legged race."

"I'm not seeing that…"

"Okay, then how about this? We could have made multiple hammocks out of them…"

"Okay, got it."

We waited.

"And remember that other time?"

"Keep going…"

"Someone removed a woman's clothes from the washing machine, placed them carefully in a basket, but when the woman came back to collect her clothes, one of her dresses had been stolen."

"And?"

"Two days later she saw someone walking on Duval wearing her dress, by the time she caught up to the woman, she had slipped in to the 801 Bar. She confronted the woman, but the woman was a man!"

"And the dress fit him?"

"The woman had snake hips."

And we waited.

Somewhere about now, a scantily attired, twitchy, high-as-a-kite twenty-something entered."

"She's spilling out everywhere!" I said.

"You can't dress up mutton," Gabrielle said.

"She's one of the lap dancers over at the private dance booths at the Red Garter," I said.

"And you are knowing this, how?"

"That's the one our old neighbor Sam used to court, remember? He thought she was duper."

"Duper?"

"Yeah, *duper*, not quite super-duper. One night they got so fucked up she had to call the ambulance right in the middle of riding the love train. Plus, I've seen her up on the balcony next store, ululating."

"*Duper. Love train. Ululating.* Where do you get this stuff from?"

I was not able to respond, because suddenly Miss Lap Duper Dancer burst into a profanity laced tirade.

"Whoa, a sailor would be impressed," Gabrielle noted.

"Who's she having a go at?"

"She's yelling at the sign that says EMPLOYEES ONLY. There must be someone back there."

"That's the drop-off/pick-up."

We couldn't make out all that was being exchanged, but it was something about the lap dancer's clothes, which she had dropped off and picked up the day before..."all smelled of sweat." And it was something about the woman employee responding with: "If you don't like it, go somewhere else."

Miss L-D yelled: "Fuck you!"

That, we heard loud and clear.

"You can take the girl out of the gutter, but..." Gabrielle said.

Miss L-D stormed out, and just thereafter, Miss Employee Woman from the back, came up to the machine that we were waiting for, removed the clothes, flung them in a basket that looked like a lobster pot, put in another load, and jammed in the required amount of quarters.

She returned to her hole in the wall.

"She didn't even ask if we were waiting," Gabrielle said. "Just went ahead and barged in."

"Should we?" Gabrielle said.

"To the other machine?" I said.

"Precisely."

"I thought you didn't want to mess with someone else's clothes?"

"I'm motivated now."

Gabrielle and I hauled our two bags of hernia-rendering clothes over to where the second machine was lying dormant.

But before we could even open the lid, Miss Employee Wench was upon us again, extracting this load and adding another one of her own.

"We were here first," I said as politely as I could, which was perhaps not so very polite.

"Listen, pal..." Miss Employee Wart said. "I got here at eight fucking AM this morning. I'm the only one with a key, I unlocked the place, I didn't see you, that makes me here first."

"You're using all the machines to do the drop-off and pick-up," Gabrielle said.

"You got a problem with that?" she spat, and she slithered back to her snake pit.

Gabrielle and I stormed out.

Out front was Oliver. He was now alone.

"Could I possibly borrow two quarters, fine sir, since you didn't get to avail of them?"

"Here," I said, "two for politeness and two more for being a wordsmith."

"I thank you both," Oliver said.

"What's the story with that woman inside?"

"She's a harridan. Just ignore her. She's disenchanted with life...or perhaps I should say *sober* life."

We bid Oliver farewell. It was now just as hot outside as it was inside the Laundromat, or nearly. We jumped on our bikes and pedaled up to the Margaret-Truman (How clever!) Launderette on the corner of...can you guess? Margaret and Truman. Well done you!

Distance four blocks.

We were now sweating-proverbial-pigs. Wait! Have you ever spent some quality time with a pig? Noooo, your fraternity roommate back at the U, doesn't count. And that voyeur in the back of the Pilates class doesn't count either. But what I'm trying to ascertain here is have you ever seen a pig work up a sweat? They're couch potatoes, they're layabouts (wallow-abouts), plus they're always covered in muck. So where does the expression come from? Perhaps I'm beating a dead pig, I just don't know.

We chained our bikes to that light pole just to the left, negotiated an assortment of polite transients and entered. *Whaaat?* They had A/C in here! We looked up. A smiley female employee was already in mid-sentence: "Yes, A/C. And soon we will have a club-card scheme."

"Say whaaat?" I said.

"Soon, we will be just like those 24 hour gyms in the big cities. We will have 24-hour Member Access. That's 24/7, bubba. You will be able to come here in the middle of the night if you want, way late, after work at the bar or the strip club, when the sun's not shining."

Well, were we ever impressed. This place was almost too good to be true.

All the machines were occupied, but when we heard our first KLUNK, the Nice Woman Employee didn't strike like a Burmese python and try to beat us to it. We spent the next two hours doing all our laundry, then stepped out of the A/C shocked how hot it had become. We pedaled the now seven blocks back to the marina, to our boat/home, and to a somewhat impatient Mr. Leroy who now wanted to be held and fed. As we were passing by the marina's small Laundromat, we both noticed that the place was now empty, all washing machines and dryers available and just beckoning for our custom. I gave Gabrielle a look.

"Sod's Law," she said, "but look how much richer we are for going up to Truman."

194

CHAPTER THIRTY-SIX

We gave Mr. Leroy his dinner, Meow Mix, the Seafood Medley (We would like to believe that Mr. Leroy likes the jingle but, in fact, it is we who like the jingle), then we showered and walked over to the Bull for *just one.* The reason I bring this up is that while we were sitting in the back corner, near the bar, we overheard the following conversation. It was between a young man, 20's, in a white T-shirt with an image of Jerry Garcia on the front, a bit hippie-esque, and a female companion of similar persuasion, tank top, a bit hippie-esque, sort of Cher without Sonny.

The Jerry Garcia T-shirt Guy was prattling on about nothing in particular, then he said this: "Was late for my job interview last week, and I didn't have time to have breakfast, so I ate a brownie my roommate had left in the fridge. Twenty minutes later I was at my job interview and I was so stoned I could barely speak."

"I'm sorry, you didn't get the job," Cher said.

"Oh, I got the job, I told my prospective boss what I'd done and he hired me for being honest. This *is* Key West, y'know."

"Why did you move down to Key West in the first place?" Cher asked.

"On account of my car insurance."

"Huh?"

"I was living in Sea Breeze, that's Jersey. My Toyota got stolen. I made a claim 'cause I needed my car for work, and the fucking gecko raised my premium right through the roof. Now that is what I call grand theft auto."

Cher laughed.

"Now I live down here and ride a bike."

"What line of work?"

"Pedicab."

Jerry and Cher hit their drinks, and I turned to Gabrielle. "He's doing what we did. Moved down here and then looked for a job that might suit him once he got here. So many people hope they can secure some great job back home and then have everything set up for them when they get here."

"Indeed," Gabrielle said. "Moving to Key West is not for the faint of heart. Many people just want a new start in life, but it doesn't hurt to have a sense of adventure."

"You're right, that's why so many people move here, but then they can't make it, get frightened and leave."

"And you need to do your homework. Remember that couple we met a few years ago? Sold everything they owned, moved down, rented a shop with extortionate rates and opened up yet another ice cream shop."

"Yeah, then low season hit, a hurricane blew through killing off about a month's revenue, and their business went in the crapper."

ALERT: Okay, folks, listen up: If you are planning to shake up your life, commit social suicide, or just hankering for the BIG CHANGE (and haven't done any research yet), I've done some for you. Here is a list of a few of the jobs available in Key West as I write this. Peruse through them and see if this helps a bit...

(ADDENDUM: If you are rich, a trust-fund brat, or about to live the life of Riley off the parents' inheritance, either stay home, or at least endeavor to embrace and integrate without flashing the cash, bling and more importantly the ego. BTW, selling drugs is *not* integrating.)

Okay, now as promised, those available jobs, and remember, this is how they appeared and the typos and syntax have not been altered or corrected by my crack editor.

A-PLUS ROOFING

196

Experience Roofers Wanted. Will train.
(**AUTHOR'S NOTE**: *Why do you need to train them if they are experienced?*)
Pay equal to experience level. Apply 8am-Noon
Monday – Friday
5686 Maloney Ave.

* * *

Experienced Veterinarian Technician/Tech Assistant
Part time, available Saturday's.
(Why *the apostrophe on Saturday's?*)
Physical work involved. Stop in at 1456 Kennedy Drive,
Key West.

* * *

Armored Car Driver/Messenger
Part-time. Must possess or able to obtain "D" Security
Guard & "G" Firearm License. For more information.
Call 305-797-xxxx.
(*Why does the messenger need the firearm?*)

* * *

Certified Pilates Instructor Needed
For Key West Spine practice. Email or
fax resume to
info@kwneurospine.com
Fax 305-296-xxxx

* * *

Certified Yoga Instructor Needed
For Key West Spine practice. Email or
fax resume to
info@kwneurospine.com

Fax 305-296-xxxx

* * *

Electricians and Experienced Helpers Wanted

Work available in Key West, Marathon and Tavernier.
Call:
305-292-xxxx
Start Immediately

* * *

EXPERIENCE PAINTERS WANTED

Must be able to lift and work with extension ladders up to
28 ft. No drugs or alcohol. Call 305-304-xxxx
(The person who wrote or took this Ad must have been high)

* * *

Full-time Physical Therapist

Director of Physical Therapy needed for busy Key West
practice. *(Probably to help the painters who threw their back out lifting
a 28-foot extension ladder.)*
email or fax resume to
info@kwneurospine.com
305-296-xxxx

* * *

Journeyman Plumbers and Experienced Apprentice Needed

Immediate employment.
Top wages and benefits! 305-296-xxxx or apply in person
at 6409 2nd Terrace

* * *

198

Key West Hammocks is looking for great Sales people. Hourly pay plus commission. You should be motivated, proactive. Will train the right person. Apply in person before Noon at 719 Duval Street (*In the afternoon, we'll all be having a siesta in our great hammocks*).

* * *

Maintenance Position
Galleon Resort is hiring a maintenance tech. Experience in plumbing, electrical and A/C (at least 5 years experience in these fields). Military welcome to apply.
Must be able to work weekends and evening shifts (3) 1-9 and (2) 8-4. Full benefit package available. Please apply in person at 617 Front Street

* * *

MOUNT SINAI MEDICAL CENTER
As Mount Sinai continues to grow, so does our legacy of caring. We are looking for top talent to join our Key West team.
This facility has exciting openings for:
*Practice Manager
*Medical Assistant
*Registered Nurse
Qualified candidates ONLY. We offer a competitive benefits package.

* * *

OFFICE ASSISTANT (Full Time – 40 hours per week)
The Monroe County Tourist Development Council (TDC) has an immediate opening for a full-time Office Assistant to support the Administrative, Sales and Finance staff. This person should have experience in Microsoft Office, specific experience with Microsoft Access will be an advantage;

have excellent organizations skills; be able to multi-task; enjoy answering phone calls; entering data into a data base; be available to assist at scheduled meetings throughout the Keys when required. Successful candidates should be prepared to take a typing test.
Previous applicants should not reapply.
(Seems a bit unfair, what if I've been studying and improving my typing skills?)
Starting Salary commensurate with experience and includes excellent benefit package
No phone calls please.

* * *

SALES ASSOCIATES
Dion C-Stores is currently accepting applications for both full and part-time for all shifts at our Key West locations and Islamorada. Applicants must be able to work nights and weekends and have 1 – 2 year previous retail.
(I used to sell my Sunset Photos down at Mallory…does that count?)
All interested candidates can stop by any Dion's or send resume.
EOE/ DFW/ M/D/V

* * *

The Basilica School of St. Mary Star of the Sea in Key West, FL, is looking to hire qualified and experienced educators for the 2017-2018 academic year. Instructional positions available in pre-kindergarten, elementary and middle school. Send resume with cover letter

* * *

The Pier House
Is hiring smiling faces for the following positions:
*Spa Receptionist

*Engineer II
*Engineer I
*Painter II,
*PT PM Line Cook (*Have you ever seen a line cook with a smiling face? Okay that guy, but who else?*)
Temporary on-call Night Auditor (with previous experience)
(*On call in case the regular guy falls asleep on duty*)
Please come to HR located at 1 Duval St. and complete an application. EOE

* * *

TROPICAL SHELL & GIFT

We are Historic Tours of America's Retail Company
Now Hiring:
Retail Store Manager
Availability:
Any day, Anytime.
Retail management experience required. Leadership skills.
Salary to be discussed at interview.
National Company with growth opportunity!
We even offer Pet Insurance (*Now we're talking!*)
*Two Weeks Paid Vacation
*Paid Sick Days
Apply online at:
www.historictours.com
EOE/DFW

* * *

OVERSEAS LUMBER SUPPLY

Is Now Accepting Applications For The
Following Positions:
YARD WORKERS AND DRIVERS. Driver applicant must have a valid Class B CDL License. Applicant must be able to load/unload building materials and work daily outside. This position is full-time with competitive pay and benefits.

RETAIL SALES

Applicant must be dependable, have a neat, clean appearance and be customer service oriented. Experience in lumber and building materials hardware and paint a plus. Position is full-time with competitive pay and benefits. Please apply in person at 30251 Overseas Hwy, Big Pine Key. EOE

(Gabrielle would like that job; she loves power tools and going to hardware stores)

* * *

AND DON'T FORGET: perhaps try to work in the marina, crew on the boats, try to get on Mallory Square during the Sunset Celebration as a crafts person, artist, or performer.

CHAPTER THIRTY-SEVEN

The dog (and cat) days of summer are coming to an end.

And there's no sign of autumn on the horizon.

The temperatures haven't dropped.

The torrential afternoon rains, which finally arrived, haven't ceased.

Nor the threat of hurricanes.

We still have almost three more months of hurricane season to go.

Believe it or not, we've already seen the arrival of the first "seasonal boat" that's cruised down to spend the winter here.

A bit early, I'm thinking, what's going on here? Perhaps some folk just like to get a jump on things. Using the strictest of nautical terms to describe the vessel: it is a big-ass powerboat.

And she's called, are you ready? The *BOOBIE BOUNCER* (such bad taste), and it's in the slip right next to us, so we hear everything that goes on.

Everything.

I wanted to write that someone likes it "deep and hard and rough," but I don't want to offend anyone (or arouse anyone), so I won't write that, just leave it at someone likes to do a *play-by-play*...or an *audio* selfie.

The owner, Mr. Rough-Provider, is a flash-the-cash asshole, somewhere between the age of forty and death, who seems bent on picking up where James Mayer, the toxic, syphilitic, former owner of Sloppy Joe's left off. (I will recount that nightmarish tale in just a few pages). Every night, Mr. Rich

Cornhole-Provider has a new woman over. We've seen him trolling in the Duval Street bars. He likes them young and zaftig.

Mr. STD-Provider is all loud and full of brio and thinks he's God's gift to women. In reality, he's God's gift to all women who will exchange a blowjob for some blow. He brings the Skank o' Night home and they "blow their brains out." There's music with a monotonous druggie bass, the aforementioned feral lovemaking, even the odd cat fight when he brings *two or more* coke-hounds home, and then the screeching begins, screeching like mandrakes being pulled out of the earth.

Mr. Flash-the-Cash is keeping us up at night, and it's ruining our peaceful, idyllic existence down here.

He's the proverbial neighbor from Hell.

And we are not happy.

We've sent an anonymous letter (they obviously work) to the dock master. Mr. KY-Jelly-Provider has received a verbal warning, and he ceased and desisted his middle-of-the-night carnal revelry for a few nights, then started it all back up again.

Problem is, he doesn't get back to his boat until two or three in the morning.

Then the orgies begin.

And the cigarette butts being dumped into the marina.

And the dock master's not on duty then.

Where's security?

The other morning we woke up and there were sacks of rotting garbage up on the dock, with an Air Force of flies, a rapacious rat, and one iguana eyeing the spoils from a nearby palm tree, waiting for the sun to warm him up enough before he could have at it.

There was no sign of our delinquent neighbor, so Gabrielle and I went up there and cleaned it all up. Had to fight the rat for the right to dispose of an oily pizza box.

We don't know what we're going to do. I would go complain to the dock master, in person, but we have CAT IN HIDING, and we're trying not to draw any unnecessary attention our way.

Having said that, the dock master *did* stop by one day.

"Thought I told you to get rid of that cat!"

Gabrielle gently picked up the sleeping stuffed cat toy and held it up for the dock master to see. "We did just as you asked," Gabrielle said. "We have him now instead. His name is Stickasockinit."

The dock master seemed decidedly confused, and then radiantly disappointed that he wasn't going to be able to bully us anymore. He just went silent and glared, then he pointed at something in the corner of the cockpit.

"What the hell's that?"

Oops.

The dock master was pointing at a kitty box filled with fresh kitty doo-dah.

"Ah, those," I said. "Those are bangers. We keep it for effect."

"You better not be lying to me…"

"Don't you have something better to do?" Gabrielle said.

"You go girl!" I wanted to shout it out…but whispered it, instead.

Stay tuned.

CHAPTER THIRTY-EIGHT

It's been raining for three straight days now. A tropical wave passed just south of the island and we're bearing the brunt.

Lower Duval is flooded, as is Front and part of Greene Street.

That's the bad news.

The good news is our friend John Rubin has just arrived. Do you remember I told you about him wanting to pay a visit?

John is from Manchester, England, and I've made mention of him before in *NAKED EUROPE*. He is quite the character, our John is. Always smiling. Always with a twinkle in his eye.

He's the fellow who, as a young lad, smuggled a live chicken into a movie theatre in Manchester during a matinee performance of Hitchcock's *THE BIRDS*, and then let it fly down from the balcony during the flappy part of the movie.

Key West will suit John Rubin just fine.

And wait till we all get together with Popcorn Joe and Johnny-Johnny.

Sparks will fly.

Just like that chicken.

John Rubin has had a successful career in the music and film business, so he's staying in a suite at the Ocean Key Resort.

For John Rubin, money is no object.

Money is also no object for Gabrielle and me, as we have no money.

John Rubin chose the Ocean Key Resort, because he likes

being close to the action.

The action being alcohol.

Good music.

And fishing.

He won't even believe the Bull when he sees it.

Or the Garden of Eden Rooftop Bar.

We may not tell him about the clothing optional side of it, just drag him up there for a nightcap.

Or send him up on his own.

See if he spots the vulva fingernails.

We have never seen John Rubin in anything other than a pinstriped business suit, and mirrors for shoes, so this should be interesting. He's a big sportsman, so presumably when he goes deep-sea fishing he will be properly kitted.

John Rubin has fished Iceland and Scotland and Ireland, but has never fished the Florida Keys. He's keen to fish the Atlantic and the Gulf, deep and shallow wrecks, and the flats, not having to switch boats or marinas. Key West allows you to do all that.

"I've done my homework," he's told us. "When the temperatures begin to drop up north, the fish migrate south. First to arrive is the bait: mullet, ballyhoo, pilchards. And the game fish are never far behind."

John Rubin goes on to tell us: "I'd like to stay on until the sailfish work their way up to the reef to chase the schools of ballyhoo. Sailfish can be caught in extremely shallow water and can be spotted by following the frigate birds that are waiting for the sails to push the 'hoos up to the surface."

"Did you say hoes?"

"No, I said 'hoos."

Hanging out with John Rubin feels like it might have felt to hang out with Hemingway and his Mob (Mike Strater and Waldo Pierce, boyhood friend Bill Smith, writer John Dos Passos, editor Maxwell Perkins, and saloonkeeper Sloppy Joe Russell.)

CHAPTER THIRTY-NINE

John Rubin is going deep-sea fishing today.

He's joined a charter on a boat out of the Galleon Marina, and they're going out in the Gulf Stream.

We will meet him for dinner tonight at the Half Shell Raw Bar. And we will take along a surprise in the form of Popcorn Joe and Johnny-Johnny.

* * *

It's a bit strange to live on a boat and not sail anywhere, but then I'm worried if we attempt to sail (with my lack of seafaring expertise), we aren't coming back.

We are not showering at the marina today, and we are not going to take a cockpit shower, we will shower at the beach.

Yes, you heard right, we are going to the beach.

Higgs Beach.

The other side of the rock.

Distance 1.5 miles.

We slapped on some sunblock, secured our snorkels and masks in our baskets, hopped on our bikes, and headed up William Street toward the Atlantic side. It was already so hot, I was only wearing my trunks and flip-flops. Gabrielle was a bit more discreet and wore a tropical top and shorts over her bikini, that plus the flippies.

At the corner of William and Windsor Lane, we swung left, then cut through the Key West cemetery, surprising a rooster, hen, and seven peeps. Despite all the chickens we see roaming around Key West, chicks have a tough time reaching adulthood. They have a wily predator who wants to eat them, Key West's many and abundant feral cats.

It was serenely quiet in the cemetery (no jokes, please), unlike Duval just a few blocks removed, although Duval can have the chickens, as well.

Did you know that plots in the Key West cemetery go for $15,000 and up? Way up? I guess, at that point, if you got the money, there's not much else you can spend it on. Having said that, the cemetery is already quite jammed and there are not many plots available, so you'd better get your skates on if this is something that you just can't go through, ah, life without.

"Look!" Gabrielle said, pointing.

Lounging in the sun on the top of a crypt was a robust iguana.

"Look at the size of that thing."

"He's got a wrestler's build."

"He must be five-feet long."

"Look at the way he's eyeing us, just the one eye, I mean."

We stayed and observed and the little scaly git must have taken exception, because he raised his spiny ridge, jerked his head up in the air a few times and hissed at us.

"How rude!"

"Don't give him the finger or piss him off in any way, those little garden-destroyers can run 21 miles per hour."

There was not much shade in the cemetery, the sun was beating down mercilessly, You Know Who was still hissing, so we pedaled like crazy past the tombstone that looks like a conch shell toward the exit over on Francis and counted 12 other iguanas scurrying about around the graves and out from under the crypts.

Creepy.

Iguanas can live up to 20 years, so maybe their menacing presence will help bring the price of a plot down a little. Wouldn't want to go in there to place some fresh flowers and come face to face with one of these evolutionary freaks.

We exited the cemetery on Francis (near Petronia) and

suddenly the skies opened and we were hit with a vicious downpour. Before we could seek shelter, we were soaked to the skin, and by the time we found shelter, the rain had abruptly stopped and the sun came back out and started to dry us out. Who needs a Laundromat?

We pedaled up Francis, turned right on Truman, then turned left on Grinnell and crossed Virginia and Catherine and United and Seminary down to South Street, and then over to Reynolds. The trip was shorter than that last sentence.

South Street and Reynolds. This is where you *don't* want to be during the middle of the night. It's one of the most dangerous areas of Key West, so give it a miss unless you get a rush negotiating with a total stranger, scoring on adulterated drugs which have been cut with baby laxative, Xanax, paracetamol, lidocaine, phenacetin (nasty pain killer which fucks up the kidneys), or levamisole (a livestock de-wormer) and you're not overly concerned about the renal failure, or the de-worming.

I cast my mind back to something I had read about crime statistics in America, a score of 100 meant a particular neighborhood was safe. The neighborhood of South Street and Reynolds in Key West scored a two.

Hard to believe it's true when you're passing through during the day, not so hard to believe it's true if you end up in there late, late at night.

There are a few other dodgy parts of Key West, such as areas of Bahama Village and over by the Bare Assets Nude Bar on Truman, but if you are so innately stupid to get pissed to the gills and go wandering around legless at 4am with **TOURON** emblazoned across your chest by the way you've dressed (and act), then perhaps you need a wake-up call.

Just saying.

We carried on riding our bikes across Washington Street, Waddell/Von Phister, then Flagler. We skirted the Waldorf Astoria's Casa Marina Resort, then stopped and straddled our bicycles.

"Oh to have been a fly on the wall in the Casa Marina back in the late 1920s and '30s and '40s?" I said.

210

"Presidents and movie stars rubbing shoulders, all sorts of affluent folk spending a few nights here before they flew Pan Am to Havana?"

"Exactly, sipping rum under the coconut palms, gazing up at a full moon. Romantic."

"Did you know that the architects were the same who designed the New York Public Library and the Metropolitan Opera House?"

"You are a fountain of knowledge."

"No, I just read about it before we came out."

"What else?"

"Well…it may have been the first clothing optional hotel in Key West, as guests were allowed to sunbathe in the nude…"

"Thus, you wanting to be the fly on the wall?"

"No, thank you, but I would like to have been a fly on the wall *inside* to see what went on in there. I'm talking about the public places only, of course, perhaps the ballroom."

"Of course."

"Or if not a fly on the wall inside, a gecko out on the terrace listening to Ezio Pinza singing *Some Enchanted Evening*."

(**Author's Note *muy importante*:** The movie industry was booming in Jacksonville, FL, long before Hollywood and many stars, and a few mafia, made the trip down from Jacksonville to Miami and then Key West. Jean Harlow and Al Capone paid a visit, both under assumed names.

By 1916, Jacksonville boasted more than 30 movie studios. One of those studios, The "Metro" as in Metro-Goldwyn-Mayer, began in a small studio alongside the St. Johns River, where *Metro*politan Park now stands.)

Who knew?

During World War II, the Navy bought the Casa Marina and converted it to officers' quarters.

In the 1950s, the grande dame was the refined refuge of other movie stars: Cary Grant, Tony Curtis, Gregory Peck, Rita Hayworth, Ethel Merman, Jennifer Jones, Gary Merrill, Richard Widmark, Miriam Hopkins and Al Jolson.

Cary Grant and Tony Curtis, along with director Blake Edwards, stayed in the Casa Marina when they were filming *Operation Petticoat* in February 1959, as most of the filming was done in and around Naval Station Key West, now Truman Annex, which substituted for the Philippines and Australia— owing to the Australian pines as a backdrop.)

Well, I'll be...

We parked our bikes just off of Atlantic Blvd., over by the foot of the Higgs Beach Pier.

Clarence S. Higgs Memorial Beach is the full name of the beach, but many locals still refer to it by its old name County Beach.

Whatever you call it, you can rest assured that the governor won't close the beach for himself and his family.

Higgs Beach is not just for sunning and splashing, historically it has much of interest to offer, as well: A Civil War era fort (the West Martello Tower, which has been the home to the Key West Garden Club for over 50 years), the largest African Refugee Burial site in the northern hemisphere, the only underwater marine park in the entire US of A that you can access from the beach and not need a boat to take you out there, the terminus of the Florida Overseas Heritage Trail, and the AIDS Memorial.

BTW: A "Martello" tower is a small defensive, usually coastal and round, fort that was first used in southeast England.

FYI: The Key West Garden Club is one of the island's last remaining *free* attractions. It's also a superb venue for a wedding (which will not be anywhere near free) as Key West never gets a frost, and glorious tropical flora abound.

AND: The African cemetery is the final resting place of Africans who died after being rescued in 1860 from captured slave ships. The cemetery was discovered in 2002 using ground-penetrating radar along Higgs Beach.

Many Africans, who were being shipped to Cuba to be sold into slavery, escaped and made their way to Key West. Those who perished were part of a trans-Atlantic trip aboard three American-owned slave ships on their way to Cuba, intercepted by the U.S. Navy in 1860. The ships, *Wildfire*, *William* and *Bogota* were captured and forced to sail to Key West. Altogether 1,432 Africans were rescued, and they were given food, clothing, housing and medical treatment by the citizens of Key West.

Key West has always welcomed diversity and always marched to its own vibrant drum. You may recall the Conch Republic's efforts to secede from the Union on April 23, 1982, so it will come as no surprise to you when I tell you that during the Civil War, Key West remained in the United States despite Florida having joined the secessionists. Africans on the island lived as free men long before it became the law of the land.

FURTHERMORE: The Underwater Marine Park is a killer spot for snorkeling. Stick your head under the warm water out by the old sunken pier, just out by those pilings where all the pelicans and cormorants are hanging out. The grassy sand flats. You will be privy to a whole new world under there and make a lot of new friends. There are over 50 species of marine life to get to know, such as starfish, sea urchins, conchs, yellow butterfly fish, nurse sharks, hogfish and parrot fish. You may even see an occasional spotted ray. Just keep a sharp eye out for jellyfish and Portuguese Men of War.

And if you see one, make a run for the dry sand.

MOREOVER: The Florida Keys Overseas Heritage Trail is a 106-mile paved trail in development in the Florida Keys. When completed, the trail will connect Key Largo to Key West. How about that! This way you can come down and not have to walk, jog, skate, or ride your bike anywhere near U.S. Highway #1. It will be part of the East Coast Greenway, a 3000-mile system of trails connecting Maine to Florida. Of course, there will be places to camp along the way.

AND FINALLY: The AIDS Memorial, near the entrance to the White Street Pier (sometimes called "the unfinished road to Cuba"), honors those who "displayed a love of Key West and the Florida Keys, by living here, working here or just visiting."

213

And it includes those who'd resided elsewhere bearing the burden of the AIDS stigma, who fled to Key West after being ostracized and persecuted by family, friends and community.

Why did they choose Key West?

They came to Key West to die with *dignity*.

They came to Key West because Key West was known for being *tolerant*.

They came to Key West because, unlike anywhere else in the country at the time, Cayo Hueso had programs in place to help people with AIDS live out their lives for as long as they had left on this earth.

Simply put, Key West was there for them, when no one else even wanted to know.

The names on the memorial are inscribed in Zimbabwe semi-precious black granite, which looks radiantly elegant and **dignified** with its gloss, polished surface.

As it should be.

We all know that Key West has long been a Mecca for gays and, sadly, many folk with their heads buried deep in the burning sand, blamed *homosexuals* for kick-starting the epidemic down here, but the disease was indiscriminate, and non-selective—and male and female, both gay and straight, from Conchs to military personnel to the service industry types, rich to poor, succumbed.

If you harbor any prejudices surrounding gays and AIDS, might I just give you a little bit of background: Clearly, it would be difficult to point the finger at just one individual for the spread of AIDS in Key West (like many did at that Canadian flight attendant), it would be unjust and unfair even … *but*, locals knew that the disease spread around the rock like the plague on account of *one* person alone. And it was not a member from the gay community who created the original AIDS panic, it was a member of the straight population, namely a certain "James Mayer," playboy, base-level bon vivant, womanizer, sex addict, pathological liar, junkie, dealer, and—former co-owner of Sloppy Joe's.

It was the late 80s, cocaine was as common as Key lime

pie and Mayer had a $500-a-day habit and an insatiable stable of coke whores and coke hounds lined up from the corner of Greene and Duval, all the way up to the University of Miami.

Mayer was a handsome rogue, a bad boy, he'd fought with the Green Berets in Vietnam, and he was full of bluster, full of himself, unrepentant, irresponsible and always goddamn right. He'd contracted AIDS from dirty needles, then became Key West's version of Typhoid Mary, infecting nearly every female he seduced, and there were many: Coeds down from Dade County to blow off steam, tourists down from the Great White North looking to try something new and, well, titillatingly sinful, singers and musicians who came down to Key West to perform up on the famous stage at Sloppy Joe's, the neighbor's wife, party-hearty girls endeavoring to reach girls-gone-wild status, any female with a pulse, really, who'd fornicate in exchange for some blow.

While the community was struggling to cope and help and prevent and counsel, Jim Mayer wasn't listening, rather he was spreading his HIV-laced seed in every motel, guest house, backseat, boat and beach on the island. He was warned by friends, warned by doctors, even warned by his wife (who eventually died of AIDS).

A real piece of work was James "Jim" Mayer.

Mayer saw himself as a sort of larger-than-life Hemingway character and soldier of fortune. Like Hemingway, he even took up boxing and built a ring inside Sloppy Joe's, where he fought and bled and infected.

By March of 1988, word on the "coconut telegraph" was that Mayer was out-of-control, dangerous, toxic, and the most promiscuous male on the island. Mayer knew damn well he had the HIV virus, but he continued to play, he continued with his hyper-active sex life ... and he never told anyone that he was a walking, talking, snorting, ticking time bomb.

Buddy Owen, aka B.O. of B.O.'s Fish Wagon noted back then: "Jim Mayer has no regard for anybody. He just doesn't listen."

Another Conch said: "He's no different than Jack the

Ripper, except he's doing it to women with his penis instead of a knife."

Young women down on holiday were infected and didn't know it, and the dominos started to tumble when their boyfriends, husbands, and sex partners back home became unknowingly infected, as well.

There was outright panic on the island. The panic spread and turned to rage. And this is when the straight party crowd on the rock realized that AIDS in Key West was not just a gay problem.

It was their problem, as well.

While I have you here, and you're thanking your lucky stars that *you* were able to slide through the height of the AIDS era without contracting the dreaded blight, might I say just one word: GONORRHEA.

Yes, gonorrhea. Don't know if you are aware, but it's making a raging comeback and it's coming to a neighborhood near you soon with a vengeance in the form of a superbug.

And it's predominantly being spread by oral sex.

Well, that leaves me out, you're saying.

Does it?

Ever cheat on your wife, husband, partner, former girlfriend, ex-boyfriend?

Ever go on holiday where no one knew you and have a one-night stand?

Ever get so wasted that you didn't even catch her (or his) name?

Or remember doing what you did?

Ever wake up in a strange bed?

Ever...not remember *anything?*

The World Health Organization warns that if someone contracts this new strain of gonorrhea, it is in some cases impossible to treat.

Impossible.

Gonorrhea can infect the genitals, rectum and throat, but it is the throat that is most concerning health officials.

The throat.

It is a very common infection, especially among young people aged 15-24 years.

Well, that leaves me out, you're thinking.

Does it?

Untreated, gonorrhea may also increase your chances of *contracting the HIV virus.*

Shiver.

CHAPTER FORTY

Okay, are you still with me?

On to something more positive, excuse the choice of words.

Gabrielle and I are still at Higgs Beach soaking up the sun. It's a scorcher as are most days this time of year, and we need to get in the water, *now*, so we grab our masks and snorkels and scamper across the hot sand, as those folk prance over hot coals, over to the pier and go out to the end, where there are steps leading down into the inviting Atlantic. Almost every piling has a cormorant or pelican sitting atop. A few of the cormorants have their wings extended, enjoying the sun and drying off.

I may try this later.

In the water just below us, entire families are snorkeling, observing a myriad of brightly colored fish. The children are wearing T-shirts so they don't get fried. Difficult to get a kid on vacation out of the ocean and quite readily compounded when there are all those curious tropical fish to make friends with. This is all new territory for them, it's not Lake Michigan, or Lake Erie, or Lake Superior, or Lake Huron, or Lake Ontario teeming with mercury, lead, cadmium and PCBs enriched perch and chinook and coho, sturgeon and walleyes.

We slip down the steps and, as always, are shocked how warm the water is. We position our masks and snorkels and plunge into the briny depths. We are in three feet of water. It's a different world under here, silent and magical and colorful, and we are surrounded by schools of fish that seem just as curious about us as we are about them. Right off we spot sergeant majors and snook and lots of parrotfish and even a small octopus, who we think we startled. Then, and you won't believe this, something black and large came darting our way and now we are being startled.

Small shark?

No.

Barracuda?

No.

A cormorant! So strange to see a bird swimming underwater. He's in hot pursuit of lunch. Never saw that before.

That made our day!

After 30 minutes, and sneezing underwater (again), we climb up the steps and out of the water to cool off, yes, cool off, and we feel blessed.

This has to be better than having psychological counseling, I'm thinking. We both feel so refreshed and, well, at peace with the world.

In the water below us, a Scottish fellow says to his wife: "Key West had over a half inch of rain yesterday..."

And the wife says: "A half inch of rain? That's a sunny day back in Glasgow!"

We watch a Hobie Cat slipping silently by, then we walk back down the pier to the molten beach. By the concession stand we find some shade for our feet, and a sign, which reads: TWO CHAIRS AND AN UMBRELLA $20.

"Such a deal," I tell Gabrielle. "That's a waste of good beer money. Why not just bring a beach towel and veg on the sand under a palm tree?"

A few slinky paddleboarders in bikinis come into view, then two Jet-skiers who feel the need to do donuts close to shore. Are they trying to impress the two girls in bikinis? Or just put them off with their testosterone-fueled display?

Right in front of us, another family from Scotland is attempting to access the warm inviting water straight off the beach, but they are having trouble wading through the Maginot

Line of seaweed and sharp rocks.

Gabrielle grew up in Scotland, so she can understand Glaswegian, *hen*, and she does the right thing by going up to them and pointing out how to avoid the Sargasso minefield by walking out on the Higgs Beach Pier and entering the warm sea taking the steps, as we did.

There's a lot more I need to tell you about this great beach: Gabrielle and I volunteered here on Earth Day, helping to pick up litter. The beach would look even better if folk DIDN'T LITTER!

Not so environmentally important, but worthy nevertheless, is the Caribbean-influenced Italian restaurant *"Salute!"* right on the beach. *Salute!* offers glorious seaside fayre, plus the all-important warm and aromatic fresh bread.

There's also kayaks and paddleboards, and snorkels for rent. There are picnic tables available (cement ones) most being used by homeless folk as an office or to sleep on, a shower (come early to avoid disappointment), public restrooms (get there early to avoid disappointment), grills for cookouts, a few tennis courts, areas to play volleyball...and, yes, pickleball.

Pickleball is a cross between badminton, ping-pong and tennis, essentially playing on a court similar to a tennis court, but smaller, with wooden paddles (or composite) and a wiffle ball, so you can avoid the frustrations of trying to get your first serve in. What I mean is, if you can swat a fly with a fly swatter, you can enjoy pickleball.

(**Urban legend** has it that pickleball got its name from the creator's dog whose name was—let's all say it together— "Pickle," who used to chase after and steal all the wiffle balls, but in fact, the family dog was named after the newfound game.

There you go.

Higgs Beach also has plenty of parking and a dog park (separate runs for the little ones) just across the street. As of this printing, it is not known if Pickle the dog has visited the dog park.)

PARKING IS FREE at Higgs Beach, so you don't need to feed the meter, but what are you doing driving over here anyway? Why aren't you riding bikes? Oh, you've come with the entire family...here's another question for you: WHAT ARE YOU DOING DRIVING OVER HERE ANYWAY?

RANT ALERT: I've heard people moan about the sand at Higgs Beach. Yes, the sand. The sand is imported from the Bahamas and somehow some folk have a problem with that. Perhaps it's just me, but I'm not seeing the problem here. Have you ever been to the Bahamas? Have you ever seen that sugar-white, super-fine sand they have over there?

Some people will moan about anything, won't they?

"Jeez, honey, these damn cigars have been imported from Havana."

"Jeez, lover-bunch, the dang wine has been imported from the Bordeaux region of France."

"Jeez, my pet, this here ice cream's been imported from Italy."

"Jeez, suckling-babe, the friggin' beer has been imported from Germany."

"Jeez, doll-fondle, the god-darn chocolate has been imported from Belgium."

"Jeez, scrotum-shrivel, the effing sand has been imported from the Bahamas."

* * *

After the beach and swim, Gabrielle and I showered and jumped back on our bikes and returned to our boat.

And we were shocked by what we saw.

The *BOOBIE BOUNCER* had a guard dog on it!

The dog was in reality a carnivorous beastie and looked to be a cross between a hyena, a wolverine, a honey badger, and the creature in the movie *ALIEN*.

As we approached, he growled viciously, sadistically, teeth dripping blood, and he was leaning out, snapping at our throats.

"He's got a head the size of a donkey!" Gabrielle shrieked,

as we scampered quickly onboard, unlocked the hatch, slid it back and undid the mahogany doors.

Mr. Leroy was not in the sink, or up on our V-bunk. Eventually, we found him cowering under the chart table/galley table.

We no longer live in the Historical Key West Bight.

We now live in the Seventh Circle of Hell.

"I thought no animals were allowed in the marina?"

"I'm going to complain. Where's that asshole's marina etiquette?"

"I thought we didn't want to bring any attention to ourselves…"

"We have no choice. I'm going."

"I'm coming with you."

We stormed over to the dock master's office. Well, that's not entirely true, I stormed, Gabrielle kept her cool.

When we got there, there was a man sitting in there that we didn't recognize. He was George Clooney with a really good tan. Wait! George Clooney always has a really good tan.

"Hi," Gabrielle said. "Do you know where the dock master is?"

"I'm the dock master."

Gabrielle and I looked at each other.

"Who's the burly fellow with the ginger hair?"

"Oh, that Kevin. He's not with us anymore. He was security."

Gabrielle and I were confused.

"He sort of led us to believe he was the dock master…" I said.

"He had a habit of doing that, one of the reasons he's gone."

We told this friendly (thank God) dock master about Mr. Rough-Provider Blowjob Guy.

We told him about the noise.

The parties.

And we told him about the dog.

"Dogs are allowed here in the marina…" he began.

"We understood that no animals were allowed?"

"Kevin told you that, right? No, not true, well-behaved animals are always welcome."

"So we could, say, get a cat?" Gabrielle asked.

"Absolutely."

Yeehaa!

Mr. Friendly Dock Master said he would note our concerns and that he would go talk to the owner of the *BOOBIE BOUNCER.*

Then he said this: "The owner of the *BOOBIE BOUNCER* has paid upfront for the entire season, so we'll get this straightened out."

"When you go speak to him," Gabrielle said. "Take along a T-bone…"

And we left on a high, and on a downer.

Mr. Leroy could stay.

But Mr. Fornicator Guy was staying, as well, with Cerberus, the hound of Hades, for a pet.

* * *

When, we got back to our boat, we received a blast of saliva-enriched hate from Flesh-Eating Hyena Dog, and we stepped in dog shit on the dock. Grrrr.

We quickly opened our boat and went below to cower and quiver, and give Mr. Leroy his fur ball medication and check him for fleas.

This calmed us down a bit. It always helps to focus on your children, then the world doesn't seem to be such a bad place.

Our method of dispensing Mr. Leroy's fur ball medication is through subterfuge. What we do is break up his pill by crushing it, then we mix it with peanut butter. What can I say? Mr. Leroy just loves peanut butter. Actually, Mr. Leroy will eat just about everything that's put in front of him (much like myself).

We gave him an extra dab of peanut butter, but we needed to monitor his intake. If he overdoes it, he gets diarrhea. Mr. Leroy doesn't fancy kitty treats, he likes human treats. He's a bit of an eating machine, so we can never leave anything around, not that you can ever leave anything around in the Key West heat.

When Gabrielle opens a can of tuna, Mr. Leroy will jump up on the counter and supervise by standing with his two front paws on Gabrielle's right hand as she opens the can. As she twists, he rocks. We're not sure if it's quality control or just feline eagerness.

Perhaps he's trying to learn how to do it himself?

When we lived back in our shack in Aronovitz Lane, Mr. Leroy would jump up in the bathroom sink and supervise if I was scrubbing tiny paw prints out of the bathtub.

Mr. Leroy has a predilection for sinks.

And cans of tuna.

FLEAS: Flea season is every season if you live in Florida. Usually, what we do with Mr. Leroy is use a flea comb. He likes this...*if* we are careful, otherwise he lets us know. We use a bucket with soapy water to rinse off the flea comb after each swipe, so the little jumping pests don't make a bid for freedom and get a foothold in our boat.

We are all about flea prevention rather than flea annihilation.

And as the saying goes: "If kitty ain't happy, ain't nobody happy."

* * *

Since I'm taking Gabrielle out to dinner tonight, we've changed into our finest clothes. Finest clothes in summer in Key West mean clean shorts, possibly underwear, and tank top or polo shirt. In winter, it could mean—drum roll, please—long trousers and a sweatshirt.

Underwear, for sure.

It will *never* mean socks.

* * *

With jangled nerves and sincere trepidation, we slide back the hatch. We peep over the top. No snarling. No baring of teeth. No blood dripping. Where is that little shit?

Is he sleeping inside in the A/C?

Chewing on a half a cow?

We quietly open the little mahogany doors and step up into the cockpit.

No explosion of teeth.

No, ah, hound's breath.

We tippy-toe to the stern and just when we're about to make good on our escape, all kinds of teethy canine-hell breaks loose about five feet from our faces, throats, carotids, sphincters.

Snarling, dripping, drooling, teeth-baring wretchedness.

Rabid Killer Dogs From Hell do that on purpose, you know. They lie in wait until you are just even with that hole in the privet hedge, or the tiny opening in the fence, or when you've just shoved the invitation for the hen party through the letter box on the front door, then they lunge, breathing fire, and give you all they've got from deep within their distended bowels.

They must train at the Kim Jong-un Blood-Thirsty Academy of Fear Mongering, and Diminishing Mental Health.

I don't know this as fact.

I'm just guessing here.

But it sort of makes sense.

* * *

It takes us three leisurely Banana Republic minutes to walk over to the Half Shell Raw Bar. It took us that long to get there from the marina, because we stopped twice to admire the view, and once to check my underwear. This is clearly one of the perks of living in the Old Town, not the checking of underwear to see if you've shit yourself, rather that you can walk everywhere. No need to hire a pedicab or taxi to convey you back home after an evening out enjoying a highly combustible mixture of the grape and the grain.

Remember, folk in Key West get arrested for riding a bike in an inebriated state, you might as well have been driving an 18-wheeler down Duval, over the legal limit.

The Half Shell Raw Bar is another example of old Key West, and that's one of the reasons we come here. We are sitting at one of the tables over by the boardwalk. It's steamy out tonight, which means it's steamy in here.

We love nights like this.

John Rubin was the first to arrive. He was well-sunburned from his deep-sea fishing adventure, and he looked the picture of health.

He pulled up a seat and gave us a quick account of his day: "Went out to the reef instead of the Gulf Stream," he said. "The wind was from the north and it was too rough in the stream, so I was told. At the reef, they chummed with hundreds of live pilchards. The pilchards actually hid under the boat for safety and that brought in barracuda and kingfish and blackfin tuna, even wahoo."

"And?"

"Didn't get skunked, that's for sure. Best fishing day I've ever had and we released them all. Let's drink."

Popcorn Joe arrived and we introduced him to John Rubin. Immediately thereafter, Johnny-Johnny arrived and after more introductions, we decided on rosé wine.

We told a few jokes, told a few war stories, then Gabrielle and I related the bad news of our new neighbor at the marina, Mr. Rich Prick, and his carnivorous pet.

"Not liking that," John Rubin said.

"Me, neither," Johnny-Johnny said.

"What can we do about it?" Gabrielle asked.

"I have an idea," Popcorn Joe said. "Go talk to him, but you can't go in all pumped up. He will just get defensive. Force against force doesn't work. You go in hard, he will give back hard. It's in a male's DNA. It's instinct. The male was meant to protect the female of the species. She'd stay in the cave and he'd go out and kill the bear. Invite him over to your boat for a coffee…"

"The bear?" John Rubin said.

Popcorn Joe gave Rubin a look, not a withering look, more a knowing twinkle.

"Anyhoo," Popcorn Joe went on. "Let Gabrielle tell him how she needs to go to work every day. Remember, force against force doesn't work."

We mulled what Popcorn Joe had just said, and then were spared responding by the arrival of our server coming over to take our order.

Our server's name was Marisol Lavavajillas, she was Cuban, and she resembled an earlier virgin, I mean, *version* of Gloria Estefan. When Marisol spoke, her accent made her sound as if she were related to Al Pacino's character Tony Montana, in *Scarface*, and that gave us all a fright. I was prepared for her to say: *"Go ahead! I take your fucking bullets! You think you kill me with bullets? I take your fucking bullets! Go ahead!"*

But she didn't, rather: "Go ahead! I take your order. Go ahead!"

Popcorn Joe was an occasional visitor to the Half Shell Raw Bar, so he knew what he wanted. We let him order first, while we perused.

"I would like the BBQ Baby Back Pork Ribs, please," Popcorn Joe said.

"With the Langy BBQ *e-sauce*?" Marisol asked, in her strong accent.

"Go ahead!" John Rubin said.

"Please," Popcorn Joe said, smiling at John Rubin.

Then Gabrielle ordered the Stuffed Shrimp Dinner.

"One *e-Stuffed e-Shrimp*," Marisol said.

"Remember the comedian George Carlin?" John Rubin said. "**JUMBO** … Shrimp. **JUMBO** … Shrimp."

"Would you like that with the Cuban bread and the ear of corn?" Marisol said.

"Please," Gabrielle said.

Then, I ordered the Seafood Combo, this means grilled shrimp, dolphin (not Flipper, rather Mahi-Mahi), and scallops (real scallops, not those popped out of shark, skate, or some other trash fish with a round cookie cutter).

"One *e-Seafood* Combo," Marisol confirmed.

Then John Rubin ordered a Bucket of Steamed Clams, Conch Chowder, and a half dozen Oysters Rockefeller. This was just for starters.

Marisol eyes were dilating.

"And now for my entrée," he said. "I would like the scallops, please."

"Broiled or fried?" Marisol asked.

"Fried, please."

"One *Bookit* of *e-Steamed* Clams, one Conch Chowder, one half dozen of Oysters Rockefeller, and one *e-Scallops.*"

Marisol turned to Johnny-Johnny. "And for you, *e-sir?*"

"If there's anything left, *mademoiselle,* I would like the Catch of the Day," he said, then under his breath: *"Although, I think you might be the catch of the day."*

"And bring us a carafe of your finest rosé," John Rubin said.

"We only have house," Marisol said.

"Then that would be your finest, thank you."

There was just the hint of a breeze and we could hear the halyards tinkling just out there.

Gabrielle said: "When we first moved onto our boat, the halyards flapping in the wind disturbed our sleep. Now we find it white noise and soothing."

"As does Mr. Leroy," I added. "Not that he has any trouble sleeping, anywhere, anytime, anyway."

Why are cats so cute when they're sleeping?

Much like children.

Here's a little tale for you: I remember Gabrielle's Auntie Dot, in Liverpool, telling us something once when we were there visiting. She had a few great nieces and nephews over and they were all curled up taking their afternoon nap. Auntie Dot led us into the spare room where they were dozing, smiled lovingly at them and said: "Aren't they adorable. If they're sleeping, they're not eating."

Later, she would tell us: "I so loved being a mum, but it

could be stressful. A mother will only ever be as happy as her least happiest child."

Auntie Dot, a wise woman.

* * *

After we'd all finished our dinners, Marisol came by. "Anyone care for any dessert?"

"I think we'll stick with the wine," John Rubin said. "Could you bring us another carafe of the rosé, please?"

"Hear! Hear!" Johnny-Johnny said.

"Of course, here," Marisol said. "Where else?"

When Marisol went to fetch the carafe, Johnny-Johnny got up from his seat. "Right back," he said.

Then John Rubin rose. "Me, too," he said.

Gabrielle and I looked over to Popcorn Joe. "What's that about?"

"They're up to something."

Marisol returned with our carafe of rosé, then aimed for the *cocina*.

At the table over by the wall plastered with the license plates, a woman's voice seems somehow familiar.

"Do you hear that?" Gabrielle asked.

"What?"

"That voice."

"Which one?"

"Wait. *That* one. That woman's voice."

"What about it?"

"Sound familiar?"

I listened. "Yeah, it does. Do you recognize her?"

Gabrielle discreetly had a peep at the woman.

"Recognize her?"

"No."

"Let me look…"

"No! She'll know you're looking at her. She's just there."

"We must know her," I said, and I got up.

"What are you doing!"

"Going to go pump the bilges. Then I'll have a squizzy."

229

I started to walk away.

"Pssst!" Gabrielle hissed.

"What?"

"The head's that way! See if Rubin and Johnny-Johnny are in there."

I turned and went the correct way, then after the obligatory pause, I returned.

"Any sign of Rubin and Johnny-Johnny?"

"Nowhere to be seen."

"Did you look at the woman?"

"I did."

"And?"

"She's sitting beneath the license plate from Vermont that says MAGOO. Never seen her before in my life."

"Perhaps she's on the radio?"

"No, she doesn't have a face for radio, she's too good looking..."

"What do you think, Giuseppe?" Gabrielle asked Popcorn Joe. "TV?"

Popcorn Joe had a good hard look. "Don't think so, she could stand to lose a few pounds and you know how the small screen puts the weight on..."

Eventually, John Rubin and Johnny-Johnny returned.

"Where were you two?" Gabrielle asked.

"Out having a cheeky fag," Johnny-Johnny said.

John Rubin just smiled a smile loaded with curious subtext.

We would soon find out that Rubin had cornered Marisol and paid for all of us. Sneaky bugger, we will get him back soon.

After dinner, we bid Popcorn Joe, John Rubin, and Johnny-Johnny farewell, then we headed the short distance home.

As we approached our boat, we both shot nervous glances at the *BOOBIE BOUNCER*. She was dark and there was no sign of Death-by-Dog, but Mr. Rich Blow Dude had come in bow first and the bow and two anchors stuck way out over the dock. Then we heard a loud SQUAWK. Mr. Rich Asshole Provider Shithead Guy Dude Prick had left the VHF radio on and every few minutes it CRACKLED loudly and spewed out indecipherable distant communications.

"How are we supposed to sleep with that on?"

We climbed onboard, I foraged in the fridge for a few minutes, then the three of us hung out in the cockpit, enjoying the intermittent tranquility in between SQUAWKS of the VHF.

The moon was just rising and it was enormous and golden.

"It's going to be a full moon tomorrow," Gabrielle said.

"Full moon in Key West."

"The perfect storm."

And the VHF CRACKLED loudly to punctuate that statement.

Then we had ten minutes of blissful silence.

Me: "Have you ever noticed that the man in the moon looks as if he has just finished telling the Wide Mouth Frog joke?"

"Funny," Gabrielle said.

About now, Gabrielle's cell phone jangled. She peered at the readout. "It's from Popcorn Joe."

"What does it say?"

"Just one word—Siri."

"Siri?" I say.

"Siri, that woman back at the Half Shell Raw Bar sounded like Siri." Then Gabrielle added: "Remember we read about the woman in Spain who is the voice of Spanish Siri?"

"Oh, yeah. Everyone recognized her voice."

"Everywhere she went, people would ask her if they had met before."

"That's right, she started by being the Spanish voice for Sat Navs, then was the voice for some bank when you dialed in, then she became the Spanish Siri."

"Even Siri likes the Half Shell Raw Bar," I said.

"Let's go to bed."

231

We went below, got undressed, turned the A/C on and got snuggled up in our V-bunk.

"Any idea what time it is?" Gabrielle asked.

"Well after two," I said.

We felt four little paws up by our head, and just before we drifted off, we heard laughter, loud, drunken laughter.

"Mr. Party-Hearty's back," Gabrielle said.

I sat up, opened the forward hatch a tad and peaked out.

"He's got four women with him!"

"What?"

"We're never going to get any sleep tonight."

Gabrielle and I lay there, waiting for that dumb pounding bass to start, followed by The Garden of Earthly Delights squeals, level 10 on the Pork-o-Meter.

But it didn't, instead we heard the engines start up.

I sneaked a peak out the forward hatch again.

"He's leaving!"

"Where could he possibly be going at this hour?"

And then our boat rocked and shook as the *BOOBIE BOUNCER* disobeyed the No Wake Zone.

CHAPTER FORTY-ONE

"I think I'm seasick…" I moaned.

"You're not seasick. We didn't sail anywhere. You overdid it on the rosé. Go back to sleep."

"But I heard waves and the ocean slapping the hull."

"We didn't go anywhere. Go back to sleep."

Moan…

CHAPTER FORTY-TWO

I rolled over in bed. Something in my addled brain was stirring and there was a low whirring noise somewhere in the distance. A *struggling* low whirring noise.

One eye popped open, then the other one tried, but it was stuck shut. I couldn't believe it, I was awake before Gabrielle. Before Mr. Leroy.

Silently, I slipped out of our V-bunk...and stepped into about a foot of water.

"We're sinking!"

No, just a dream.

Nothing but a bad dream.

See...I could have said "wet dream," but I won't say that or stoop that low so as to receive raised eyebrows and a groan from you.

CHAPTER FORTY-THREE

Mr. Leroy was the first one up the next morning.

And he was peckish.

No surprise there.

We didn't need an alarm clock, we had Cat-A-Larm. Seven a.m. sharp. You could set your watch to Mr. Leroy.

And he was always polite: He'd jump up by Gabrielle's face and gently touch her cheek with a paw. If that didn't work, he would softly head-butt her face.

There are worse ways to wake up of a morning.

Gabrielle stirred, then both eyes popped open.

"I'm on it, Mr. Leroy," she said, then scooted down the V-berth so she could escape.

She turned toward me: "How did you sleep?"

"Like a drunken sailor. Did Mr. STD Risk-Factor leave early this morning, or did I dream it?"

"He buggered off." Then: "Did you hear the rain last night?"

"I heard nothing."

"It was a real tropical downpour. Lots of lightning."

"Really? I thought I was having an optical migraine."

"Hangover?"

"Ye-esss," I said. "I think as I get older I get hangovers more easily. If this keeps up it could have a detrimental effect on the Bull's yearly take."

"But we didn't go to the Bull last night."

"We didn't?"

"No, the Half Shell Raw Bar."

"I knew that."

Meow! Mr. Leroy was wrapping himself around Gabrielle's leg. Gabrielle had to get a move on. I got up out of *bunk*, tossed our one lonely sheet back to straighten it. "That's the bed made," I said to absolutely no one.

"Just got a text from John Rubin," Gabrielle yelled over. "The wind's still from the north, he says, so he's going out on the flats. He's hoping for a Grand Slam."

"A Grand Slam of what?"

"No idea. He'll probably tell us tonight."

I went to the head. I performed my ablutions, then peered into our one mirror to make sure my eyes weren't bleeding. When I was sure they weren't, I decided there was no better time than now to attempt to get the contacts in. At least I'd remembered to take them out the previous night when we got back to the boat, so I wasn't a complete, hopeless drunk.

No comments, please.

I fetched my little contact holder from under the sink and opened the right lens side. I always opened the right side first and I was worried that I was becoming Sheldon. Right contact lens first. Right sock first. Right leg in trousers or shorts.

But there was no contact lens in the right compartment. I looked in the sink. I looked all around the sink. Had I been so pissed to the gills that I sent the little bugger flying? They're like drones, aren't they? They'll go just about anywhere.

I opened the left side of the contact case. No contact. Shit! I hadn't taken them out when I got home last night.

At least I wasn't like that 67-year-old woman in the UK who had 27 contact lenses in one eye.

FYI: from *The Manchester Guardian*: A 67-year-old woman has had 27 contact lenses removed from one eye.

The discovery was made after the woman went to Solihull hospital in the West Midlands for routine cataract surgery. In a report for the *British Medical Journal* (BMJ), experts from the hospital said "a bluish foreign body" emerged during the procedure "as a hard mass of 17 contact lenses bound together by mucus".

(Author's Note: Yuk!)

Ten more were found under further examination.

(Author's Note: WTF!)

The experts wrote: "The patient had worn monthly disposable lenses for 35 years. She had poorer vision in the right eye and deep-set eyes, which might have contributed to the unusually large number of retained foreign bodies."

(Author's Note: No shit!)

Rupal Morjaria, a specialist trainee in ophthalmology, told *Optometry Today*: "None of us have ever seen this before.

"It was such a large mass. All the 17 contact lenses were stuck together.

"We were really surprised that the patient didn't notice it because it would have caused quite a lot of irritation.

"She was quite shocked. She thought her previous discomfort was just part of old age and dry eyes."

(Author's Note: Hmmm…)

* * *

"What do you want for breakfast?" came a voice from the galley.

"Aspirin," I moaned.

Gabrielle sorted out Mr. Leroy, then me, then we went over to the showers in the marina.

After showering I felt marginally better. Marginally.

When we got back onboard our boat, we both stopped.

"Ewww, smell that?" Gabrielle said.

"Where's that coming from? Down below?"

We went down into the galley. The smell was worse. I pulled up the floorboards and grimaced. "The bilge is almost overflowing. Rank! Why wasn't the bilge pump working?"

Gabrielle and I looked at each other as both of our minds raced for an explanation, and don't forget, boats are foreign objects to us.

Finally, we both came to the same conclusion at the same time: "Popcorn Joe!"

Because it was an emergency, we grabbed our rarely used

cell phone to call Giuseppe, but couldn't get a signal, so we pedaled over to Truman Annex and knocked on his door.

"Not home. Maybe he's rollerblading around the island."

"Or he's at the gym."

"Or he's finished rollerblading and he's over at the Conch Seafood Restaurant cleaning his popcorn cart."

We jumped back on our bikes and pedaled over to the Conch Seafood Restaurant and found Popcorn Joe in the shed out back, cleaning his Pretty Good Popcorn cart, just as we'd surmised.

"Giuseppe!"

"What's up, B's?"

We explained our dilemma.

"And the backup bilge pump didn't work?"

"We have a backup bilge pump?" I said.

"When's the last time you checked the bilge?"

"A week ago," I said. "Same day I checked the air in our bike tires."

"I'll be there in half an hour, let me just finish here."

Popcorn Joe arrived and the first thing he said was: "Where's your neighbor from hell? His boat's gone?"

"He buggered off in the middle of the night."

"Middle of the night?" Popcorn Joe said. "That's weird."

"Thank God," Gabrielle said. "Let's hope he stays away for a while. Couldn't have taken much more."

"What comes around, sometimes goes," Popcorn Joe said, putting a new twist on the expression.

Within minutes, Popcorn Joe was peering down at a very robust bilge. Hovering over his shoulder, trying to make sense of it all was Mr. Leroy.

"Coffee, Giuseppe?" Gabrielle offered.

"Black. Thanks."

Popcorn Joe studied the situation some more then said. "It rained a lot last night. First thing we have to do is determine if this is fresh water or saltwater. Water can get in here a million ways: through deck joints, hatches, seals, rod holders if you had 'em, screws, through bolts, anchor lockers if you had one, through the hull, any seam or crack really."

"So how do we check if it's fresh water or saltwater?" Gabrielle asked.

"I'm going to taste it. Get me a cup, will you, please."

"Really?"

Gabrielle handed Popcorn Joe his coffee and another cup to check the bilge water.

"Thanks, Gabrielle," Popcorn Joe said, then he scooped the empty cup into the filthy, somewhat oily bilge water, then pointed out toward our dock box at a pelican who had just perched on top.

"You have a new friend!"

"That's Helen the Pelican," Gabrielle said.

When we looked back at Popcorn Joe, he was sipping, indeed, savoring the bilge water.

"Jesus, you were serious!"

"About what?"

"Tasting the bilge water."

"No, this is the coffee, who'd want to taste bilge water?"

Always the comedian, Popcorn Joe got up. "Let's go up in the cockpit."

We all followed Popcorn Joe out, even Mr. Leroy, who seemed to now be more interested in the pelican than the bilge water. Couldn't blame him really, Helen the Pelican had a regal bearing.

Popcorn Joe poured a small amount of bilge water on the deck.

"Now what do we do?" Gabrielle asked.

"We wait," Popcorn Joe said.

Popcorn Joe pulled out his cell phone and thumbed in a few numbers, then, said: "Johnny-Johnny? Got a favor, get me a hand bilge pump ASAP." Popcorn Joe listened. "On the *Mr. Leroy* with the B's. Later!"

"We'll need to get that water out of there if you want to sleep onboard tonight."

"If the bilge pump is buggered, is that expensive to repair?"

"Got a friend at the marine store, he'll source a rebuilt one."

Ten minutes later, Johnny-Johnny pulled up on his bicycle. In his basket was a manual bilge pump. Johnny-Johnny was wearing a black T-shirt with red lettering, which stated quite accurately: **SURELY NOT EVERYONE WAS KUNG FU FIGHTING**.

"Monsieur, Madame, Popcorn Man," he said, as he climbed aboard. He gave Mr. Leroy a quick scratch under the chin. "Mr. Leroy."

Johnny-Johnny spotted the empty slip. "Where's the fuckwit?"

"That's the question of the day," Gabrielle said.

Johnny-Johnny looked off toward the horizon, toward the Gulf, then he said: "Turn me loose. Pumping bilges is free on Wednesdays, if you buy me a beer the next time you see me in the Bull."

"When will you be there next?"

"I will be there tonight."

"Tonight it is, then," I said, always looking for a reason to spend some quality time in my office.

"Count me in," Popcorn Joe said. "I'll be there after sunset."

"And bring John Rubin," Johnny-Johnny said. "Man's a hoot."

Johnny-Johnny set up the manual bilge pump and began the work at, ah, hand. And, just so you know, if you've never had the opportunity to pump a bilge out by hand, this is decidedly labor intensive.

After twenty minutes, Johnny-Johnny noted: "Feel as if I'm pumping all the water out of the marina, through this bilge." By the time Johnny-Johnny was finished, he was dripping in sweat. "Won't need to go to the gym today," he said.

"How do you know boats?" Gabrielle asked. "Thought you were stationed in the desert?"

"C'est vrai, Madame, but I was brought up near Belfast and

240

Belfast is all about boats. And ships. Remember, the *Titanic* was built in Belfast."

"The *Titanic* sunk," I said, then wished I hadn't.

Johnny-Johnny went on: "Then, as a youth, I was stationed on a merchant ship for a while..."

"Did you like that?"

"No, a mate and I jumped ship in Galveston. Not so easy to hide there in those days when you have an Irish accent. The local sheriff caught us eventually. By then, the ship was on its way to San Diego, so the sheriff was instructed to drive us all the way to San Diego. The sheriff was thrilled to get to go out to California...

"In San Diego, we were thrown in the *brig* because we'd arrived in California a few days before our ship. The police officer there had never met anyone from Ireland, so he let us out one night to show us the town and to introduce some local girls to two nice lads from Belfast. Nice town, San Diego. Really good craic, it was."

"When your ship arrived, were you punished?" I asked.

"No, *promoted*. The crew member, who was supposed to be our superior, jumped ship in San Diego."

Johnny-Johnny peered into the bilge. "Be so kind and get me a torch."

Gabrielle handed Johnny-Johnny our trusty police zoomable waterproof flashlight with handy wrist strap that we had purchased on eBay.

Johnny-Johnny switched it on then shone the beam around the bilge "Got any rags or old towels? Let's get it as dry as we can, then I can lay down some talcum powder and perhaps we can see where the leak is coming from."

"You carry talcum powder with you?"

"Today I did."

Well, were we ever impressed. *Friends, contacts,* what a difference they made when your home was on its way to Davy Jones' locker.

It took a while to get the bilge dry enough to lay down some talcum powder.

"While we're waiting, and dying of the heat and smell down here," Popcorn Joe said. "Let's go look at my little experiment."

We went up above (*note use of nautical terminology again*) to check on the little splash of water that Popcorn Joe had spilled out. Popcorn Joe got his nose right up close to the now dry spot and adjusted his glasses. "Saltwater!" he proclaimed. "I see residue."

"I can verify that."

We all looked over at Johnny-Johnny who now had Mr. Leroy on his lap.

"How?" Gabrielle asked.

"How what?"

"How can you verify if it was salt or fresh from way over there?"

"I tasted it."

"Gross!"

"No so awful, *Madame*, as you probably know, drinking is *de rigueur* in the Legion. From time to time, we would brew up our own hooch. We'd get right bladdered. This'd probably do much the same."

"*Eau-de-Vie?*" I said.

"Oh, you know about *Eau-de-Vie?* No, ours was much more inhumane."

"*Pisse de chat?*" I said.

Johnny-Johnny laughed. "*Mais oui*, more like *pisse de chat*."

* * *

Later that day, after I returned home from doing some sanding on a boat over at Garrison Bight, I found Johnny-Johnny hanging out with Mr. Leroy.

"I put down a layer of talcum powder in the bilge, but nothing yet, which I guess is good. Let's keep an eye on it. Gabrielle's at Fausto's."

"She'll be buying dinner. Care to dine with us, then we'll head over to the Bull afterwards?"

"It would be a pleasure."

242

"Coffee?"

"Hoping you were going to say that. *Merci.*"

I rustled up two *con leches*, then Johnny-Johnny and I sat out in the cockpit. "While you were gone, I checked for dry rot. Boat of this age could have it…"

"And do we?"

"None that I found yet, but we've got to keep on top of that."

FYI: I Googled dry rot and this is what I learned: dry rot is a "fungus amongus" that arises from wet wood. It only needs a miniscule amount of water to gain a foothold and send out rhizomorphic runners in search of more moisture. (sounds sinister, doesn't it?)

It thrives in poorly ventilated areas (our bilge), grows in temperatures above 40 degrees Fahrenheit, and literally eats up the cellulose of its host, destroying the wood in the process. Unless stopped, the fungus can spread like wildfire.

FY-botany-**I:** Cellulose is an important structural component of the primary cell walls of green plants, for example, cotton fiber is 90% cellulose. Who knew?

Dry rot is not actually dry at all, but instead requires about 20% moisture to get going. It is a spore-based killer of wood and once it gets chomping is very tricky to get it to cease and desist. I'm probably stating the obvious here, but it usually requires the removal of all infected wood.

Gabrielle pulled up on her bicycle, chained it to mine, then stepped onboard, carrying *one* can of food.

Gabrielle was laughing. "The guy at the cash register said 'paper or plastic,' and I said I'd be paying with cash. But he didn't get it."

"Is that dinner?"

Gabrielle said. "It's for Mr. Leroy."

"You feed Mr. Leroy tuna?" Johnny-Johnny said.

"Mr. Leroy loves the juice…plus this brand is 'dolphin friendly.'"

"Don't believe everything you read and hear," Johnny-Johnny said. "Since the 1990s, tuna fishermen were supposed to use nets with special hatches so unwanted fish could escape. But tuna are wide-ranging and fast and powerful, so catching them is not so easy. Plus, they're big, six-to-seven feet long and can go over 900 pounds. This is the highly prized bluefin, I'm talking about."

"The Japanese love their sushi and sashimi," Gabrielle said.

"Indeed they do. Previously, fishing fleets used harpoons, but that is time consuming, so fleets have had to develop new techniques. Some use vast purse-like seine nets to scoop them out of the sea. Japanese vessels trail lines of baited hooks many miles long, but they don't just catch tuna. The by-catch routinely includes sharks, turtles, even albatrosses, and they're brought in dead and just dumped. The ratio is about four sharks caught for every tuna.

"Do you remember earlier this year? One bluefin tuna fetched £517,000 at a market in Japan. That's three-quarters-of-a-million dollars. They're getting the big bucks because bluefin are on the wane. Over-fishing is taking the species to the brink of extinction."

"How much did that tuna weigh?" Gabrielle asked.

"Nearly 450 pounds."

"So what does the world do?"

"Moratorium, bluefin population is down 97%. The tuna are being harvested when they're too young, and they haven't reached maturity and the ability to reproduce."

"Jeez, Johnny-Johnny, how do you know so much about it?"

"I covet life and I despise greed," was Johnny-Johnny's response.

Dead silence for a while, then Gabrielle spoke. "Okay, I've learned something new. Taking this tuna back tomorrow and no more tuna. Anyone up for pizza? Without the anchovies?"

* * *

As we walked along the harbor walk, Johnny-Johnny suddenly

stopped and became reflective. "I love nights like this, reminds me of Casablanca."

"Isn't Casablanca hot and dry?"

"Casablanca is along the coast, so you get your fair share of rain and humidity. Deeper inland you get all that dry heat. Walking along the Boulevard de la Corniche at night, a night like tonight, looking at all the boats, that was blissful."

Johnny-Johnny was lost for a moment, probably slipped back in time.

"There was a girl, wasn't there?" Gabrielle said.

Johnny-Johnny smiled. "Oh, there's always a girl, *Madame*..."

"And?"

"You want the story?"

"If you want to tell it."

"Well, her name was ZiZi. She was from Marseilles, but was working in Casablanca..."

"Doing what?"

"She was a tattoo artist." Johnny-Johnny pulled up his T-shirt in the back. There was a tattoo of a young woman, naked, lying on a bed of cushions.

"Zizi did that?"

"*Oui, Madame*, she did."

"Tattoos were allowed in the French Foreign Legion?" I asked.

"Since forever. A hundred years ago, only legionnaires, mariners and prisoners were known in France for being tattooed."

"The girl in the tattoo, that's ZiZi, isn't it?" Gabrielle said.

Johnny-Johnny smiled. *"Oui, Madame."*

"And that's how you really learned your French..." I said.

"The best way to learn a language is in bed," Johnny-Johnny said. "ZiZi thought I had the morals of an alley cat, and she somehow found that appealing...but..."

"Go on," Gabrielle coaxed.

"I was in the Legion. I had four more years. I was being deployed. She was in Casablanca."

"And she didn't wait for you?" Gabrielle asked.

"She waited," Johnny-Johnny said. "But I had changed."

"Nothing wrong with change."

"I *transformed*..." Johnny-Johnny said.

Johnny-Johnny slipped back into the past for a moment, then said. "I don't mind visiting the past from time to time, because I'm now content with myself in the present..."

And then he said no more.

And we didn't probe.

We aimed up Greene Street and walked over to the little hole-in-the-wall pizza joint just across from Sloppy's back door.

The place is called Paradise Pizza & Pasta.

Surprisingly, the joint was dead.

We ordered slices of pizza and beverages from the bloke behind the counter. When he turned his back to us, we could read on the back of his T-shirt: IF YOU ARE NOT MEANT TO HAVE MIDNIGHT SNACKS, WHY IS THERE A LIGHT IN THE FRIDGE?

We were handed our slices and drinks, and then repaired to a booth back near the Pepsi machine. Johnny-Johnny and Gabrielle each ordered a massive Supreme Slice of pizza. I ordered two (piglet). The place was a furnace, as it always seems to be.

Johnny-Johnny gnawed on his pizza and then held it up the way a scientist holds up a beaker in the lab.

"For a bloke who usually drinks his dinner, I had the Half Shell Raw Bar the other night, and now this, I'm probably good until the end of hurricane season. And I am thankin' ye."

"We come in here from time to time," I said to Johnny-Johnny, "but that guy behind the counter has never been too friendly. Tonight he was all charm."

Johnny-Johnny gnawed again on his pizza.

"Locals say it's a great place to come to if you're really wasted late, because they're open till 1am, and if you're really blootered you won't notice how rude that guy is," I went on.

Gnaw.

I looked at Gabrielle.

Gnaw.

"It's your doing, isn't it, Johnny-Johnny," Gabrielle said. "You've scared some manners into that man."

Gnaw.

After dinner, we exited out onto Greene Street, crossed over to the back door of Sloppy's.

"Let's cut through here," Johnny-Johnny said. "Bloke owes me some money and he's been avoiding me like the clergy avoided the Black Death in Dublin in 1348. Until I get my money back, I'll toy with his brain and that will bring me great joy."

I looked over at Gabrielle.

"How do you know he's here?"

"I looked at the bar webcam before I came out. He's sitting in the back corner to the right of the stage, under the blue marlin. He's hard to miss, he's got a face like a slapped behind."

We penetrated Sloppy's. Even hotter in here.

Johnny-Johnny cased Sloppy's as we wove our way through a packed house, and then out the front door.

"Did you see him?" I said.

"*Mais, oui*, but he reckons I didn't clock him. He thinks he's safe and he will drop his guard. I'll go back later and collect."

I looked over at Gabrielle.

We crossed Duval, watched as two drunken tourons stopped in the middle of the street to tongue wrestle and almost got flattened by a pink taxi.

"Get a room!" Johnny-Johnny yelled.

Then a car with Vermont plates crawled slowly past. Just as it got even with us, the driver threw his still burning cigarette butt out the window. In a flash, Johnny-Johnny scooped up the offending cigarette butt and threw it back in the open window.

"Go back to Vermont and shit in your own nest!"

Wow, walking down Duval with Johnny-Johnny was quite exciting.

We strode through the balmy night and a heady aroma of conflicting smells, past Rick's and Durty Harry's, and as we did Gabrielle yelled: "I GOT SHOTGUN!"

Okay, this is a need-to-know. *I GOT SHOTGUN* is what we yell when we are going anywhere on Duval where there is a balcony overhead that we have to pass under. What this means is, "SHOTGUN" entitles you to walk closest to the wall and out of reach of anyone spilling beer on you from above…or throwing beer on you…or urinating on you. Yes, *urinating*.

It was too early for the working girls and their posse to be out on the balcony above Durty Harry's and Rick's blowing kisses and misbehaving, but we kept one eye up there, just in case.

"Once upon a time, it was chamber pots being emptied out windows, not much has changed," Johnny-Johnny said, eyeing the balcony.

"The night is young," Gabrielle said.

"Indeed, *Madame*."

We maintained a steady course, only tacking once to avoid a vomit slick, and soon saw a fashionably corpulent woman strolling toward us. She had a face that jiggled, multiple curves working in her favor, and a T-shirt which read: **A RECENT STUDY HAS FOUND THAT WOMEN WHO CARRY A LITTLE EXTRA WEIGHT LIVE LONGER THAN MEN … WHO MENTION IT.**

All three of us laughed then I stopped and said: "Look!"

Right there in front of us was the blind German student. He was wearing his dark sunglasses, sitting on his small folding chair, cloth across lap, and the sign proclaiming his blindness was at his feet.

"There he is again," I said. "He still hasn't gone back to Germany."

"I don't think he's blind," Gabrielle said.

"I'm going to do something," I said.

Gabrielle was horrified, but Johnny-Johnny wasn't: "Go for it!" he said.

I walked up and stopped right in front of the blind

German.

He continued to stare down at his lap.

I didn't move.

He didn't budge or flinch. Perhaps I was mistaken and he was indeed blind. I decided to try one last thing. I raised my right arm to give him a wave, but owing to my rotator cuff injury and stiff shoulder, I could only raise my arm at a forty-five degree angle.

A very distinctive *Heil Hitler* salute.

"Fuck you!" came the explosive response. "Fuck you!"

* * *

We scarpered and disappeared into the Duval Street crowd, and soon arrived at the entrance to the Bull. We fought our way in through a miasma of tourists and locals. It was as easy to recognize the differences between the two cultural ends of the spectrum as it was to tell the difference between the Atlantic and the Gulf Stream when you're out past the reef.

Our favorite seats over by the window and front door were taken, *again*, so we aimed for our second favorite seats over by the back door which leads out to Caroline, but it was occupied by a lone soul. We did a double take, it was John Rubin.

"Rubin!" I yelled.

"Breakfield!" he yelled back. "I came early. Had a stroll on Duval and couldn't take it anymore. I was getting all twitchy, somewhere between frightened and aroused. First, I saw some woman touting for Brazilian Bum Lifts...*touting!*"

We started laughing.

"Then a busty woman, and I mean busty, in a diaphanous top, approached me with two cockatoos. Asked me if I wanted to hold them and have my photo taken. I was cheeky and said okay, but who's going to hold the cockatoos? She gave me a long look and I thought she was going to slap me about, but she said 'No, problem, but that'll be twenty dollars extra.'"

Now we were losing it.

"Reminds me of a street back home in Manchester,"

Rubin said. "It's called Canal Street."

"Canal Street?" Gabrielle said, "Isn't that the Gay Village of Manchester?"

"It is, indeed, Gabbers, it's packed at night with gays, lesbians, transsexuals and transvestites who have flocked to the area from all over the world. Everyone had a good laugh when some wag painted over the 'C' of Canal and the 'S' of Street. Gay references aside, the whole village is very mixed, very straight-friendly. A bit like here, but without the cockatoos."

We heard a scream come from out on Duval. We rubbernecked to see what was going on. No need, Popcorn Joe was suddenly entering and laughing.

The spider is back!" Popcorn Joe said.

"Spider?" John Rubin said. "What spider? I like spiders."

"We have a local bloke who dangles a big rubber spider off the balcony to frighten all the girls..." Johnny-Johnny said.

"Was it a group of coeds from the University of Miami?" I asked.

"Not this time," Popcorn Joe said. "It was a group of gays dressed as the Village People."

"Colorful, indeed," John Rubin mused.

"Okay, listen up amigos, it's our shout," I said. "What's your poison?"

"Pastis, please, large," Johnny-Johnny said.

"Pastis, large," I repeated.

"Rubin?"

"Wine. Red. All of it."

"Wine, red, all of it," I repeated.

"Gabrielle?"

"House red."

"House red," I repeated.

"For you, Giuseppe?"

"Alcohol."

"Alcohol, I'm on it," I said. I knew Popcorn Joe liked Michelob, so no need to waste precious drinking time through discussion.

I rose and was shocked not to see a scrum formed around

the bar. I ordered our beverages from Debbie behind the bar. As always Debbie was the best example of multi-tasking. She was able to get our drinks, point out where the toilets were to a patron, and tell some rude prick to fuck off, pretty much all at the same time. And with a smile.

Then she turned to her bar-back, and I could just make out her saying: "You can't make everyone happy, you are not pizza."

I returned with our drinks, twice, and sat down. Had to pull up an extra chair and squeeze in the corner.

Up on the stage, the Fabulous Spectrelles, yes, you heard right the Divas of Doo-Wop, were just finishing "Where the Boys Are."

I've written about the Fabulous Spectrelles before, and I just have to say it again, if you are in town (after all, it's where the boys are), GO SEE THEM! They are an absolute institution here, a downright hoot, and so much damn fun.

"They are fabulous, indeed," John Rubin said. "Never seen anything like it, and I've been around…"

"Say no more," Gabrielle said. "You've been to Canal Street."

John Rubin winked knowingly at Gabrielle.

We lapped at our drinks with commendable lust.

The Spectrelles were now singing "I met him on a Monday and my heart stood still."

And Baby Tracy was *killing it* with her hips.

So good.

It was hot and sultry in the Bull. There was no movement of air—other than the ceiling fans overhead and Baby Tracy's hips—but there's something exotic about the Bull in the sultry throes of Key West's version of Indian summer, something end of the world, end of the line, end of a previous life that just wasn't working. Can't put my finger on it so well right now, but I think you know what I'm shooting for.

I raised my plastic glass of Bud, and we toasted.

"Thanks for helping us today, Johnny-Johnny," Gabrielle said. "That's the second time you saved us from peril."

"Mon plaisir."

"Question, Johnny-Johnny?" I said.

"Hit it," he said.

"Where do the soldiers come from who end up in the Legion?"

"All over the world…all over."

"And who makes the best soldiers, then?" John Rubin asked.

"It helps if you're a misfit, a sadist, a masochist, and get off by fighting, but if you are asking which nationality, let me start by saying the Chinese make the worst legionnaires…"

"But they're good in the kitchen," Popcorn Joe said.

"That they are, and that's where they usually end up—in the kitchen. Perhaps it's safer there. The Americans and British are always a pain in the arse, because they get upset about the living conditions. They endure it at the start, then they go AWOL. Not all, but most. You would think that the selection board by now would have figured this out. The French are flaky, the Serbs are tough motherfuckers, begging your pardon, *Madame*, the Koreans are the best of the Asians, and the Brazilians are the best of all. *C'est tout.*"

"You speak French a lot," I said. "You must miss the Legion."

"You now know why I speak French, for memories and just for fun, but I don't miss the Legion. When I was in, the light at the end of the tunnel was always another train coming."

"Which means?"

"I'd had enough of armed conflict. With the Legion, there is always another war."

"Why did you join in the first place?"

"The Legion gave me a chance to start a new life. Key West has afforded me the same opportunity all over again."

"Why'd you get out?" John Rubin asked.

"I was getting old. Sex with prostitutes, heavy drinking and fighting were encouraged. One general told me 'We do not build empires with virgins.'"

"Fair enough," John Rubin said. "I can see the logic behind that."

Johnny-Johnny went on: "In the Legion, no one cared what your social status was. It's a bit like that here in Key West. Sure, there are some people here who feel they are above others. I just laugh at them along with all the other people who are laughing at them. Which are a fair many."

"We used to have a friend here in Key West, God rest his soul," I said. "His name was Captain Jerry. He used to pee on the grills of the cars of folk who talked down to him."

"I like his style," Johnny-Johnny said. "I may have to add that to my arsenal."

We listened to the Spectrelles for a moment, just basking in the glow brought on by having the freedom (and guts) to live your life the way you wish, and being able to share it all with good friends of like-minded ilk.

Someone's cell phone rang. The ring tone was the *Marseillaise*.

"Gotta go!" Johnny-Johnny announced, and he jumped up. *Salut!*" And he was out the front door heading toward Sloppy's, talking into his cell.

Popcorn Joe turned to us: "Johnny-Johnny, he's been around the block a few times."

"What does Johnny-Johnny do?" John Rubin asked.

"You mean for work?"

"Yes, for work."

"He's a professional *gofer*."

"A what?"

"A professional gofer. You know, he goes for this and he goes for that. He takes care of things for people who hire him."

"What kind of things."

"Anything."

"A good man to know?"

"He's always looked out for me. Helped me a few times and I've never forgotten that."

"Getting that same feeling," Gabrielle said.

Popcorn Joe went on: "Before I came down to Key West, I owned a gym, then when I arrived here I had to reinvent myself, so I got on the pier down at Mallory by selling popcorn. Then I bought the Pineapple Apartments. None of that would have happened if I had stayed up north. Same with Johnny-Johnny, he came to the rock to get a fresh start on life and reinvented himself, became a professional gofer. When folk move down here they dig down deep inside and find a talent they didn't know they had, or they simply go after something that was always a dream and just out of reach. If you have a bit of an entrepreneurial spirit, you can make it work...if you can control your partying, that is."

"Is it running away from your past?" Gabrielle asked.

"Don't see it that way. I see it as running toward a new beginning."

"I like the sound of that," John Rubin said.

"Mr. Rubin..." Gabrielle said, changing topics.

"Oh, oh, by the sound of your voice, I'm in for it now."

"We have an assignment for you. Are you up for some adventure?"

"Does it involve alcohol?"

"It will when you return."

"I'm all ears."

"We will have a large glass of the *finest* red waiting for you upon your return."

"I'm going. I'm motivated now."

"This is your first time to Key West and we would like your impression of something," Gabrielle said.

"I think I can just manage that, please continue..."

"We would like you to go upstairs, not one flight to the Whistle Bar, but up two flights to the Garden of Eden Rooftop Bar."

"Garden of Eden? And Eve, any chance of her being there?"

"More likely than not," Popcorn Joe said.

"Indeed, we would like you to go up there, observe, take mental notes, and then report back."

254

John Rubin slid his chair back.

"One other thing," Gabrielle said, freezing John Rubin. "Your mobile, hand it over."

"I can't take my mobile with me? What kind of a place are you sending me to?"

"Not allowed," Gabrielle said. "Plus, we don't want you to run afoul of an Apple Picker."

"Apple Picker?"

"People who steal cell phones."

Rubin pulled his cell out of his pocket, then pulled a funny face.

"What?" Gabrielle said.

"I sent a pocket text."

"A what?"

"A pocket text. When I stuff my cell phone in my pocket, something goes nuts…wait, bad choice of words. When I stick my mobile in my pocket, it somehow types out all the common words, but jumbled together, throws in some emojis, then invariably it gets sent to EVERYONE on my phone list."

"You need to upgrade."

"I paid over a hundred quid for this Smartphone."

"Then downgrade," Popcorn Joe said. "Mine was ten dollars and I have no problems."

"Simplicity," Rubin said. "I think I like the sound of that."

"Go!" Gabrielle commanded.

Rubin handed his cell to Gabrielle, rose and turned to go toward the front door. "I just love stuff like this," he said.

Gabrielle stopped him. "Rubin, back door, turn right, climb the wooden staircase to the top."

Rubin gave us all a big smile and the Magnum, P.I. eyebrows.

"Godspeed!" Popcorn Joe said.

Twenty-five minutes later, Rubin stumbled in the back door. He was laughing and he went straight for his promised large glass of red which was waiting for him.

We watched gobsmacked as he downed nearly the entire glass without coming up for air.

"Funny!" I said.

"Not trying to be funny," he said sincerely. "I need this."

Rubin drained the rest of his wine glass, then blew out his cheeks and addressed us: "Bloody hell! It's a long way to the top if you want to rock and roll."

We all laughed.

"First of all," he began. "There was the world's largest bouncer at the door. A chappie the size of an American refrigerator."

"Was it the Refrigerator himself," I asked?

"Who?"

"Never mind."

"First thing I saw when I walked in, other than the lady vomiting over the side of the rooftop, was the sign that said: NO SEX ON THE PREMSES. They misspelled premises. But I was encouraged by the sign, you don't need to erect a Stop Sign on the corner if the people are stopping."

"I hear you there," Popcorn Joe said.

"There were a lot of bras and panties hanging above the bar," Rubin said. "Whatever happened to dollar bills and license plates?"

"Wrong bar," Popcorn Joe said.

"Then I noticed that the bartender was gay?"

"How could you tell?" Gabrielle said.

"I've been to Canal Street, remember?" Then: "There were a bunch of military types, as well. They were staring at a naked woman having her body painted."

"What was he painting on her?" Popcorn Joe asked.

"A naked woman."

"What?"

"He was painting a naked body over her naked body. Worked for me. When he was done she looked about eighteen."

"Anything else?" I asked.

"There were a few turtle dicks hanging out, so to speak, by the bar, they were old, creepy men, sweating their junk on the barstools. Oh, and there was a bald man about forty, who was only wearing a dressing gown and flip-flops. What was that about? Was he at home showering and he decided to pop over for a quick drink and a flash?"

Rubin grabbed my beer and took an Olympic gulp.

"Only downside was, the toilet was downstairs in the Whistle Bar and you had to get dressed to go down."

We all roared.

"What?" Rubin said innocently. "And there were two topless women on the dance floor. They were all over each other and that made it a bit more interesting."

John Rubin wiped some perspiration and sat back down.

"How was the DJ?" Popcorn Joe asked.

"I heard some couple moan that they thought the DJ couldn't mix a bag of concrete, but I thought he was alright."

"You did well," Gabrielle said. "You passed with flying colors."

"Thank you, Gabbers," he said, then pointed at her wine. "Are you planning on finishing that wine?"

* * *

We were enjoying the Spectrelles, when Johnny-Johnny suddenly reappeared through the back door. He gave Popcorn Joe a "yes" shake of his head and then sat back down.

"Good timing, Johnny-Johnny," John Rubin said. "My shout everyone."

"But you treated all of us to dinner the other night," Gabrielle said.

"Indeed, I did, but I feel after that baptism up there in the Garden of Eden, I should somehow give thanks."

"It can be a religious experience for some," Johnny-Johnny said.

The Spectrelles were now singing "DANCING IN THE STREET."

Outside on Duval, folk had stopped to listen to the Spectrelles and now they were dancing in the streets.

257

We settled deeper into the evening. We told jokes and we told stories and Johnny-Johnny showed John Rubin his tattoo of Zizi and before we knew it, it was well after midnight.

The Bull was still heaving and everyone was feeling no pain and there wasn't a care or worry in the world and Duval still was one pulsing daisy-chain of flesh peddlers.

"I like Key West," John Rubin said. "I like Key West a lot...

* * *

I'm not so sure, but I think we closed the Bull. Popcorn Joe turned right and walked back down Caroline to his home in Truman Annex. Johnny-Johnny walked up Duval toward his flat and a rendezvous with Manxsie. John Rubin headed down Duval to his apartment in the Ocean Key Resort. Gabrielle and I held hands and crossed over Duval, wobbled down Caroline, turned left on Margaret and entered the Key West Bight.

In the distance, heat lightening splintered the sky above the Gulf. It was still warm and balmy. There was nearly no breeze. The night was still and agreeable.

We walked on, hoping that Mr. Leroy wouldn't scold us because we were gone so long.

Suddenly, Gabrielle grabbed my arm. "Look!"

The *BOOBIE BOUNCER* was back.

"There are lights on," Gabrielle said. "But it's quiet. And no dog. For sure he's home. Perhaps the dock master's pounded some sense into him."

We climbed silently onboard and unlocked our boat. Mr. Leroy was already up in our V-bunk waiting for us. He had been asleep, but he turned his head toward us and gave us a sleepy, silent meow.

We locked up the boat, turned on the A/C, got undressed and crawled into bed, adjusting Mr. Leroy up by our heads.

But neither of us could fall asleep.

We kept waiting for all hell to break loose next door.

CHAPTER FORTY-FOUR

We must have eventually fallen asleep, because we were unceremoniously wrenched from glorious, albeit *short*, blissful slumber early the next morning by a strange sound.

Gabrielle looked over at me: "What's that noise?"

"It sounds like water running. What's going on?"

We opened the forward hatch, kneeled on our V-bunk and peeped out. There was a blush of pink and magenta in the eastern sky.

But now there was no noise. No running water. Then it started back up again. And we heard laughter.

Even Mr. Leroy now seemed to be interested.

"There!" Gabrielle said. "You won't believe it!"

Mr. Shit-for-Brains Guy and a topless Bow Bunny were standing on their swim platform, letting a manatee drink fresh water from a hose.

"They haven't even been to bed yet!"

CHAPTER FORTY-FIVE

For the next few days, Mr. Rich Rough Freshwater-Provider was quiet at night, but pissing us off during the day. He was taking his boat out and never obeying the NO Wake Zone. When he would yank the lines and depart, the boats in our area would rock and bang...and then there was that manatee. A friendly manatee that comes for a fresh drink of water would have no chance against a powerboat's screws.

I decided to complain.

"I'm going to go talk to the dock master," I told Gabrielle.

"No, you'll get upset if it goes south, I'll go."

So Gabrielle went.

She was gone about twenty minutes, when she returned, she had this to say: "He told me he had talked to the owner about keeping the noise down. Said the dog was friendly and well-behaved..."

"What? That's because the owner was there. When the owner is not there he becomes Godzilla on crack."

"Then, I told him about the guy not observing the 'idle speed and no wake', and about the manatee. He said he'd look into it when he got back."

"Back from what?"

"Vacation."

"When's he coming back?"

"I asked him that. He said not till next week."

CHAPTER FORTY-SIX

We decided to call a meeting of the War Cabinet.

That evening, we met in the back corner of our HQ—the Bull.

In attendance, Popcorn Joe, Johnny-Johnny, John Rubin, Gabrielle and me.

First action of order was ordering drinks.

Gabrielle, juice.

Johnny-Johnny, club soda.

Popcorn Man and me, coffee.

Sometimes you need to take a break.

John Rubin is super-human, so he took one for the team and ordered a large red.

It was still hot, but there was just the hint of autumn in the air, if there is such a thing in Key West.

As always, everyone was dressed in shorts and T-shirts, except John Rubin. He was dressed like a charter boat captain, complete with khaki baseball cap with fish hooks in the bill.

Sallie Foster was up on stage. She was playing "STAND BY ME." Someone had requested it.

Sallie is the queen of requests.

Just love that about her.

I held up my cup of coffee. "To coming up with a plan!" And we toasted.

Popcorn Joe raised his hand: "Can't you just move slips?"

"We asked about that, all booked until the spring."

Momentary silence.

"I have a plan," Johnny-Johnny announced. "Let's use

261

poena cullei!"

"Let's use what?"

"*Poena cullei*...the 'punishment of the sack.' It's a kind of torture..."

"We're listening," Gabrielle said.

"It was used in ancient Rome. What it basically is, the guilty is sewn into a leather sack with a rabid dog, a viper, a rooster, and a monkey."

We were all temporarily stunned into silence.

"You can't bring a spoon to a knife fight," Johnny-Johnny went on. "This'll work!"

"I'm sure we can all agree that it has a certain appeal," I noted. "Finding a rabid dog in Key West won't be a problem, a rooster will be easy enough, the viper we could trade out with a five-foot iguana, or in a pinch, no pun, a Burmese python...but the monkey, where would we get a monkey?"

"At Bobby's Monkey Bar."

'That's a gay bar."

"Alright, then forget that, I have another idea..."

"We're listening," Gabrielle said.

"Let's kill him, tie a square grouper around his neck, and feed him to the sharks!" This said with much brio and conviction.

And we all laughed.

"What?"

We stopped laughing.

"Gotcha!"

And we all laughed again, sort of.

"Okay, okay, okay, what I really think we should do, and I'm being conservative here, is sink the *BOOBIE BOUNCER.*"

"And how would we manage that?" Popcorn Joe asked.

"I'll shoot a few holes in it!"

"We're impressed with your passion," Gabrielle said, then she wrote down on a small notepad she had brought with her: KILL THE *BOOBIE BOUNCER.*

"Next!" Gabrielle said.

We sipped our beverages, then one by one, we took turns

coming up with a plan.

I went next.

"When I used to crew on yachts in Antibes, on the Côte d'Azur, we had a skipper who needed some extra cash, so he poured sugar in the engine of our seventy-footer. Then he rang the owner back in London and told him that the engine had packed up and it would need to be overhauled. The skipper called his mechanic buddy to come over and service the engine, then the skipper and the mechanic split the money the owner had wired down."

"How will we get onboard to put sugar in the engine?" Popcorn Joe asked.

"Haven't figured that one out yet, but it shouldn't be too difficult. The next night he goes on the hunt, we follow, use cell phones, break in…"

And Sallie sang Ben E. King's "Stand By Me."

Gabrielle gave me a look and blew out her cheeks, then she wrote down: SUGAR IT.

It was Popcorn Joe's turn to go: "We could untie it, and I'll tow it out into the flats. We'll do it as the tide's going out, then we'll leave it up on a sandbar."

UNTIE IT, Gabrielle wrote.

"Just had a thought," Gabrielle said. "Are there any CCTV cameras in the marina? Perhaps this idiot has security onboard."

"I'll get a hold of a dinghy and putt about and see what I can see," Johnny-Johnny said.

SURVEILLANCE, Gabrielle wrote down.

Then John Rubin spoke: "Why not go after him and not the boat?"

We all put our beverages down and gave our full attention to John Rubin.

"What do you mean?" I said.

"Hire a young lady to go back to the boat with him. From what you say, he thinks through his johnson."

"His what?" Popcorn Joe said.

"His tallywacker…" John Rubin clarified.

263

His what?" Popcorn Joe said.

John Rubin sighed: "Two countries separated by a common language. You know, his todger, his plonker, his bell-end, his wedding tackle, his pork sword, his willy, his giggle stick, his trouser snake…Get it?"

"Pork sword?" I said.

"Giggle stick?" Gabrielle said.

"Oh, now I get it," Popcorn Joe said.

"I like your style, *monsieur* Rubin, absolutely brilliant," Johnny-Johnny said. "And I know just the *demoiselle* who could do it…"

We all looked to Johnny-Johnny.

"Who?" I said.

"Me, I'm a master of disguises."

"But as a woman?" John Rubin said.

"In the Merchant Navy, we had a pantomime every Christmas. We all had to dress in drag. Believe me when I say I can rock a pair of high heels."

"I'm not seeing it," John Rubin said.

"Girls get prettier at last call," Johnny-Johnny said.

"Okay, now I'm seeing it," John Rubin said.

"But, what if?" Popcorn Joe said.

"Yes, what if?" Gabrielle said.

"Indeed, WHAT IF?!" I said.

"Well, I'm not about to go that far! Listen, once I'm onboard, I can slip him a Mickey and we can do it all, sugar in the engine, square grouper *in situ*, tow it out to the flats, sink it…"

"Oh, shit," Popcorn Joe said. "We're all gonna get arrested."

"Only if we're caught," Johnny-Johnny said.

ALL THE ABOVE, Gabrielle wrote down, and then she added ARRESTED.

"Fuck me," John Rubin said. "Let's order some proper plonk and give this some serious thought."

Gabrielle and I took orders and we gladly paid for the round. We felt we should pay now, in case we needed to be bailed later.

Having said that, we knew no one was really serious, this was all waffle, and we were just having a bit of fun.

We sipped and supped.

Then we returned to our quest.

"Perhaps we should come up with an alternative plan?" I said. "Something more realistic, something less likely to get us all thrown in the big house."

"You don't like my plan?" Johnny-Johnny said.

"I, ah, love your plan, but maybe…we should brainstorm a bit more. See where it takes us."

Johnny-Johnny looked at me for the longest time, saying nothing, and the place went quiet. At least in our table in the corner.

It was getting late.

Well after midnight now.

Still too hot to hang meat.

Up on stage, Sallie was now singing another request, Muddy Waters' "HOOCHIE COOCHIE MAN."

"If we don't come up with a fool-proof plan," John Rubin said. "We'll all be swimming in muddy waters."

"Good one, Rubin!" Gabrielle said.

Then we finished our beverages and hung out listening to Sallie. I looked over at Gabrielle and our eyes met. We were on the same page. We each knew what the other was thinking: nothing was going to happen, and we still didn't have the slightest clue what to do with the *BOOBIE BOUNCER*.

CHAPTER FORTY-SEVEN

Gabrielle and I were asleep up in the bow of our boat. Mr. Leroy had his paws on our heads.

KNOCK, KNOCK, KNOCK. "Breakfield!"

KNOCK, KNOCK, KNOCK. "Breakfield!"

KNOCK, KNOCK, KNOCK. "Breakfield!"

Someone was doing the Sheldon/Penny thing on our hull. Who could it be at this hour?

I slipped from the V-bunk, trying not to wake Gabrielle or Mr. Leroy.

I padded through the galley, quietly slid back the hatch, and opened the door to our cockpit.

"Oh, my God!" I must have said it out loud.

Standing on the dock were John Rubin, Johnny-Johnny and Popcorn Joe.

John Rubin was holding a chicken.

Johnny-Johnny was dressed as Baby Tracy from the Spectrelles, awesome hair, tight sequined dress, fashionable high heels.

Popcorn Joe was wearing his rollerblades and holding a square grouper.

"It's time," John Rubin said.

"Now?"

"Now," John Rubin said.

"Nooo!" I screamed. "Don't make us do it!"

And then I woke up.

As did Gabrielle.

As did Mr. Leroy.

"You were having a nightmare," Gabrielle said.

"Was I ever!"

I told Gabrielle about my dream. I knew she would soothe me and comfort me, perhaps even offer to make me a cup of tea.

But she didn't, rather she said: "Where would Popcorn Joe get the square grouper?"

CHAPTER FORTY-EIGHT

When we finally woke up the next morning, I needed my Tums. My stomach had been churning the entire night, and it was now a witch's cauldron of agro.

Life was too short for this kind of shit.

I turned off the A/C, slid the hatch back, opened the little door to the cockpit and stepped out into a refreshing morning mist.

I yawned, I stretched, I looked behind me, Mr. Leroy was there, yawning and stretching, as well.

Gabrielle popped her head out: "Coffee?"

"Strong, please," I said.

Gabrielle brought out the entire cafetière and we poured ourselves two strong cups and sat in the cockpit with Mr. Leroy.

We sipped our coffees and rued the day Mr. Rich Prick Dude had arrived on the scene.

"Ever since we changed the name of the boat, we've had bad luck," I said.

"We'll have to shake the boat down. Maybe there's a name on something that we didn't spot before."

"What are you saying?"

"Remember one important rule that must be followed through to perfection when changing the name?"

I had to think for a few minutes. "Something about ensuring that there's no mention of the old name anywhere?"

"Exactly."

"And you think we missed something?"

"I think we missed something…"

"Let's ring Tina and ask her to go back through her old papers."

So we rang Tina. She said she would check and call us back later that afternoon.

Then we scoured the boat. Nothing.

Our brains were short-circuiting, so we took a bike ride through the Old Town, up to the cemetery, right on Petronia, deep into Bahama Village then back, finally stopping in at Pepe's for a second infusion of caffeine.

We sat in the second booth just to the right when you walk in, under that cool painting of Pepe's itself, and gave a wave to photographer Henry Fuller who was sitting in the fourth booth with an eclectic group of locals.

Gabrielle and I had a *con leche* each and did some quality head scratching.

"I've got it!" Gabrielle almost shouted it out.

"What?"

Gabrielle jabbed a hand into the pocket of her shorts and extracted her cell phone.

"Here!" She swiped her cell phone and thumbed it for a few seconds. "Look!"

I was staring at the photos we had taken of our boat when we first took possession. Lovely photos from all angles, and one was from astern, and in great big letters, the transom read: *RESTLESS*.

"Delete it, then we'll be good to go," I said.

"Not so fast. Remember we sent it to John Rubin. If he still has it on his mobile, then he'll need to delete it as well."

We tried John Rubin's cell, but he wasn't answering (probably wrestling a marlin and having seawater poured over his head to keep him cooled down), so we left a message at the Ocean Key Resort for him to meet us at the Bull after he returned from fishing.

* * *

Through the magic of prose we are now sitting in the back

269

corner of the Bull. Popcorn Joe is here, Johnny-Johnny is here and John Rubin is just walking in the front door. There he is, right over there.

"My shout!" Rubin yells over to us, and he's already sorting out the first round.

One by one, Rubin hands our drinks to us, then he pulls up a seat.

"How was fishing?" Gabrielle asks.

"Went out into the flats and caught my first tarpon. They're not keen on coming in the boat, are they? This one must have leapt ten feet out of the water. It was rattling its gills like a rattlesnake and doing all sorts of acrobatics. Couldn't wait to get him next to the boat for a photo op."

"Did you release him?"

"Not only wanted to, had to. It's the law since September 2013 in the state of Florida. What a gorgeous impressive creature, he was."

After we, ah, wet our whistles at the Bull, we told everyone of our discovery about the photos and John Rubin told us: "Crap, I must have sent that photo to everyone in my contact list…"

Oh, no, this is not what we wanted to hear…

"Ahhh, you should see your faces, redder than mine…JUST JOKING. Let's drink…no wait, you drink and I'll delete the photo."

Drink, GULP, GULP, GLUG…

Delete, CLICK, CLICK, PUNCH…

CHAPTER FORTY-NINE

The next day we re-christened the boat. In attendance, the usual suspects: John Rubin, Popcorn Joe, Johnny-Johnny, Patty and Tina, dog Sasha, and Mr. Leroy up on the boom.

The re-christening all went well and not long after it seemed that our luck began to change, Mr. Rough-STD-Provider cleaned out his dock box, pulled the spring lines and chugged out of the Bight.

Coincidence? I think not.

CHAPTER FIFTY

A few days later, Johnny-Johnny and Popcorn Joe stopped by.

We welcomed them onboard, Gabrielle made Cuban coffee and we all sat out in the cockpit. Mr. Leroy greeted and sniffed Popcorn Joe and Johnny-Johnny, then took his position up on the boom.

I pointed at the *BOOBIE BOUNCER*'s empty slip.

"He's upped sticks," I said. "Wonder what lit a fire under his ass?"

Silence from Popcorn Joe and Johnny-Johnny.

Curious subtext.

"What's going on?" Gabrielle said.

Silence.

Finally Johnny-Johnny spoke: "I've been a bad boy..."

"How so?"

"I called in a favor to someone I did some work for..."

"Gofer work?"

"Oh, you know about that, eh? *Mais oui*, and the friend owed me big time. The person works for the DMV. He dug around a bit, turned over a few coconuts, made a few calls..."

"And?"

"The *BOOBIE BOUNCER* was not the boat's original name."

"What was it?"

"*CIRROHIS OF THE RIVER...*"

"A real comedian, this guy."

"If your friend at the DMV saw this, then that means not all references to the original boat's name have been purged?"

272

"You got that right."

"And that means bad luck."

"And bad luck is coming his way…the home port of the *BOOBIE BOUNCER* is listed as Naples, but the home port of the *CIRRHOSIS OF THE RIVER* is Everglades City."

"Where do they get 'river' from?" I asked.

"The Everglades is known as the River of Grass, and in the early 1980s, Everglades City meant drugs. But most of that's been cleaned up. Guess the *BOOBIE BOUNCER*'s owner thought no one was paying attention anymore. He's been running drugs down from Everglades City to Stock Island. To a whole family over there. They're all thick as thieves. Father, sons, a whole den of snakes. Purportedly, the DEA was about to chew the *BOOBIE BOUNCER*'s owner a new asshole, beggin' your pardon, *Madame*, and he took her back up into the maze that is the 10,000 islands that shield Everglades City. He's hiding out there, but I reckon he'll be getting the ejector seat soon enough."

DENOUEMENT

Gabrielle and I are celebrating the departure of the *BOOBIE BOUNCER and* the Hyena from Hell at the Bull & Whistle.

And...shock of shocks, we are not downstairs at one of our favorite seats, we are upstairs at the Whistle at the moment, sitting outside on the corner of the Havana-influenced wraparound balcony.

The temperature is in the low 80s.

The night air is sweet with jasmine and sweat and stale beer.

And somehow it all feels right.

John Rubin is here with us. He requested a drink up here before we repair downstairs to listen to Sallie Foster. John Rubin says he has a surprise for us, but he will wait till Popcorn Joe and Johnny-Johnny arrive.

The Mob.

John Rubin is now tanned black and looks like Hemingway would if he had shaved his beard and had been deep-sea fishing in, ah, earnest. He's kitted in all khaki and has a few new hooks in his baseball cap.

"Hello, B's! Hello, Rubin!"

We look up and it's Popcorn Joe. He grabs a stool and sits down to join us.

About now, a slinky young "thang" sashays up and sits just on the other side of John Rubin. A waft of pungent perfume slaps us in the face.

"Do you mind if I smoke?" the young thang asks, but the voice is not the ilk of any such young thang, the voice is deep baritone and rich.

"Johnny-Johnny!" John Rubin says.

"Told you I could rock a pair of heels."

And we all laugh.

We could hear loud music coming from up the street, to the right. We all leaned forward and looked over the balcony. Coming down Duval were eight young men dressed in white T-shirts emblazoned with a small British ensign, and white shorts. They were making as if they were running, but doing it in SLOW MOTION. The music was emanating from a ghetto-box one of them was carrying. It was the theme song from the movie *Chariots of Fire*.

"You've got to love Key West," John Rubin said.

We ordered drinks and just watched Duval pass by below.

"Check it out," Johnny-Johnny said.

Now coming down the street were four rather androgynous looking young men or was it young women? Each one sported a different color T-shirt: one red, one purple, one yellow, one green. And each one had a large letter painted on the front. The letters were T and B and L and G.

We watched them pass by below.

"What's that all about?" Popcorn Joe says.

"Who knows, but they're up to something," I say.

"Okay, we're all here now," Gabrielle says. "John Rubin has a surprise for us."

"I do, indeed," Rubin says, and he reaches into a pocket and pulls out about fifteen feet of monofilament fishing line...and a large, hairy rubber spider!

And we all laugh again.

"I like Key West," John Rubin says slowly lowering the spider over the railing. "There's something special about it, isn't there? Key West has a good feel to it. It's exciting, but in a way gentle and forgiving and accepting. And it's fun. I could live here, I think. Yes, I think I could live here and be very happy, indeed."

And on that, John Rubin lets the big, hairy spider drop

down.

We waited.

We didn't have to wait long.

Here came the screams.

And not long after the screams dissipated we spotted the four androgynous young men/young women coming back.

But they were in a different order now.

And it was very clear what this was all about.

Now the letters read: LGBT.

* * *

Gabrielle and I are downstairs in the Bull now.

We scored on our favorite window seat up by the front door.

John Rubin has gone back to his suite at the Ocean Key Resort.

Popcorn Joe has gone back home to Truman Annex.

Johnny-Johnny has transitioned over to Bobby's Monkey Bar, the place heaves with locals, late, and he says he finds comfort and kindred spirits there.

Up on stage, Sallie Foster has the whole place rocking, dancing, singing, drinking with "DON'T STOP ME NOW."

And…to keep you in the loop, I'm happy to report that an older couple from Mobile have taken the slip next to ours. They are on a 65-foot Chris-Craft Commander that was designed for the DuPont family. The boat is the epitome of marine opulence as it sports *two* heads. The elderly couple are quiet as mice, and respect the marina rules and regulations. They spend a lot of time sitting out on the afterdeck nursing rum beverages and working on crosswords and Sudoku.

We like them, they like us.

And Mr. Leroy likes them…because they have a cat!

The cat's name is Bulldog (I know) and he's a little fur ball of purring, wide-eyed joy. Bulldog loves to just stare at you and he never seems to blink. He has grand, round eyes like an owl. Bulldog and Mr. Leroy spend a lot of time gazing fondly at one another.

Gabrielle and I are over the moon that it's all worked out for us, and we blessed to be able to live in Key West, FL, not quite the USA, and not:

Anus, France (population 24).

Pussy, France (population 276).

Fucking, Austria (population 104).

Wank, Germany (population about the same as your sperm count).

Horni Police, Czech Republic (population 690).

North Piddle, England (population 80).

Dildo, Canada (population 1198).

After those, Hell, Michigan, Intercourse, Pennsylvania, and French Lick, Indiana, aren't looking so bad now, are they?

Just ask Larry Bird.

There's nothing at all wrong with these places (except, perhaps, Fucking, Austria), it's just that Key West works for us.

Gives us what we want.

Gives us what we need.

Key West has its many flaws and imperfections, but if you can find it in your heart to deem them quirky and charming, rather than off-putting and offensive, you'll fit right in and have a new home.

And a new, glorious life.

Just like we have.

As you've suspected, our lives are back on track…or, perhaps I should stick with nautical terminology and sailing maneuvers, and say our lives are back on *tack*.

We have our home, we have our jobs, and we have each other.

And we have Mr. Leroy.

We had to start all over again, but clearly it was all worth it. Starting over is better than giving up.

I lift my plastic glass of Bud to you, Dear Reader.

And Gabrielle lifts her mojito to you.

This chapter in our lives, which is indeed this very book, has come to an end, and I thank you for getting this far and not nodding off.

I wish you the very best through happiness and health, both physical and mental.

And Sallie carries on singing the Freddy Mercury classic "DON'T STOP ME NOW," which is really the whole idea, isn't it?

AFTERWORD

Hi, it's me again.

We're still at the Bull. You weren't expecting that, were you? Well, join the club, neither were we, but Sallie is still killing it, and we are not about to bolt while she's up there.

Can't do it.

Shouldn't do it.

Wouldn't do it.

So, let's have one for the Yellow Brick, what say you?

I have one eye out the window watching the foot traffic crawl slowly by on Duval. And I have the other eye on Sallie Foster up on stage. It's like sitting mid-court and watching a tennis match between a drunk and a rock star.

It's hot in here and the ceiling fans are giving it the ol' college try.

Everyone is knocking back the plonk and singing along with Sallie.

Some are dancing.

I look over at my wife and a glow sweeps over me. As it always does.

Gabrielle is enjoying the music and pecking away at her cell phone.

She can multi-task.

I can't.

"What's up?" I ask.

"Checking the Weather Channel," she says. "See what tomorrow holds for us."

"We'd be lost without the Weather Channel down here in

Key West, end of the line, not quite the USA," I say.

Gabrielle laughs.

Then, she goes quiet for a moment.

"What?" I ask.

"Remember that tropical wave that came off the African coast?"

"There's been so many this year…"

"The one that developed into a tropical storm and then just became a Category 1 hurricane?"

"And the reason you are telling me this is?"

"It's intensified rapidly and is now a Category 5."

"Well not to worry, it'll jog north like the others and be no threat," I said.

"But it's not swinging north," Gabrielle says. "It's maintaining a path to the west."

"Where's it headed?"

"It's on a collision course with the Florida Keys…"

AND FINALLY

May I leave you with this:

We never know what life has in store for us.

Sometimes life gets in the way of life.

Sometimes Mother Nature gets in the way of life.

Hurdles are erected in our path as we are beavering away trying to better our existence.

Obstacles stand tall and threatening, blocking quests, blocking dreams, blocking health, blocking happiness.

But we must soldier on.

We must endeavor to improve our lot for ourselves and our loved ones.

We must stand strong and respond resolutely in the face of adversity.

We must never quit no matter what nasty curve life throws our way, just make adjustments, hang in there and swing for the fences.

And let us be good and kind to others.

Let us lead by example.

Forgive me for pontificating here and once again using up all my clichés, but with each passing day, it becomes more and more clear that…LIFE IS SHORT.

And we only get one shot at it.

Unless, you're Mr. Leroy.

Also by Jon Breakfield:

NON-FICTION

The KEY WEST SERIES:

ALSO

FICTION:

SHORT STORY

EDITED

KEY WEST ROGUE DIARIES by Will Soto

TWENTY-ONE AGAIN by Kate Vann

THE LASCAR by Shahida Rahman